*Everyman, I will go with thee,
and be thy guide*

Elizabeth Barrett Browning

SELECTED POEMS

Edited by
COLIN GRAHAM
University of Huddersfield

EVERYMAN
J. M. DENT · LONDON
CHARLES E. TUTTLE
VERMONT

Selected Poems of Elizabeth Barrett Browning first published by
Everyman Paperbacks in 1988
This edition first published in 1996
Selection, introduction and other critical material © J. M. Dent 1996

J. M. Dent
Orion Publishing Group
Orion House
5 Upper St Martin's Lane
London WC2H 9EA
and
Charles E. Tuttle Co. Inc.
28 South Main Street
Rutland, Vermont 05701, USA

Typeset in Sabon by CentraCet Limited, Cambridge

Printed in Great Britain by
The Guernsey Press Co. Ltd, Guernsey, C. I.

British Library Cataloguing-in-Publication Data is available
upon request.

ISBN 0 460 87425 X

CONTENTS

NOTE ON THE AUTHOR

ELIZABETH BARRETT was born on 6 March 1806 at Coxhoe Hall, County Durham, the first of eleven children. When she was three years old the family moved to Hope End, Herefordshire. Her writing career began in earnest at the age of eleven when she began composing *The Battle of Marathon*, which was published privately three years later. At fifteen she had published for the first time in a magazine. It was also at around the age of fifteen that she began to feel the effects of an illness and possible hypochondria which was to recur for the rest of her life, and which may have been connected with her consumption of laudanum.

Her next volume of poetry, *An Essay on Mind, with Other Poems*, was published in 1826, again with the aid of family money. By this time she had determined to turn poetry into a career. In 1827 she began a correspondence with the scholar Hugh Stuart Boyd, who she felt was the intellectual interlocutor she had always needed and who encouraged her writing.

Her next volumes, *Prometheus Bound* (1833) and *The Seraphim, and Other Poems* (1838), proved to be relatively successful and led to the publication, despite long periods of illness and convalescence, of *Poems* (in 2 volumes) in 1844. The following year she received the first of many letters from Robert Browning, whose poetry she had mentioned approvingly in 'Lady Geraldine's Courtship' in *Poems*. In May 1845 Robert Browning made his first visit to Elizabeth Barrett and the two married secretly, against the wishes of Elizabeth's father, on 12 September 1845. One week later they eloped to Italy.

Elizabeth Barrett Browning spent most of the remainder of her life in Italy, punctuated by visits to London. It was during this period that her major poetical works were written: *Casa Guidi Windows* (1851) and her long poem *Aurora Leigh* (1857). Her passionate interest in Italian nationalism, the inspiration for *Casa Guidi Windows*, was also apparent in the last volume published during her lifetime, *Poems Before Congress* (1860).

Elizabeth Barrett Browning died, after a winter of illness, in Florence on 29 June 1861. She was buried in the Protestant cemetery in Florence two days later. In 1862 Elizabeth Barrett Browning's *Last Poems*, arranged by Robert Browning, were published.

NOTE ON THE EDITOR

COLIN GRAHAM is lecturer in English Literature at the University of Huddersfield. He has written on nineteenth-century poetry, Irish literature and post-colonial theory. He has edited Robert Browning, *Men and Women and Other Poems* (Everyman, 1993) and is currently writing *An Introduction to Irish Studies*.

CHRONOLOGY OF ELIZABETH
BARRETT BROWNING'S LIFE

Year	Age	Life
1806		Elizabeth Barrett born 6 March at Coxhoe Hall, Durham
1809	3	Barrett family move to Hope End, Herefordshire
1815	9	Elizabeth Barrett and her parents in Paris
1817	11	Begins writing *The Battle of Marathon*
1820	14	*The Battle of Marathon* printed privately. 'Bro' (her brother Edward) goes to Charterhouse
1821	15	Her poetry is published in a magazine for the first time (*New Monthly Magazine*)
1822	16	Returns to Hope End after a stay in Gloucester
1823	17	Holiday in France
1825	19	Stays with her grandmother in Hastings
1826	20	*An Essay on Mind, with Other Poems* published (25 March)
1827	21	Begins her correspondence with Hugh Stuart Boyd
1828	22	Mary Moulton-Barrett, Elizabeth's mother, dies on 7 October

CHRONOLOGY OF HER TIMES

Year	Artistic Context	Historical Events
1806		Grenville replaces Pitt as Prime Minister
1807	Wordworth, *Poems in Two Volumes*	
1809	Birth of Tennyson	Beginning of commercial boom
1811	Jane Austen, *Sense and Sensibility*	Luddites in Yorkshire and Nottinghamshire
1812	Births of Dickens and Browning	Napoleon enters Russia. America declares war on Britain
1813	Jane Austen, *Pride and Prejudice*	East India Company abolished
1814	Wordsworth, *The Excursion*	
1816	Lord Byron, *Childe Harold* Canto I	
1817	Death of Jane Austen	Economic slump follows boom of previous two years
1818	Keats, *Endymion*	
1819		Peterloo massacre
1820	Shelley, *Prometheus Unbound*	Accession of George IV
1821	Death of Keats	
1822	Birth of Arnold Death of Shelley	Famine in Ireland
1824	Death of Byron	
1825		Trades Unions legalised
1827	Clare, *The Shepherd's Calendar*	
1829		Catholic Emancipation

Year	Age	Life
1830	24	Death of her paternal grandmother
1831	25	Keeps a diary during this year
1832	26	Hope End is sold; the Barretts move to Sidmouth in Devon
1833	27	*Prometheus Bound* published
1835	29	Barrett family move to London
1838	32	*The Seraphim, and Other Poems* published. Elizabeth goes to Torquay for a period of convalescence
1840	34	Her brother Edward drowns
1841	35	Returns to London
1844	38	*Poems* (two volumes) published
1845	39	In January Robert Browning writes his first letter to Elizabeth Barrett. Visits her first in May
1846	40	Elizabeth Barrett and Robert Browning marry secretly on 12 September. They leave clandestinely for Italy one week later
1847	41	Brownings live in Pisa, then Florence
1848	42	Begins writing *Casa Guidi Windows*
1849	43	Birth of Elizabeth's son 'Pen' (Robert Weidemann Browning)
1850	44	New edition of *Poems* published
1851	45	The Brownings return to London for the first time since their elopement. *Casa Guidi Windows* published
1852	46	Visits London again, staying at Paris on the return journey to Florence
1853	47	Begins writing *Aurora Leigh*

Year	Artistic Context	Historical Events
1830	Tennyson, *Poems, Chiefly Lyrical*	Accession of William IV. Revolutions in Europe
1832	Death of Walter Scott	First Reform Act
1833	Carlyle, *Sartor Resartus*	Abolition of slavery in British Empire
1834	Death of Coleridge	Trial of 'Tolpuddle Martyrs'
1837	Dickens, *Oliver Twist*	Accession of Victoria
1838	Dickens, *Nicholas Nickleby*	Anti-Corn Law League established
1840	Dickens, *The Old Curiosity Shop*	
1841	Carlyle, *On Heroes and Hero-Worship* Browning, *Pippa Passes*	Robert Peel becomes Prime Minister
1842	Tennyson, *Poems*	Chartist riots
1843	Death of Southey Wordsworth becomes Poet Laureate	
1844		Railway boom
1846		Corn Law abolished
1847	Charlotte Brontë, *Jane Eyre* Emily Brontë, *Wuthering Heights*	
1848	Thackeray, *Vanity Fair* Pre-Raphaelite Brotherhood founded	Revolutions in Europe
1849	Ruskin, *Seven Lamps of Architecture*	
1850	Death of Wordsworth Tennyson publishes *In Memoriam* and becomes Poet Laureate	
1851	Ruskin, *Stones of Venice*	Great Exhibition
1852	Thackeray, *Henry Esmond* Harriet Beecher Stowe, *Uncle Tom's Cabin*	Fall of French Republic
1853	Arnold, *Poems*	

Year	Age	Life
1854	48	Returns to Florence after travels around Italy
1855	49	After an illness early in the year, visits London
1856	50	*Aurora Leigh* completed
1857	51	Death of Edward Moulton-Barrett, Elizabeth's father. *Aurora Leigh* published
1858	52	Holiday in France
1859	53	Returns to Florence from Rome. Illness
1860	54	*Poems Before Congress* published. Death of her sister Henrietta
1861	55	Winter brings on illness while in Rome. Returns to Florence in June. Death of Elizabeth Barrett Browning on 29 June. Buried 1 July in Protestant cemetery in Florence

Year	Artistic Context	Historical Events
1854	Dickens, *Hard Times*	Crimean War begins
1855	Arnold, *Poems, Second Series* Browning, *Men and Women*	Palmerston becomes Prime Minister
1856	Thomas Hughes, *Tom Brown's Schooldays*	Treaty of Paris
1857	Trollope, *Barchester Towers*	Indian Mutiny
1858	George Eliot, *Scenes of Clerical Life*	British Crown assumes control of India
1859	Darwin, *Origin of Species*	Construction of Suez Canal begins
1860	George Eliot, *The Mill on the Floss* Wilkie Collins, *The Woman in White*	
1861	J. S. Mill, *Utilitarianism*	Prince Albert dies. American Civil War begins

INTRODUCTION

The feminist recuperation of Elizabeth Barrett Browning in recent years has convincingly shown how she confronted the problems facing a woman poet in the nineteenth century.[1]

As David Riede's comment above suggests (and as Elizabeth Barrett and Her Critics at the end of this edition shows), recent critical understanding of Elizabeth Barrett Browning's importance for Victorian women's poetry, and Victorian poetry in general, has been constituted by a series of developing feminist readings of her work. Moving from discussion of Barrett Browning's explicit interest in the role of the female poet/writer to her attempts to write as a woman poet in relation to the influence of male poetics, feminist readings have laid increasing stress on the centrality of Barrett Browning in recuperating Victorian women's poetry. The sense of recovery involved in such readings has been overtaken in recent years by a closer examination of Barrett Browning's texts in the light of feminist criticism, and this seems likely to produce ever more complex readings of her work.

Elizabeth Barrett's early life (which might even be thought of as the time before she corresponded with Robert Browning in 1845) was dominated by the presences of three men: her father, her brother Edward (known as 'Bro') and Hugh Boyd, a classical scholar who heavily influenced her reading and early intellectual development. Her devotion to these men was intense and they may be seen to represent the emotional and intellectual fetters which were to restrict, or at the very least dominate, her early poetry. Edward Barrett Moulton-Barrett, Elizabeth's father, is most notable for his attempt to prevent his children entering into marriage (see discussion of 'The Runaway Slave at Pilgrim's Point' below), and it has been usual to see this as an exaggerated, near paranoid, extension of the affection between the father and his children. Margaret Forster, in her biography of Barrett Browning, writes:

The love and affection between Elizabeth and her father was [just after her mother's death] . . . free-flowing and almost untroubled. [His children], for their part, felt secure in his love. 'I feel how dearly he loves us,' wrote Elizabeth, but significantly, she began to think he loved them 'too well'.[2]

'To My Father on His Birthday', published in *An Essay on Mind, with Other Poems* (1826) seems at first sight a reflection of this devotion, couched in a classicised poetic form attempting to gain the recognition of the father. As the quotation from Horace which stands as an epigraph to this poem suggests, 'my father was the reason for these things', and superficially the poem plays on the near-divine inspiration of the paternal in Elizabeth Barrett's poetry:

> No thoughts of fondness e'er appear
> *More* fond, than those I write of here!
> No name can e'er on tablet shine,
> My Father! more beloved than *thine*!

Dorothy Mermin says of this poem: 'In this book obsessed with naming, she names her father first',[3] and the poem tends to justify the notion that Edward Barrett Moulton-Barrett's influence was all-encompassing. Yet the poem may also contain the germ of the uneasiness Forster alludes to when she notes that Elizabeth Barrett 'began to think he loved them "too well"'. The poem is replete with emphatic, often near-trite statements of affection, which, as the poem progresses, tend towards hollowness. The poem ends:

> But still my Father's looks remain
> The best Maecenas of my strain;
> My gentlest joy, upon his brow
> To read the smile, that meets me now –
> To hear him, in his kindness, say
> The words, – perchance he'll speak today!

The final couplet borders on awkwardness, even toying with parody, while stressing the importance of the father's speech and language for the poetry of his daughter. The 'strain' here may have a double-edge and it is tempting to read this as a foreshadowing of Aurora Leigh (whose education is consciously set out in her father's as opposed to her mother's 'tongue') discovering her father's library:

> Books! books! books!
> I had found the secret of the garret-room
> Piled high with cases in my father's name,
> Piled high, packed large . . .
> (*Aurora Leigh*, First Book [see extracts from *Aurora Leigh*, pp. 269–301, line 228ff.])

By the time of *Aurora Leigh* Barrett Browning was registering a much more conscious recognition that it is the 'father's name' which presides over knowledge and poetry. The encouraging Maecenas who is Moulton-Barrett is transformed into the metaphoric sets of secret knowledge hidden from Aurora. Poetry changes from being sanctioned by the father to become an intellectual experience which has secretly to be wrested from closed packing cases, significantly placed in the deliberately poetically clichéd garret-room, and labelled paternally. If we read back to 'To My Father on His Birthday' the 'strain' of those final lines becomes all the more ambiguous.

Elizabeth Barrett's early life was, then, deeply affected by this series of relationships with men, all of which were vitally important to her intellectual development, but all of which were deeply unsatisfactory. Her relationship with the elderly Boyd gave her a knowledge of and almost an awe for classicism (an influence also apparent in 'To My Father on His Birthday'), while her affection for 'Bro' was certainly intellectually vital and at times passionate. Elizabeth Barrett's relationships with these men made concrete early on what became a central focus for her poetry later: the problem of the apparent necessity to address her poetry at least partially *to* men. *Aurora Leigh* and *Sonnets from the Portuguese* explore this problem in complex ways, both in terms of poetic form and in their interwoven narratives and contemplations. Negotiating her position as a female poet with these paternal and masculine influences led in two directions; in personal terms, her reaction was to shut herself off from any event which might earn the 'disapprobation' of her father – in doing so she took his ethos, and the unexpressed dictum against marriage, to an extreme of seclusion and her 'illness' during this period, whether psychosomatic or otherwise, is easily read as an extension of this process.[4]

In poetic terms, Barrett Browning was faced with the dilemma forced upon the female poet by an apparent lack of satisfactory

predecessors and the pressure to write, for the sake of accept-
ance, in recognised 'male' forms. In her 'Introduction I' to
Victorian Women Poets, Margaret Reynolds notes Barrett
Browning's 'much quoted line "I look everywhere for grand-
mothers and see none"'. While Reynolds acknowledges the
forcefulness of this statement out of context, she sees its full
impact as more complex:

> ... look again at Barrett Browning's two letters on the subject,
> and they tell quite a different story. When she said that she longed
> for 'grandmothers' Barrett Browning didn't mean that she couldn't
> find any women poets. She could think of plenty and she lists
> them ... But of all these only Joanna Baillie, she says, is in the
> very highest sense a true poet. The rest are 'versifiers'.[5]

The method employed in *Sonnets from the Portuguese* to
overcome these difficulties of audience, influence and the charge
of 'versification', is one partly embodied in the dramatic mono-
logue form used by both Robert and Elizabeth Barrett Browning;
masks and elisions are used to open new perspectives and at
times to call the bluff of standard practices. The *Sonnets* are
both deliberately authorless (or authoressless) and *not* 'from the
Portuguese', creating a double remove from a direct engagement
of the female poet with the extended analysis of passion which
the *Sonnets* undertake. This creates a space and an ambiguity
exploited by Barrett Browning, but notably she explores these
new possibilities within two recognised forms: the sonnet itself,
made into a finely honed and exact form of poetic expression in
the *Sonnets*, and the sonnet sequence, drawing its model primar-
ily from Shakespeare's sonnets.

This method of exact and overtly skilful use of poetic form to
channel the issues most pressing on the woman poet is repeated,
in modified way, in *Aurora Leigh*, a poem which addresses its
own form and its relationship to 'male' epic, and which is
written in an 'assured technique ... [of] "Shakespearean"
iambic pentameter in blank verse with suppleness', yet which
has a narrative tackling the issues of 'socialism, rape, prostitu-
tion'.[6] *Aurora Leigh* is remarkable enough for its ability to
undertake its narrative through its chosen poetic structure. But
as feminist critics from Cora Kaplan onwards (see *Elizabeth
Barrett Browning and Her Critics*) have hinted at and in places
examined, *Aurora Leigh* involves complexly evolving attempts

to formulate a feminist poetics – forms of poetic expression apt
to the woman poet, and capable of addressing the issues of the
pressures of masculinity in poetic discourse and the need for
'difference' in female poetic expression. As an example of this
one can take the opening lines (1–42) of the Fifth Book,
pp. 281–2. Here, the repeated 'Aurora Leigh, be humble' signals
the beginning of a contemplation of the new and unsettled – this
phrase is used constantly in the poem to mark both the extent
to which Aurora feels awkward in assuming her role as a thinker
and the ability she has to retrace her thoughts and revise the
'newness' she uncovers. The sentence which follows is one of
the most tortuous in the poem, made up of a series of clauses
each reformulating and asking a parallel question to 'Shall I
hope/To speak my poems in mysterious tune/With man and
nature?', a set of questions which are then restated in 'can I
speak my verse ...'. The sentence is finally brought to a
conclusion at line 445 (in this edition) and like the end of a
parenthesis is enclosed by the repeated (though more positively
expressed) phrase 'Go,/ Aurora Leigh: be humble.' This gram-
matical awkwardness and difficulty is no accident. The series of
clauses which make up the bulk of the sentence may be
grammatically parallel, but they build on each other for specific
effects. Take, for example, the lines:

> With spring's delicious trouble in the ground,
> Tormented by the quickened blood of roots,
> And softly pricked by golden crocus sheaves
> In token of the harvest-time of flowers?

The question is explicitly about the 'mysterious tune' which the
female poet must write in; the harmony which she needs to
achieve between 'nature' and 'man' (a term used ironically here
– is it male or human?). In putting together this fundamental
question about whether feminist poetics are possible Aurora
begins to show that they are. Standard poetic images of spring
are celebratory (both the opening of Chaucer's *Canterbury Tales*
and Wordsworth's 'I wandered lonely as a cloud' are obvious
sources here); Aurora's rendition of spring adds a different
dimension – 'delicious trouble' appears to be in 'mysterious
tune' with nature on particular terms, so that the regeneration
of spring is close to pregnancy and childbirth, involving pain
and ecstasy. The notion of spring as regenerative and reproduc-

tive, yet close to the feminine, is furthered by images of menstruation in 'Tormented by the quickened blood of roots' and loss of virginity in 'softly pricked by golden crocus-sheaves'. This feminised revision of staid poetic imagery culminates in the extraordinary lines:

> . . . with all that strain
> Of sexual passion, which devours the flesh
> In a sacrament of souls? with mother's breasts
> Which, round the new-made creatures hanging there,
> Throb luminous and harmonious like pure spheres?

Here the standard poetic image (the usually metaphysical 'spheres' which represent the universe and its harmonies in totality) is made radically female, a process which the previous revision of spring prepared the reader for. If *Aurora Leigh*'s achievement is to be fully understood beyond its narrative impact, then points such as this, at which it begins to address the very substance of feminist poetics, will be vital.

One danger of this sort of analysis could be to lead critics and readers of Barrett Browning to read her in celebratory rather than analytic terms, and only to read her in the context of the particular issue of women's poetry and poetics. This would reduce the complex nature of her poetry in the very ways Aurora herself tries to resist. Reading class issues in Barrett Browning in relation to gender is, for example, crucial, and the passages of *Aurora Leigh* describing Aurora's first meeting with Marian Erle, or her slightly disparaging mention of 'your common men/ [Who] Lay telegraphs, gauge railroads . . . / And dust the flaunty carpets of the world', need to be closely examined in order to comprehend how class issues may cut across the gender obsessions of the poetry.

Most recently the issues of race and colonialism have appeared to offer pressing new perspectives on Barrett Browning's poetry, especially in the light of Julia Markus's assertions on the subject in *Done and Dared: The Marriage of Elizabeth Barrett and Robert Browning*. Markus did not so much uncover new findings as put together already existing knowledge of Barrett Browning in a way only previously hinted at. Markus carefully delineates the Barrett family lineage and its origins in Jamaican plantations. The argument Markus puts forward hinges on evidence that there were fears in the Barrett family that Creole 'blood' would show itself eventually in the family line. Markus ties this to Edward Barrett Moulton-Barrett's restrictions on marriage for his children:

> A father who insists on his daughters' purity is not an unfamiliar type. One who insists that his sons not marry is a unique type.[7]

Markus also quotes from Elizabeth herself, who seems to have believed, as Markus states, that 'she had African blood through her grandfather Charles Moulton'. Writing in 1845 to Robert, Elizabeth said:

> My true initials are E.B.M.B. – my long name as opposed to my short one, being: ... Elizabeth Barrett Moulton Barrett! – there's a full length to take away one's breath! [...] Nevertheless it is true that I would give ten towns in Norfolk (if I had them) to own some purer lineage than that of the blood of the slave! – Cursed we are from generation to generation![8]

Whether Barrett Browning is being more metaphorical than autobiographical here may still be debatable, but it seems less likely after Markus's book. For the reader of Barrett Browning's poetry this is interesting in biographical terms, but more crucially it could affect the way in which certain poems are read. Marian, for example, in *Aurora Leigh*, is described 'not white nor brown,/ But could look either' (ll. 388–9 in this edition), lines which could lead to many possible readings. Markus herself points to the most obvious poem affected by these revelations, 'The Runaway Slave at Pilgrim's Point':

> The impetus for 'The Runaway Slave', the passion behind it, was a particular evil of slavery. The poem exposes the rapes and mixed blood that resulted, and the psychotic disorientation this could engender. Had Elizabeth, with the eerie closeness of an eldest daughter to a once-devoted father, 'written out' her father's deepest, most unspoken fear?[9]

That this poem can be read as in any way autobiographical entirely changes the context and voice of the poem from liberal anti-slavery to a deeply troubled Western consciousness. The murder of the child by the mother is carried out because the child had the '*master's* look'; rape, genetics, race, violence and children become loaded themes in the poem. We could take this further biographically, as Markus does, to make more sense of

Barrett Browning's worries over her pregnancies; we could look more closely at poems with similar themes – 'Hiram Powers' Greek Slave' suddenly has entirely different connotations; most usefully perhaps, we can see the poem as an indication of the ways in which imperialism was often a successfully hidden aspect of Victorian literature and society.

Elizabeth Barrett Browning's poetry can be read in gender terms, in post-romantic terms, in class terms, or in post-colonial terms. Her poetry embodies ideas and energies which all of these ways of reading will find useful; to apply any single reading exclusively may be to reduce aspects of her poetry but, equally, such readings have furthered the ideas she tried to address in her writing. Any critic of Barrett Browning is confronted with a poet who writes (often self-consciously) in an intellectual way, exploring and creating 'neologisms' (as Aurora calls new thinking) within carefully and skilfully crafted verse forms. While Barrett Browning's poetry should thus prove to be a vital meeting place for Victorian attitudes to gender, race and class, to see these issues fully scrutinised and uncovered in her poetry we need to pay attention to the forms in which she expresses herself. This combination of poetics and ideas becomes an interdependent relationship in her poetry, and makes Barrett Browning one of the most challenging and rewarding Victorian poets.

COLIN GRAHAM

References

1 David G. Riede, 'Elizabeth Barrett: Poet as Angel', *Victorian Poetry*, 32:2 (Summer 1994), 121–39 (p. 121).

2 Margaret Forster, *Elizabeth Barrett Browning* (London: Paladin, 1988), p. 54.

3 Dorothy Mermin, *Elizabeth Barrett Browning: The Origins of a New Poetry* (London: University of Chicago Press, 1989), p. 37.

4 This period is vividly described in Julia Markus, *Dared and Done: The Marriage of Elizabeth Barrett and Robert Browning* (London: Bloomsbury, 1995).

5 Margaret Reynolds, 'Introduction I' in Angela Leighton and Mar-

garet Reynolds (eds), *Victorian Women Poets: An Anthology* (Oxford: Blackwell, 1995), p. xxix.

6 Angus Calder, with Lizbeth Goodman, 'Gender and Poetry' in Lizbeth Goodman (ed.), *Literature and Gender* (London: Routledge, 1996), p. 52.

7 Markus, *Dared and Done*, p. 105.

8 Ibid.. p. 106.

9 Ibid., p. 107.

NOTE ON THE TEXT

This edition is based on the selection and text of the previous Everyman *Selected Poems* edited by Margaret Forster. The selection has been slightly changed from that edition; 'The Runaway Slave at Pilgrim's Point' and selections from *Aurora Leigh* replace poems previously included. Minor textual errors have also been corrected. The source text from which the poems are taken is the *Oxford Complete Edition of the Poetical Works of Elizabeth Barrett Browning* (Oxford University Press, 1908); 'A True Dream' appeared in *New Poems by Robert and Mrs Browning* ed. F. G. Kenyon (1914). The version of *Aurora Leigh* used is taken from *The Poetical Works of Elizabeth Barrett Browning* (London: Smith, Elder & Co., 1897).

'De Profundis' was written in 1841 but first appeared in *Last Poems*; here it is placed chronologically. 'Question and Answer' and 'A Denial' were first included in the 1856 edition of *Poems* (1850). Sonnet XLII in *Sonnets from the Portuguese* was added in 1856.

SELECTED POEMS

From

AN ESSAY ON MIND,
WITH OTHER POEMS
(1826)

TO MY FATHER ON HIS BIRTHDAY

Causa fuit Pater his.
HORACE

Amidst the days of pleasant mirth,
That throw their halo round our earth;
Amidst the tender thoughts that rise
To call bright tears to happy eyes;
Amidst the silken words that move
To syllable the names we love;
There glides no day of gentle bliss
More soothing to the heart than *this*!
No thoughts of fondness e'er appear
More fond, than those I write of here!   10
No name can e'er on tablet shine,
My Father! more beloved than *thine*!
  'Tis sweet, adown the shady past,
A lingering look of love to cast –
Back th' enchanted world to call,
That beamed around us first of all;
And walk with Memory fondly o'er
The paths where Hope had been before –
Sweet to receive the sylphic sound
That breathes in tenderness around,   20
Repeating to the listening ear
The names that made our childhood dear –
For parted Joy, like Echo, kind,
Will leave her dulcet voice behind,
To tell, amidst the magic air,
How oft she smiled and lingered there.
Oh! let the deep Aonian shell
Breathe tuneful numbers, clear and well,
While the glad Hours, in fair array,
Lead on this buxom Holiday;   30
And Time, as on his way he springs
Hates the last bard who gave him wings;
For 'neath thy gentleness of praise,
My Father! rose my early lays!
And when the lyre was scarce awake,
I loved its strings for *thy* loved sake;

Wooed the kind Muses – but the while
Thought only how to win thy smile –
My proudest fame – my dearest pride –
More dear than all the world beside!   40
And now, perchance, I seek the tone
For magic that is more its own;
But still my Father's looks remain
The best Maecenas of my strain;
My gentlest joy, upon his brow
To read the smile, that meets me now –
To hear him, in his kindness, say
The words, – perchance he'll speak today!

SONG

Weep, as if you thought of laughter!
Smile, as tears were coming after!
Marry your pleasures to your woes;
And think life's green well worth its rose!

No sorrow will your heart betide,
Without a comfort by its side;
The sun may sleep in his sea-bed,
But you have starlight overhead.

Trust not to Joy! the rose of June,
When opened wide, will wither soon;   10
Italian days without twilight
Will turn them suddenly to night.

Joy, most changeful of all things,
Flits away on rainbow wings;
And when they look the gayest, know,
It is that they are spread to go!

THE DREAM

A FRAGMENT

I had a dream! – my spirit was unbound
From the dark iron of its dungeon, clay,
And rode the steeds of Time; – my thoughts had sound,
And spoke without a word, – I went away
Among the buried ages, and did lay
The pulses of my heart beneath the touch
Of the rude minstrel Time, that he should play
Thereon a melody which might seem such
As musing spirits love – mournful, but not too much!

I had a dream – and there mine eyes did see   10
The shadows of past deeds like present things –
The sepulchres of Greece and Hespery,
Aegyptus, and old lands, gave up their kings,
Their prophets, saints, and minstrels, whose lute-strings
Keep a long echo – yea, the dead, white bones
Did stand up by the house whereto Death clings,
And dressed themselves in life, speaking of thrones,
And fame, and power, and beauty, in familiar tones!

I went back further still, for I beheld
What time the earth was one fair Paradise –   20
And over such bright meads the waters welled,
I wot the rainbow was content to rise
Upon the earth, when absent from the skies!
And there were tall trees that I never knew,
Whereon sate nameless birds in merry guise,
Folding their radiant wings, as the flowers do,
When summer nights send sleep down with the dew.

*   *   *

Anon there came a change – a terrible motion,
That made all living things grow pale and shake!
The dark Heavens bowed themselves unto the ocean,   30
Like a strong man in strife – Ocean did take
His flight across the mountains; and the lake
Was lashed into a sea where the winds ride –
Earth was no more, for in her merry-make
She had forgot her God – Sin claimed his bride,
And with his vampire breath sucked out her life's fair tide!

Life went back to her nostrils, and she raised
Her spirit from the waters once again –
The lovely sights, on which I erst had gazed,
Were *not* – though she was beautiful as when   40
The Grecian called her 'Beauty' – sinful men
Walked i' the track of the waters, and felt bold –
Yea, they looked up to Heaven in calm disdain,
As if no eye had seen its vault unfold,
Darkness, and fear, and death! – as if a tale were told!

And ages fled away within my dream;
And still Sin made the heart his dwelling-place,
Eclipsing Heaven from men; but it would seem
That two or three dared commune face to face,
And speak of the soul's life, of hope, and grace.   50
Anon there rose such sounds as angels breathe –
For a God came to die, bringing down peace –
'Pan *was not*'; and the darkness that did wreathe
The earth, passed from the soul – Life came by Death!

*   *   *

From

PROMETHEUS BOUND
AND MISCELLANEOUS POEMS
(1833)

EPITAPH

Beauty, who softly walkest all thy days
In silken garment to the tunes of praise; –
Lover, whose dreamings by the green-banked river,
Where once she wandered, fain would last for ever; –
King, whom the nations scan, adoring scan,
And shout 'a god,' when sin hath marked thee man; –
Bard, on whose brow the Hyblan dew remains,
Albeit the fever burneth in the veins; –
Hero, whose sword in tyrant's blood is hot; –
Sceptic, who doubting, wouldst be doubted not; –   10
Man, whosoe'er thou art, whate'er thy trust; –
Respect thyself in me; – thou treadest *dust*.

THE IMAGE OF GOD

I am God, and there is none like me.
ISAIAH xlvi.9

Christ, who is the image of God.
2 CORINTHIANS iv.4

Thou! art thou like to God?
(I asked this question of the glorious sun)
Thou high unwearied one,
Whose course in heat, and light, and life is run?

Eagles may view thy face – clouds can assuage
Thy fiery wrath – the sage
Can mete thy stature – thou shalt fade with age.
Thou art not like to God.

Thou! art thou like to God?
(I asked this question of the bounteous earth)   10
O thou, who givest birth
To forms of beauty and to sounds of mirth?

In all thy glory works the worm decay –
Thy golden harvests stay
For seed and toil – thy power shall pass away.
Thou art not like to God.

Thou! art thou like to God?
(I asked this question of my deathless soul)
O thou, whose musings roll
Above the thunder, o'er creation's whole?   20

Thou art not. Sin, and shame, and agony
Within thy deepness lie:
They utter forth their voice in thee, and cry,
'*Thou* art not like to God.'

Then art Thou like to God;
Thou, who didst bear the sin, and shame, and woe –
O Thou, whose sweat did flow –
Whose tears did gush – whose brow was dead and low?

No grief is like Thy grief; no heart can prove
Love like unto Thy love;   30
And none, save only Thou, – below, above, –
O God, is like to God!

A SEA-SIDE MEDITATION

Ut per aquas quae nunc rerum simulacra videmus.
LUCRETIUS

Go, travel 'mid the hills! The summer's hand
Hath shaken pleasant freshness o'er them all.
Go, travel 'mid the hills! There, tuneful streams
Are touching myriad stops, invisible;
And winds, and leaves, and birds, and your own thoughts
(Not the least glad) in wordless chorus, crowd
Around the thymele of Nature.
                              Go,
And travel onward. Soon shall leaf and bird,
Wind, stream, no longer sound. Thou shalt behold

Only the pathless sky, and houseless sward; 10
O'er which anon are spied innumerous sails
Of fisher vessels like the wings o' the hill,
And white as gulls above them, and as fast, –
But sink they – sink they out of sight. And now
The wind is springing upward in your face;
And, with its fresh-toned gushings, you may hear
Continuous sound which is not of the wind,
Nor of the thunder, nor o' the cataract's
Deep passion, nor o' the earthquake's wilder pulse;
But which rolls on in stern tranquillity, 20
As memories of evil o'er the soul; –
Boweth the bare broad Heaven. – What view you? sea – and
    sea!

The sea – the glorious sea! from side to side
Swinging the grandeur of his foamy strength,
And undersweeping the horizon, – on –
On – with his life and voice inscrutable.
Pause: sit you down in silence! I have read
Of that Athenian, who, when ocean raged,
Unchained the prisoned music of his lips
By shouting to the billows, sound for sound. 30
I marvel how his mind would let his tongue
Affront thereby the ocean's solemnness.
Are we not mute, or speak restrainedly,
When overhead the trampling tempests go,
Dashing their lightning from their hoofs? and when
We stand beside the bier? and when we see
The strong bow down to weep – and stray among
Places which dust or mind hath sanctified?
Yea! for such sights and acts do tear apart
The close and subtle clasping of a chain, 40
Formed not of gold, but of corroded brass,
Whose links are furnished from the common mine
Of every day's event, and want, and wish;
From work-times, diet-times, and sleeping-times:
And thence constructed, mean and heavy links
Within the pandemonic walls of sense
Enchain our deathless part, constrain our strength,
And waste the goodly stature of our soul.

Howbeit, we love this bondage; we do cleave
Unto the sordid and unholy thing,   50
Fearing the sudden wrench required to break
Those clasped links. Behold! all sights and sounds
In air, and sea, and earth, and under earth,
All flesh, all life, all ends, are mysteries;
And all that is mysterious dreadful seems,
And all we cannot understand we fear.
Ourselves do scare ourselves: we hide our sight
In artificial nature from the true,
And throw sensation's veil associative
On God's creation, man's intelligence;   60
Bowing our high imaginings to eat
Dust, like the serpent, once erect as they;
Binding conspicuous on our reason's brow
Phylacteries of shame; learning to feel
By rote, and act by rule (man's rule, not God's!),
Unto our words grow echoes, and our thoughts
A mechanism of spirit.
                            Can this last?
No! not for ay. We cannot subject ay
The heaven-born spirit to the earth-born flesh.
Tame lions *will* scent blood, and appetite   70
Carnivorous glare from out their restless eyes.
Passions, emotions, sudden changes, throw
Our nature back upon us, till we burn.
What warmed Cyrene's fount? As poets sing,
The *change* from light to dark, from dark to light.

All that doth force this nature back on us,
All that doth force the mind to view the mind,
Engend'reth what is named by men, *sublime*.
Thus when, our wonted valley left, we gain
The mountain's horrent brow, and mark from thence   80
The sweep of lands extending with the sky;
Or view the spanless plain; or turn our sight
Upon yon deep's immensity; – we breathe
As if our breath were marble: to and fro
Do reel our pulses, and our words are mute.
We cannot mete by parts, but grapple all;
We cannot measure with our eye, but soul;

And fear is on us. The extent unused,
Our spirit, sends, to spirit's element,
To seize upon abstraction: first on space, 90
The which *eternity in place* I deem;
And then upon eternity; till thought
Hath formed a mirror from their secret sense,
Wherein we view ourselves, and back recoil
At our own awful likeness; ne'ertheless,
Cling to that likeness with a wonder wild,
And while we tremble, glory – proud in fear.
So ends the prose of life: and so shall be
Unlocked her poetry's magnific store.
And so, thou pathless and perpetual sea, 100
So, o'er thy deeps, I brooded and must brood,
Whether I view thee in thy dreadful peace,
Like a spent warrior hanging in the sun
His glittering arms, and meditating death;
Or whether thy wild visage gath'reth shades,
What time thou marshall'st forth thy waves who hold
A covenant of storms, then roar and wind
Under the racking rocks; as martyrs lie
Wheel-bound; and, dying, utter lofty words!
Whether the strength of day is young and high, 110
Or whether, weary of the watch, he sits
Pale on thy wave, and weeps himself to death; –
In storm and calm, at morn and eventide,
Still have I stood beside thee, and out-thrown
My spirit onward on thine element, –
Beyond thine element, – to tremble low
Before those feet which trod thee as they trod
Earth, – to the holy, happy, peopled place,
Where there is no more sea. Yea, and my soul,
Having put on thy vast similitude, 120
Hath wildly moaned at her proper depth,
Echoed her proper musings, veiled in shade
Her secrets of decay, and exercised
An elemental strength, in casting up
Rare gems and things of death on fancy's shore,
Till Nature said 'Enough.'
                    Who longest dreams,
Dreams not for ever; seeing day and night

And corporal feebleness divide his dreams,
And on his elevate creations weigh
With hunger, cold, heat, darkness, weariness: 130
Else should we be like gods; else would the course
Of thought's free wheels, increased in speed and might
By an eterne volution, oversweep
The heights of wisdom, and invade her depths:
So, knowing all things, should we have all power;
For is not Knowledge power? But mighty spells
Our operation sear; the Babel must,
Or ere it touch the sky, fall down to earth:
The web, half formed, must tumble from our hands,
And, ere they can resume it, lie decayed.   140
Mind struggles vainly from the flesh. E'en so,
Hell's angel (saith a scroll apocryphal)
Shall, when the latter days of earth have shrunk
Before the blast of God, affect his heaven;
Lift his scarred brow, confirm his rebel heart,
Shoot his strong wings, and darken pole and pole, –
Till day be blotted into night; and shake
The fevered clouds, as if a thousand storms
Throbbed into life! Vain hope – vain strength – vain flight!
God's arm shall meet God's foe, and hurl him back!   150

THE TEMPEST

A FRAGMENT

Mors erat ante oculos.
LUCAN lib. ix

The forest made my home – the voiceful streams
My minstrel throng: the everlasting hills, –
Which marry with the firmament, and cry
Unto the brazen thunder, 'Come away,
Come from thy secret place, and try our strength,' –
Enwrapped me with their solemn arms. Here, light
Grew pale as darkness, scarèd by the shade
O' the forest Titans. Here, in piny state,

Reigned Night, the Aethiopian queen, and crowned
The charmèd brow of Solitude, her spouse.   10

*   *   *

A sign was on creation. You beheld
All things encoloured in a sulph'rous hue,
As day were sick with fear. The haggard clouds
O'erhung the utter lifelessness of air;
The top boughs of the forest, all aghast,
Stared in the face of Heaven; the deep-mouthed wind,
That hath a voice to bay the armèd sea,
Fled with a low cry like a beaten hound;
And only that askance the shadows flew
Some open-beakèd birds in wilderment,   20
Naught stirred abroad. All dumb did Nature seem,
In expectation of the coming storm.

It came in power. You soon might hear afar
The footsteps of the martial thunder sound
Over the mountain battlements; the sky
Being deep-stained with hues fantastical,
Red like to blood, and yellow like to fire,
And black like plumes at funerals; overhead
You might behold the lightning faintly gleam
Amid the clouds which thrill and gape aside,   30
And straight again shut up their solemn jaws,
As if to interpose between Heaven's wrath
And Earth's despair. Interposition brief!
Darkness is gathering out her mighty pall
Above us, and the pent-up rain is loosed,
Down trampling in its fierce delirium.

Was not my spirit gladdened, as with wine,
To hear the iron rain, and view the mark
Of battle on the banner of the clouds?
Did I not hearken for the battle-cry,   40
And rush along the bowing woods to meet
The riding Tempest – skyey cataracts
Hissing around him with rebellion vain?
Yea! and I lifted up my glorying voice
In an 'All hail'; when, wildly resonant,
As brazen chariots rushing from the war,

As passioned waters gushing from the rock,
As thousand crashèd woods, the thunder cried:
And at his cry the forest tops were shook
As by the woodman's axe; and far and near   50
Staggered the mountains with a muttered dread.

All hail unto the lightning! hurriedly
His lurid arms are glaring through the air,
Making the face of Heaven to show like hell!
Let him go breathe his sulphur stench about,
And, pale with death's own mission, lord the storm!
Again the gleam – the glare: I turned to hail
Death's mission: at my feet there lay the dead!

The dead – the dead lay there! I could not view
(For Night espoused the storm, and made all dark)   60
Its features, but the lightning in its course
Shivered above a white and corpse-like heap,
Stretched in the path, as if to show his prey,
And have a triumph ere he passed. Then I
Crouched down upon the ground, and groped about
Until I touched that thing of flesh, rain-drenched,
And chill, and soft. Nathless, I did refrain
My soul from natural horror! I did lift
The heavy head, half-bedded in the clay,
Unto my knee; and passed my fingers o'er   70
The wet face, touching every lineament,
Until I found the brow; and chafed its chill,
To know if life yet lingered in its pulse.
And while I was so busied, there did leap
From out the entrails of the firmament,
The lightning, who his white unblenching breath
Blew in the dead man's face, discovering it
As by a staring day. I knew that face –
His, who did hate me – his, whom I did hate!

I shrunk not – spake not – sprang not from the ground!   80
But felt my lips shake without cry or breath,
And mine heart wrestle in my breast to still
The tossing of its pulses; and a cold,
Instead of living blood, o'ercreep my brow.

Albeit such darkness brooded all around,
I had dread knowledge that the open eyes
Of that dead man were glaring up to mine,
With their unwinking, unexpressive stare;
And mine I could not shut nor turn away
The man was my familiar. I had borne   90
Those eyes to scowl on me their living hate,

Better than I could bear their deadliness:
I had endured the curses of those lips
Far better than their silence. Oh, constrained
And awful silence! – awful peace of death!
There is an answer to all questioning,
That one word – *death*. Our bitterness can throw
No look upon the face of death, and live.
The burning thoughts that erst my soul illumed
Were quenched at once; as tapers in a pit   100
Wherein the vapour-witches weirdly reign
In charge of darkness. Farewell all the past!
It was out-blotted from my memory's eyes
When clay's cold silence pleaded for its sin.

Farewell the elemental war! farewell
The clashing of the shielded clouds – the cry
Of scathèd echoes! I no longer knew
Silence from sound, but wandered far away
Into the deep Eleusis of mine heart,
To learn its secret things. When armèd foes   110
Meet on one deck with impulse violent,
The vessel quakes thro' all her oaken ribs,
And shivers in the sea; so with mine heart:
For there had battled in her solitudes,
Contrary spirits; sympathy with power,
And stooping unto power; – the energy
And passiveness, – the thunder and the death!

Within me was a nameless thought: it closed
The Janus of my soul on echoing hinge,
And said 'Peace!' with a voice like War's. I bowed,   120
And trembled at its voice: it gave a key,
Empowered to open out all mysteries

Of soul and flesh; of men, who doth begin,
But endeth not; of life, and *after life*.

      *   *   *

Day came at last: her light showed grey and sad,
As hatched by tempest, and could scarce prevail
Over the shaggy forest to imprint
Its outline on the sky – expressionless,
Almost sans shadow as sans radiance:
An idiocy of light. I wakened from   130
My deep unslumb'ring dream, but uttered naught.
My living I uncoupled from the dead,
And looked out, 'mid the swart and sluggish air,
For place to make a grave. A mighty tree
Above me, his gigantic arms outstretched,
Poising the clouds. A thousand muttered spells
Of every ancient wind and thund'rous storm
Had been off-shaken from his scatheless bark.
He had heard distant years sweet concord yield,
And go to silence; having firmly kept   140
Majestical companionship with Time.
Anon his strength waxed proud: his tusky roots
Forced for themselves a path on every side,
Riving the earth; and, in their savage scorn,
Casting it from them like a thing unclean,
Which might impede his naked clambering
Unto the heavens. Now blasted, peeled, he stood.
By the gone night, whose lightning had come in
And rent him, even as it rent the man
Beneath his shade: and there the strong and weak   150
Communion joined in deathly agony.
There, underneath, I lent my feverish strength,
To scoop a lodgement for the traveller's corse.
I gave it to the silence and the pit,
And strewed the heavy earth on all: and then –
I – I, whose hands had formed that silent house, –
I could not look thereon, but turned and wept!

      *   *   *

O Death – O crownèd Death – pale-steedèd Death!
Whose name doth make our respiration brief,
Muffling the spirit's drum! Thou, whom men know   160
Alone by charnel-houses, and the dark

Sweeping of funeral feathers, and the scath
Of happy days, – love deemed inviolate!
Thou of the shrouded face, which to have seen
Is to be very awful, like thyself! –
Thou, whom all flesh shall see! – thou, who dost call,
And there is none to answer! – thou, whose call
Changeth all beauty into what we fear,
Changeth all glory into what we tread,
Genius to silence, wrath to nothingness,   170
And love – not love! – thou hast no change for love!
Thou, who art Life's betrothed, and bear'st her forth
To scare her with sad sights, – who hast thy joy
Where'er the peopled towns are dumb with plague, –
Where'er the battle and the vulture meet, –
Where'er the deep sea writhes like Laocoon
Beneath the serpent winds, and vessels split
On secret rocks, and men go gurgling down,
Down, down, to lose their shriekings in the depth!
O universal thou! who comest ay   180
Among the minstrels, and their tongue is tied;
Among the sophists, and their brain is still;
Among the mourners, and their wail is done;
Among the dancers, and their tinkling feet
No more make echoes on the tombing earth;
Among the wassail rout, and all the lamps
Are quenched, and withered the wine-pouring hands!
Mine heart is armèd not in panoply
Of the old Roman iron, nor assumes
The Stoic valour. 'Tis a human heart,   190
And so confesses, with a human fear; –
That only for the hope the cross inspires,
That only for the MAN who died and lives,
'Twould crouch beneath thy sceptre's royalty,
With faintness of the pulse, and backward cling
To life. But knowing what I soothly know,
High-seeming Death, I dare thee! and have hope,
In God's good time, of showing to thy face
An unsuccumbing spirit, which sublime

May cast away the low anxieties   200
That wait upon the flesh – the reptile moods;
And enter that eternity to come,
Where live the dead, and only Death shall die.

From

THE SERAPHIM,
AND OTHER POEMS
(1838)

A TRUE DREAM

(Dreamed at Sidmouth, 1833)

I had not an evil end in view,
   Tho' I trod the evil way;
And why I practised the magic art,
   My dream it did not say.

I unsealed the vial mystical,
   I outpoured the liquid thing,
And while the smoke came wreathing out,
   I stood unshuddering.

The smoke came wreathing, wreathing out,
   All mute, and dark, and slow,   10
Till its cloud was stained with a fleshly hue,
   And a fleshly form 'gan show.

Then paused the smoke – the fleshly form
   Looked steadfast in mine ee,
His beard was black as a thundercloud,
   But I trembled not to see.

I unsealed the vial mystical,
   I outpoured the liquid thing,
And while the smoke came wreathing out,
   I stood unshuddering.   20

The smoke came wreathing, wreathing out,
   All mute, and dark and slow,
Till its cloud was stained with a fleshly hue,
   And a fleshly form 'gan show.

Then paused the smoke – but the mortal form
   A garment swart did veil,
I looked on it with fixed heart,
   Yea – not a pulse did fail!

I unsealed the vial mystical,
  I outpoured the liquid thing,   30
And while the smoke came wreathing out,
  I stood unshuddering.

The smoke came wreathing, wreathing out,
  And now it was faster and lighter,
And it bore on its folds the rainbow's hues,
  Heaven could not show them brighter.

Then paused the smoke, the rainbow's hues
  Did a childish face express –
The rose in the cheek, the blue in the eyne
  The yellow in the tress.   40

The fair young child shook back her hair,
  And round me her arms did wreathe,
Her lips were hard and cold as stone,
  They sucked away my breath.

I cast her off as she clung to me,
  With hate and shuddering;
I brake the vials, and foresware
  The cursed, cursed thing.

Anon outspake a brother of mine –
  'Upon the pavement, see,   50
Besprent with noisome poison slime,
  Those twining serpents three.'

Anon outspake my wildered heart
  As I saw the serpent train –
'I have called up three existences
  I cannot quench again.

'Alas! with unholy company,
  My lifetime they will scathe;
They will hiss in the storm, and on sunny days
  Will gleam and thwart my path.'   60

Outspake that pitying brother of mine –
  'Now nay, my sister, nay,
I will pour on them oil of vitriol,
  And burn their lives away.'

'Now nay, my brother, torture not,
  Now hold thine hand, and spare.'
He poured on them oil of vitriol,
  And did not heed my prayer.

I saw the drops of torture fall;
  I heard the shriekings rise,
While the serpents writhed in agony
  Beneath my dreaming eyes.

And while they shrieked, and while they writhed,
  And inward and outward wound,
They waxed larger, and their wail
  Assumed a human sound.

And glared their eyes, and their slimy scales
  Were roundly and redly bright,
Most like the lidless sun, what time
  Thro' the mist he meets your sight.

And larger and larger they waxed still,
  And longer still and longer;
And they shrieked in their pain, 'Come, come to us,
  We are stronger, we are stronger.'

Upon the ground I laid mine head,
  And heard the wailing sound;
I did not wail, I did not writhe –
  I laid me on the ground.

And larger and larger they waxed still
  And longer still and longer;
And they shrieked in their pangs, 'Come, come to us,
  We are stronger, we are stronger.'

70

80

90

Then up I raised my burning brow,
   My quiv'ring arms on high;
I spake in prayer, and I named aloud
   The name of sanctity.

And as in my anguish I prayed and named
   Aloud the holy name,
The impious mocking serpent voice
   Did echo back the same.   100

And larger and larger they waxed still,
   And stronger still and longer!
And they shrieked in their pangs, 'Come, come to us,
   We are stronger, we are stronger.'

Then out from among them arose a form
   In shroud of death indued –
I fled from him with wings of wind,
   With whirlwinds he pursued.

        *   *   *

I stood by a chamber door, and thought
   Within its gloom to hide;   110
I locked the door, and the while forgot
   That I stood on the outer side.

And the knell of mine heart was wildly tolled
   While I grasped still the key;
For I felt beside me the icy breath,
   And knew that *that* was *he*.

I heard these words, 'Whoe'er doth *taste*,
   Will *drink* the magic bowl;
So her body may do my mission here
   Companioned by her soul.'   120

Mine hand was cold as the key it held,
   Mine heart had an iron weight;
I saw a gleam, I heard a sound –
   The clock was striking eight.

MAN AND NATURE

A sad man on a summer day
Did look upon the earth and say –

'Purple cloud, the hill-top binding,
Folded hills, the valleys wind in,
Valleys, with fresh streams among you,
Streams, with bosky trees along you,
Trees, with many birds and blossoms,
Birds, with music-trembling bosoms,
Blossoms, dropping dews that wreathe you
To your fellow flowers beneath you,   10
Flowers, that constellate on earth,
Earth, that shakest to the mirth
Of the merry Titan ocean,
All his shining hair in motion!
Why am I thus the only one
Who can be dark beneath the sun?'

But when the summer day was past,
He looked to heaven and smiled at last,
Self-answered so –
                    'Because, O cloud,
Pressing with thy crumpled shroud   20
Heavily on mountain top, –
Hills, that almost seem to drop
Stricken with a misty death
To the valleys underneath, –
Valleys, sighing with the torrent, –
Waters, streaked with branches horrent, –
Branchless trees, that shake your head
Wildly o'er your blossoms spread
Where the common flowers are found, –
Flowers, with foreheads to the ground, –   30
Ground, that shriekest while the sea
With his iron smiteth thee –
I am, besides, the only one
Who can be bright *without* the sun.'

THE DESERTED GARDEN

I mind me in the days departed,
How often underneath the sun
With childish bounds I used to run
  To a garden long deserted.

The beds and walks were vanished quite;
And wheresoe'er had struck the spade,
The greenest grasses Nature laid,
  To sanctify her right.

I called the place my wilderness,
For no one entered there but I;
The sheep looked in, the grass to espy,
  And passed it ne'ertheless.

The trees were interwoven wild,
And spread their boughs enough about
To keep both sheep and shepherd out,
  But not a happy child.

Adventurous joy it was for me!
I crept beneath the boughs, and found
A circle smooth of mossy ground
  Beneath a poplar tree.

Old garden rose-trees hedged it in,
Bedropt with roses waxen-white
Well satisfied with dew and light
  And careless to be seen.

Long years ago it might befall,
When all the garden flowers were trim,
The grave old gardener prided him
  On these the most of all.

Some lady, stately overmuch,
Here moving with a silken noise,
Has blushed beside them at the voice
  That likened her to such.

And these, to make a diadem,
She often may have plucked and twined,
Half-smiling as it came to mind
   That few would look at *them*.

Oh, little thought that lady proud,
A child would watch her fair white rose,
When buried lay her whiter brows,
   And silk was changed for shroud! —   40

Nor thought that gardener (full of scorns
For men unlearned and simple phrase),
A child would bring it all its praise
   By creeping through the thorns!

To me upon my low moss seat,
Though never a dream the roses sent
Of science or love's compliment,
   I ween they smelt as sweet.

It did not move my grief to see
The trace of human step departed: 50
Because the garden was deserted,
   The blither place for me!

Friends, blame me not! a narrow ken
Has childhood 'twixt the sun and sward:
We draw the moral afterward —
   We feel the gladness then.

And gladdest hours for me did glide
In silence at the rose-tree wall;
A thrush made gladness musical
   Upon the other side.   60

Nor he nor I did e'er incline
To peck or pluck the blossom white;
How should I know but roses might
   Lead lives as glad as mine?

To make my hermit-home complete,
I brought clear water from the spring
Praised in its own low murmuring, –
    And cresses glossy wet.

And so, I thought, my likeness grew
(Without the melancholy tale)   70
To 'gentle hermit of the dale,'
    And Angelina too.

For oft I read within my nook
Such minstrel stories; till the breeze
Made sounds poetic in the trees, –
    And then I shut the book.

If I shut this wherein I write
I hear no more the wind athwart
Those trees, – nor feel that childish heart
    Delighting in delight.   80

My childhood from my life is parted,
My footstep from the moss which drew
Its fairy circle round: anew
    The garden is deserted.

Another thrush may there rehearse
The madrigals which sweetest are;
No more for me! – myself afar
    Do sing a sadder verse.

Ah me, ah me! when erst I lay
In that child's-nest so greenly wrought,   90
I laughed unto myself and thought
    'The time will pass away.'

And still I laughed, and did not fear
But that, whene'er was past away
The childish time, some happier play
    My womanhood would cheer.

I knew the time would pass away,
And yet, beside the rose-tree wall,
Dear God, how seldom, if at all,
   Did I look up to pray!   100

The time is past; – and now that grows
The cypress high among the trees,
And I behold white sepulchres
   As well as the white rose, –

When graver, meeker thoughts are given,
And I have learnt to lift my face,
Reminded how earth's greenest place
   The colour draws from heaven, –

It something saith for earthly pain,
But more for Heavenly promise free,   110
That I who was, would shrink to be
   That happy child again.

THE SEA-MEW

I

How joyously the young sea-mew
Lay dreaming on the waters blue
Whereon our little bark had thrown
A little shade, the only one,
But shadows ever man pursue.

II

Familiar with the waves and free
As if their own white foam were he,
His heart upon the heart of ocean
Lay learning all its mystic motion,
And throbbing to the throbbing sea.   10

III

And such a brightness in his eye
As if the ocean and the sky
Within him had lit up and nurst
A soul God gave him not at first,
To comprehend their majesty.

IV

We were not cruel, yet did sunder
His white wing from the blue waves under,
And bound it, while his fearless eyes
Shone up to ours in calm surprise,
As deeming us some ocean wonder.   20

V

We bore our ocean bird unto
A grassy place where he might view
The flowers that curtsey to the bees,
The waving of the tall green trees,
The falling of the silver dew.

VI

But flowers of earth were pale to him
Who had seen the rainbow fishes swim;
And when earth's dew around him lay
He thought of ocean's wingèd spray,
And his eye waxèd sad and dim.   30

VII

The green trees round him only made
A prison with their darksome shade;
And drooped his wing, and mournèd he
For his own boundless glittering sea –
Albeit he knew not they could fade.

VIII

Then One her gladsome face did bring,
Her gentle voice's murmuring,
In ocean's stead his heart to move
And teach him what was human love:
He thought it a strange mournful thing.   40

IX

He lay down in his grief to die,
(First looking to the sea-like sky
That hath no waves) because, alas!
Our human touch did on him pass,
And with our touch, our agony.

A SEA-SIDE WALK

I

We walked beside the sea
After a day which perished silently
Of its own glory – like the princess weird,
Who, combating the Genius, scorched and seared,
Uttered with burning breath, 'Ho! victory!'
And sank adown, an heap of ashes pale:
        So runs the Arab tale.

II

The sky above us showed
A universal and unmoving cloud,
On which the cliffs permitted us to see   10
Only the outline of their majesty,
As master-minds, when gazed at by the crowd!
And shining with a gloom, the water gray
        Swang in its moon-taught way.

III

Nor moon, nor stars were out:
They did not dare to tread so soon about,
Though trembling, in the footsteps of the sun;
The light was neither night's nor day's, but one
Which, life-like, had a beauty in its doubt,
And Silence's impassioned breathings round   20
    Seemed wandering into sound.

IV

O solemn-beating heart
Of nature! I have knowledge that thou art
Bound unto man's by cords he cannot sever –
And, what time they are slackened by him ever,
So to attest his own supernal part,
Still runneth thy vibration fast and strong
    The slackened cord along:

V

For though we never spoke
Of the gray water and the shaded rock,   30
Dark wave and stone unconsciously were fused
Into the plaintive speaking that we used
Of absent friends and memories unforsook;
And, had we seen each other's face, we had
    Seen haply each was sad.

MY DOVES

O Weisheit! Du red'st wie eine Taube!
GOETHE

My little doves have left a nest
   Upon an Indian tree,
Whose leaves fantastic take their rest
   Or motion from the sea;
For, ever there, the sea-winds go
With sunlit paces to and fro.

The tropic flowers looked up to it,
   The tropic stars looked down,
And there my little doves did sit,
   With feathers softly brown,   10
And glittering eyes that showed their right
To general Nature's deep delight.

And God them taught, at every close
   Of murmuring waves beyond,
And green leaves round, to interpose
   Their choral voices fond,
Interpreting that love must be
The meaning of the earth and sea.

Fit ministers! Of living loves,
   Theirs hath the calmest fashion,   20
Their living voice the likest moves
   To lifeless intonation,
The lovely monotone of springs
And winds, and such insensate things.

My little doves were ta'en away
   From that glad nest of theirs,
Across an ocean rolling grey,
   And tempest-clouded airs:
My little doves, – who lately knew
The sky and wave by warmth and blue!   30

And now, within the city prison,
　　In mist and chillness pent,
With sudden upward look they listen
　　For sounds of past content –
For lapse of water, swell of breeze,
Or nut-fruit falling from the trees.

The stir without the glow of passion,
　　The triumph of the mart,
The gold and silver as they clash on
　　Man's cold metallic heart –   40
The roar of wheels, the cry for bread, –
These only sounds are heard instead.

Yet still, as on my human hand
　　Their fearless heads they lean,
And almost seem to understand
　　What human musings mean,
(Their eyes, with such a plaintive shine,
Are fastened upwardly to mine!)

Soft falls their chant as on the nest
　　Beneath the sunny zone;   50
For love that stirred it in their breast
　　Has not aweary grown,
And 'neath the city's shade can keep
The well of music clear and deep.

And love that keeps the music, fills
　　With pastoral memories:
All echoings from out the hills,
　　All droppings from the skies,
All flowings from the wave and wind,
Remembered in their chant, I find.   60

So teach ye me the wisest part,
　　My little doves! to move
Along the city-ways with heart
　　Assured by holy love,
And vocal with such songs as own
A fountain to the world unknown.

'Twas hard to sing by Babel's stream –
  More hard, in Babel's street!
But if the soulless creatures deem
  Their music not unmeet   70
For sunless walls – let *us* begin,
Who wear immortal wings within!

To me, fair memories belong
  Of scenes that used to bless,
For no regret, but present song,
  And lasting thankfulness,
And very soon to break away,
Like types, in purer things than they.

I will have hopes that cannot fade,
  For flowers the valley yields!   80
I will have humble thoughts instead
  Of silent, dewy fields!
My spirit and my God shall be
My seaward hill, my boundless sea.

NIGHT AND THE MERRY MAN

NIGHT

'Neath my moon what doest thou.
With a somewhat paler brow
Than she giveth to the ocean?
He, without a pulse or motion,
Muttering low before her stands,
Lifting his invoking hands,
Like a seer before a sprite,
To catch her oracles of light.
But thy soul out-trembles now
Many pulses on thy brow!   10
Where be all thy laughters clear,
Others laughed alone to hear?

Where, thy quaint jests, said for fame?
Where, thy dances, mixed with game?
Where, thy festive companies,
Moonèd o'er with ladies' eyes,
All more bright for thee, I trow?
'Neath my moon, what doest thou?

THE MERRY MAN

I am digging my warm heart,
Till I find its coldest part;   20
I am digging wide and low,
Further than a spade will go;
Till that, when the pit is deep
And large enough, I there may heap
All my present pain and past
Joy, dead things that look aghast
By the daylight. – Now 'tis done.
Throw them in, by one and one!
I must laugh, at rising sun.

Memories – of fancy's golden   30
Treasures which my hands have holden,
Till the chillness made them ache;
Of childhood's hopes, that used to wake
If birds were in a singing strain,
And for less cause, sleep again;
Of the moss-seat in the wood,
Where I trysted solitude;
Of the hill-top, where the wind
Used to follow me behind,
Then in sudden rush to blind   40
Both my glad eyes with my hair
Taken gladly in the snare;
Of the climbing up the rocks, –
Of the playing 'neath the oaks,
Which retain beneath them now
Only shadow of the bough;
Of the lying on the grass
While the clouds did overpass,
Only they, so lightly driven,

Seeming betwixt me and Heaven!   50
Of the little prayers serene,
Murmuring of earth and sin;
Of large-leaved philosophy
Leaning from my childish knee;
Of poetic book sublime,
Soul-kissed for the first dear time, –
Greek or English, – ere I knew
Life was not a poem too.
Throw them in, by one and one!
I must laugh, at rising sun.   60
Of the glorious ambitions,
Yet unquenched by their fruitions;
Of the reading out the nights;
Of the straining at mad heights;
Of achievements, less descried
By a dear few, than magnified;
Of praises, from the many earned,
When praise from love was undiscerned;
Of the sweet reflecting gladness,
Softened by itself to sadness –   70
Throw them in, by one and one!
I must laugh, at rising sun.

What are these? more, more than these!
Throw in, dearer memories! –
Of voices – whereof but to speak,
Makes mine own all sunk and weak;
Of smiles, the thought of which is sweeping
All my soul to floods of weeping;
Of looks, whose absence fain would weigh
My looks to the ground for ay;   80
Of clasping hands – ah me! I wring
Mine, and in a tremble fling
Downward, downward, all this paining!
Partings, with the sting remaining;
Meetings, with a deeper throe,
Since the joy is ruined so;
Changes, with a fiery burning –
(Shadows upon all the turning);
Thoughts of – with a storm they came –

Them, I have not breath to name.   90
Downward, downward, be they cast
In the pit! and now at last
My work beneath the moon is done,
And I shall laugh, at rising sun.

But let me pause or ere I cover
All my treasures darkly over.
I will speak not in thine ears,
Only tell my beaded tears
Silently, most silently!
When the last is calmly told,   100
Let that same moist rosary
With the rest sepùlchred be.
Finished now. The darksome mould
Sealeth up the darksome pit.
I will lay no stone on it:
Grasses I will sow instead,
Fit for Queen Titania's tread;
Flowers, encoloured with the sun,
And αι αι written upon none.
Thus, whenever saileth by   110
The Lady World of dainty eye,
Not a grief shall here remain,
Silken shoon to damp or stain;
And while she lisps, 'I have not seen
Any place more smooth and clean' . . .
Here she cometh! – Ha, ha! – who
Laughs as loud as I can do?

THE ROMAUNT OF MARGRET

Can my affections find out nothing best,
But still and still remove?
QUARLES

I

I plant a tree whose leaf
    The yew-tree leaf will suit;
But when its shade is o'er you laid,
    Turn round and pluck the fruit.
Now reach my harp from off the wall
    Where shines the sun aslant!
The sun may shine and we be cold –
O hearken, loving hearts and bold,
    Unto my wild romaunt,
                Margret, Margret.   10

II

Sitteth the fair ladye
    Close to the river side,
Which runneth on with a merry tone
    Her merry thoughts to guide.
    It runneth through the trees,
        It runneth by the hill,
Nathless the lady's thoughts have found
    A way more pleasant still.
                Margret, Margret.

III

The night is in her hair   20
    And giveth shade to shade,
And the pale moonlight on her forehead white
    Like a spirit's hand is laid;
  Her lips part with a smile
    Instead of speakings done:
I ween, she thinketh of a voice,
    Albeit uttering none.
                Margret, Margret.

IV

All little birds do sit
    With heads beneath their wings: 30
Nature doth seem in a mystic dream,
    Absorbed from her living things.
  That dream by that ladye
    Is certes unpartook,
For she looketh to the high cold stars
    With a tender human look.
                Margret, Margret.

V

The lady's shadow lies
    Upon the running river;
It lieth no less in its quietness,   40
    For that which resteth never:
  Most like a trusting heart
    Upon a passing faith, –
Or as, upon the course of life,
    The steadfast doom of death.
                Margret, Margret.

VI

The lady doth not move,
    The lady doth not dream,
Yet she seeth her shade no longer laid
    In rest upon the stream.   50
It shaketh without wind,
    It parteth from the tide,
It standeth upright in the cleft moonlight,
    It sitteth at her side.
                    Margret, Margret.

VII

Look in its face, ladye,
    And keep thee from thy swound!
With a spirit bold, thy pulses hold,
    And hear its voice's sound.
For so will sound thy voice,   60
    When thy face is to the wall;
And such will be thy face, ladye,
    When the maidens work thy pall.
                    Margret, Margret.

VIII

'Am I not like to thee?' –
    The voice was calm and low;
And between each word you might have heard
    The silent forests grow.
'*The like may sway the like,*'
    By which mysterious law   70
Mine eyes from thine and my lips from thine
    The light and breath may draw.
                    Margret, Margret.

IX

'My lips do need thy breath,
My lips do need thy smile,
And my pallid eyne, that light in thine
Which met the stars erewhile.
Yet go with light and life,
If that thou lovest one
In all the earth, who loveth thee   80
As truly as the sun,
Margret, Margret.

X

Her cheek had waxèd white
Like cloud at fall of snow;
Then like to one at set of sun
It waxèd red alsò;
For love's name maketh bold,
As if the loved were near.
And then she sighed the deep long sigh
Which cometh after fear.   90
Margret, Margret.

XI

'Now sooth, I fear thee not –
Shall never fear thee now!'
(And a noble sight was the sudden light
Which lit her lifted brow.)
'Can earth be dry of streams?
Or hearts, of love?' she said;
'Who doubteth love, can know not love:
He is already dead.'
Margret, Margret.   100

XII

'I have' . . . and here her lips
    Some words in pause did keep,
And gave the while a quiet smile,
    As if they paused in sleep, –
'I have . . . a brother dear,
    A knight of knightly fame!
I broidered him a knightly scarf
    With letters of my name.
                Margret, Margret.

XIII

'I fed his grey goss-hawk,   110
    I kissed his fierce bloodhound,
I sate at home when he might come
    And caught his horn's far sound:
I sang him hunters' songs,
    I poured him the red wine –
He looked across the cup and said,
    I love thee, sister mine.'
                Margret, Margret.

XIV

IT trembled on the grass,
    With a low, shadowy laughter;   120
The sounding river which rolled for ever,
    Stood dumb and stagnant after.
'Brave knight thy brother is!
    But better loveth he
Thy chaliced wine than thy chanted song,
    And better both, than thee,
                Margret, Margret.'

XV

The lady did not heed
   The river's silence while
Her own thoughts still ran at their will,   130
   And calm was still her smile.
'My little sister wears
   The look our mother wore:
I smooth her locks with a golden comb,
   I bless her evermore.'
                  Margret, Margret.

XVI

'I gave her my first bird,
   When first my voice it knew;
I made her share my posies rare,
   And told her where they grew.   140
I taught her God's dear name
   With prayer and praise, to tell –
She looked from heaven into my face,
   And said, *I love thee well.*'
                  Margret, Margret.

XVII

IT trembled on the grass
   With a low, shadowy laughter:
You could see each bird as it woke and stared
   Through the shrivelled foliage after.
'Fair child thy sister is!   150
   But better loveth she
Thy golden comb than thy gathered flowers,
   And better both, than thee,
                  Margret, Margret.'

XVIII

The lady did not heed
    The withering on the bough:
Still calm her smile, albeit the while
    A little pale her brow.
'I have a father old,
    The lord of ancient halls;   160
An hundred friends are in his court,
    Yet only me he calls.
                Margret, Margret.

XIX

'An hundred knights are in his court,
    Yet read I by his knee;
And when forth they go to the tourney show,
    I rise not up to see.
'Tis a weary book to read,
    My tryst's at set of sun,
But loving and dear beneath the stars   170
    Is his blessing when I've done.'
                Margret, Margret.

XX

IT trembled on the grass
    With a low, shadowy laughter;
And moon and star, though bright and far,
    Did shrink and darken after.
'High lord thy father is!
    But better loveth he
His ancient halls than his hundred friends,
    His ancient halls, than thee,   180
                Margret, Margret.'

XXI

The lady did not heed
    That the far stars did fail:
Still calm her smile, albeit the while . . .
    Nay, but she is not pale!
  'I have a more than friend
    Across the mountains dim:
No other's voice is soft to me,
    Unless it nameth *him*.'

Margret, Margret.   190

XXII

'Though louder beats mine heart
    I know his tread again,
And his far plume ay, unless turned away,
    For the tears do blind me then.
  We brake no gold, a sign
    Of stronger faith to be, –
But I wear his last look in my soul,
    Which said, *I love but thee!*'

Margret, Margret.

XXIII

IT trembled on the grass
    With a low, shadowy laughter;
And the wind did toll, as a passing soul
    Were sped by church-bell after;
  And shadows, 'stead of light,
    Fell from the stars above,
In flakes of darkness on her face
    Still bright with trusting love.

Margret, Margret.

200

XXIV

'He *loved* but only thee!
  That love is transient too: 210
The wild hawk's bill doth dabble still
  I' the mouth that vowed thee true.
Will he open his dull eyes,
  When tears fall on his brow?
Behold, the death-worm to his heart
  Is a nearer thing than *thou*,
      Margret, Margret.'

XXV

Her face was on the ground –
  None saw the agony,
But the men at sea did that night agree   220
  They heard a drowning cry;
And when the morning brake,
  Fast rolled the river's tide,
With the green trees waving overhead,
  And a white corse laid beside.
      Margret, Margret.

XXVI

A knight's bloodhound and he
  The funeral watch did keep;
With a thought o' the chase he stroked its face
  As it howled to see him weep.   230
A fair child kissed the dead,
  But shrank before its cold;
And alone yet proudly in his hall
  Did stand a baron old.
      Margret, Margret.

XXVII

Hang up my harp again!
    I have no voice for song:
Not song, but wail, and mourners pale,
    Not bards, to love belong.
    O failing human love!
      O light, by darkness known!
O false, the while thou treadest earth!
      O deaf beneath the stone!
               Margret, Margret.

240

A ROMANCE OF THE GANGES

I

Seven maidens 'neath the midnight
    Stand near the river-sea,
Whose water sweepeth white around
    The shadow of the tree.
The moon and earth are face to face,
    And earth is slumbering deep;
The wave-voice seems the voice of dreams
    That wander through her sleep.
               The river floweth on.

II

What bring they 'neath the midnight,
    Beside the river-sea?
They bring the human heart wherein
    No nightly calm can be, –
That droppeth never with the wind,
    Nor drieth with the dew:
Oh, calm it, God! Thy calm is broad
    To cover spirits, too.
               The river floweth on.

10

III

The maidens lean them over
  The waters, side by side,   20
And shun each other's deepening eyes,
  And gaze adown the tide;
For each within a little boat
  A little lamp hath put,
And heaped for freight some lily's weight
  Or scarlet rose half shut.
                The river floweth on.

IV

Of shell of coco carven,
  Each little boat is made:
Each carries a lamp, and carries a flower,   30
  And carries a hope unsaid;
And when the boat hath carried the lamp
  Unquenched, till out of sight,
The maiden is sure that love will endure, –
  But love will fail with light.
                The river floweth on.

V

Why, all the stars are ready
  To symbolize the soul,
The stars untroubled by the wind,
  Unwearied as they roll;   40
And yet the soul by instinct sad
  Reverts to symbols low –
To that small flame, whose very name
  Breathed o'er it, shakes it so!
                The river floweth on.

VI

Six boats are on the river,
  Seven maidens on the shore,
While still above them steadfastly
  The stars shine evermore.
Go, little boats, go soft and safe,   50
  And guard the symbol spark! –
The boats aright go safe and bright
  Across the waters dark.
                    The river floweth on.

VII

The maiden Luti watcheth
  Where onwardly they float:
That look in her dilating eyes
  Might seem to drive her boat!
Her eyes still mark the constant fire,
  And kindling unawares   60
That hopeful while, she lets a smile
  Creep silent through her prayers.
                    The river floweth on.

VIII

The smile – where hath it wandered?
  She riseth from her knee,
She holds her dark, wet locks away –
  There is no light to see!
She cries a quick and bitter cry –
  'Nuleeni, launch me thine!
We must have light abroad to-night,   70
  For all the wreck of mine.'
                    The river floweth on.

IX

'I do remember watching
  Beside this river-bed,
When on my childish knee was laid
  My dying father's head;
I turned mine own, to keep the tears
  From falling on his face:
What doth it prove when Death and Love
  Choose out the self-same place?'   80
                      The river floweth on.

X

'They say the dead are joyful
  The death-change here receiving:
Who say – ah, me! – who dare to say
  Where joy comes to the living?
Thy boat, Nuleeni! look not sad –
  Light up the waters rather!
I weep no faithless lover where
  I wept a loving father.'
                      The river floweth on.   90

XI

'My heart foretold his falsehood
  Ere my little boat grew dim:
And though I closed mine eyes to dream
  That one last dream of *him*,
They shall not now be wet to see
  The shining vision go:
From earth's cold love I look above
  To the holy house of snow.'
                      The river floweth on.

XII

'Come thou – thou never knewest   100
    A grief, that thou shouldst fear one!
Thou wearest still the happy look
    That shines beneath a dear one;
Thy humming-bird is in the sun,
    Thy cuckoo in the grove,
And all the three broad worlds, for thee
    Are full of wandering love.'
                          The river floweth on.

XIII

'Why, maiden, dost thou loiter?
    What secret wouldst thou cover?   110
That peepul cannot hide thy boat,
    And I can guess thy lover.
I heard thee sob his name in sleep . . .
    It was a name I knew;
Come, little maid, be not afraid,
    But let us prove him true!'
                          The river floweth on.

XIV

The little maiden cometh,
    She cometh shy and slow,
I ween she seeth through her lids,   120
    They drop adown so low;
Her tresses meet her small bare feet –
    She stands and speaketh nought,
Yet blusheth red, as if she said
    The name she only thought.
                          The river floweth on.

XV

She knelt beside the water,
　　She lighted up the flame,
And o'er her youthful forehead's calm
　　The fitful radiance came: –　　　　　　　　130
'Go, little boat, go, soft and safe,
　　And guard the symbol spark!'
Soft, safe, doth float the little boat
　　Across the waters dark.
　　　　　　　　　　　The river floweth on.

XVI

Glad tears her eyes have blinded,
　　The light they cannot reach;
She turneth with that sudden smile
　　She learnt before her speech –
'I do not hear his voice! the tears　　　　　140
　　Have dimmed my light away!
But the symbol light will last to-night,
　　The love will last for ay.'
　　　　　　　　　　　The river floweth on.

XVII

Then Luti spake behind her,
　　Outspake she bitterly,
'By the symbol light that lasts to-night,
　　Wilt vow a vow to me?' –
Nuleeni gazeth up her face,
　　Soft answer maketh she:　　　　　　　　150
'By loves that last when lights are past,
　　I vow that vow to thee!'
　　　　　　　　　　　The river floweth on.

XVIII

An earthly look had Luti
   Though her voice was deep as prayer:
'The rice is gathered from the plains
   To cast upon thine hair.
But when *he* comes, his marriage-band
   Around thy neck to throw,
Thy bride-smile raise to meet his gaze,   160
And whisper, – *There is one betrays,*
   While Luti suffers woe.'
                The river floweth on.

XIX

'And when in seasons after,
   Thy little bright-faced son
Shall lean against thy knee and ask
   What deeds his sire hath done,
Press deeper down thy mother-smile
   His glossy curls among –
View deep his pretty childish eyes,   170
And whisper, – *There is none denies,*
   While Luti speaks of wrong.'
                The river floweth on.

XX

Nuleeni looked in wonder,
   Yet softly answered she:
'By loves that last when lights are past,
   I vowed that vow to thee.
But why glads it thee that a bride-day be
   By a word of *woe* defiled?
That a word of *wrong* take the cradle-song   180
   From the ear of a sinless child?' –
'Why?' Luti said, and her laugh was dread,
   And her eyes dilated wild –
'That the fair new love may her bridegroom prove,
   And the father shame the child.'
                The river floweth on.

XXI

'Thou flowest still, O river,
  Thou flowest 'neath the moon!
Thy lily hath not changed a leaf,
  Thy charmèd lute a tune!   190
He mixed his voice with thine – and *his*
  Was all I heard around;
But now, beside his chosen bride,
  I hear the river's sound.'
                    The river floweth on.

XXII

'I gaze upon her beauty
  Through the tresses that enwreathe it;
The light above thy wave, is hers –
  My rest, alone beneath it.
Oh, give me back the dying look   200
  My father gave thy water!
Give back! – and let a little love
  O'erwatch his weary daughter!'
                    The river floweth on.

XXIII

'Give back!' she hath departed –
  The word is wandering with her;
And the stricken maidens hear afar
  The step and cry together.
Frail symbols? None are frail enow
  For mortal joys to borrow! –   210
While bright doth float Nuleeni's boat,
  She weepeth, dark with sorrow.
                    The river floweth on.

From

POEMS
(1844)

DE PROFUNDIS

I

The face which, duly as the sun,
Rose up for me with life begun,
To mark all bright hours of the day
With hourly love, is dimmed away, –
And yet my days go on, go on.

II

The tongue which, like a stream, could run
Smooth music from the roughest stone,
And every morning with 'Good day'
Make each day good, is hushed away, –
And yet my days go on, go on.   10

III

The heart which, like a staff, was one
For mine to lean and rest upon,
The strongest on the longest day
With steadfast love, is caught away, –
And yet my days go on, go on.

IV

And cold before my summer's done,
And deaf in Nature's general tune,
And fallen too low for special fear,
And here, with hope no longer here, –
While the tears drop, my days go on.   20

V

The world goes whispering to its own,
'This anguish pierces to the bone';
And tender friends go sighing round,
'What love can ever cure this wound?'
My days go on, my days go on.

VI

The past rolls forward on the sun
And makes all night. O dreams begun,
Not to be ended! Ended bliss,
And life that will not end in this!
My days go on, my days go on.   30

VII

Breath freezes on my lips to moan:
As one alone, once not alone,
I sit and knock at Nature's door,
Heart-bare, heart-hungry, very poor,
Whose desolated days go on.

VIII

I knock and cry, – Undone, undone!
Is there no help, no comfort, – none?
No gleaning in the wide wheat-plains
Where others drive their loaded wains?
My vacant days go on, go on.   40

IX

This Nature, though the snows be down,
Thinks kindly of the bird of June:
The little red hip on the tree
Is ripe for such. What is for me,
Whose days so winterly go on?

X

No bird am I, to sing in June,
And dare not ask an equal boon.
Good nests and berries red are Nature's
To give away to better creatures, –
And yet my days go on, go on.   50

XI

I ask less kindness to be done, –
Only to loose these pilgrim-shoon
(Too early worn and grimed), with sweet
Cool deathly touch to these tired feet,
Till days go out which now go on.

XII

Only to lift the turf unmown
From off the earth where it has grown,
Some cubit-space, and say, 'Behold,
Creep in, poor Heart, beneath that fold,
Forgetting how the days go on.'   60

XIII

What harm would that do? Green anon
The sward would quicken, overshone
By skies as blue; and crickets might
Have leave to chirp there day and night
While my new rest went on, went on.

XIV

From gracious Nature have I won
Such liberal bounty? may I run
So, lizard-like, within her side,
And there be safe, who now am tried
By days that painfully go on?   70

XV

– A Voice reproves me thereupon,
More sweet than Nature's when the drone
Of bees is sweetest, and more deep
Than when the rivers overleap
The shuddering pines, and thunder on.

XVI

God's Voice, not Nature's! Night and noon
He sits upon the great white throne
And listens for the creatures' praise.
What babble we of days and days?
The Dayspring He, whose days go on.　　　　　80

XVII

He reigns above, He reigns alone;
Systems burn out and leave His throne:
Fair mists of seraphs melt and fall
Around Him, changeless amid all, –
Ancient of Days, whose days go on.

XVIII

He reigns below, He reigns alone,
And, having life in love forgone
Beneath the crown of sovran thorns,
He reigns the Jealous God. Who mourns
Or rules with Him, while days go on?　　　　　90

XIX

By anguish which made pale the sun,
I hear Him charge His saints that none
Among His creatures anywhere
Blaspheme against Him with despair,
However darkly days go on.

XX

Take from my head the thorn-wreath brown!
No mortal grief deserves that crown.
O súpreme Love, chief Misery,
The sharp regalia are for THEE
Whose days eternally go on!   100

XXI

For us, – whatever's undergone,
Thou knowest, willest what is done.
Grief may be joy misunderstood;
Only the Good discerns the good.
I trust Thee while my days go on.

XXII

Whatever's lost, it first was won:
We will not struggle nor impugn.
Perhaps the cup was broken here,
That Heaven's new wine might show more clear.
I praise Thee while my days go on.   110

XXIII

I praise Thee while my days go on;
I love Thee while my days go on:
Through dark and dearth, through fire and frost,
With emptied arms and treasure lost,
I thank Thee while my days go on.

XXIV

And having in Thy life-depth thrown
Being and suffering (which are one),
As a child drops his pebble small
Down some deep well, and hears it fall
Smiling – so I. THY DAYS GO ON.   120

PAST AND FUTURE

My future will not copy fair my past
On any leaf but Heaven's. Be fully done,
Supernal Will! I would not fain be one
Who, satisfying thirst and breaking fast
Upon the fullness of the heart, at last
Says no grace after meat. My wine has run
Indeed out of my cup, and there is none
To gather up the bread of my repast
Scattered and trampled, – yet I find some good
In earth's green herbs, and streams that bubble up   10
Clear from the darkling ground, – content until
I sit with angels before better food.
Dear Christ! when Thy new vintage fills my cup,
This hand shall shake no more, nor that wine spill.

GRIEF

I tell you, hopeless grief is passionless;
That only men incredulous of despair,
Half-taught in anguish, through the midnight air
Beat upward to God's throne in loud access
Of shrieking and reproach. Full desertness
In souls, as countries, lieth silent-bare
Under the blanching, vertical eye-glare
Of the absolute Heavens. Deep-hearted man, express
Grief for thy Dead in silence like to death: –
Most like a monumental statue set   10
In everlasting watch and moveless woe,
Till itself crumble to the dust beneath.
Touch it: the marble eyelids are not wet;
If it could weep, it could arise and go.

TEARS

Thank God, bless God, all ye who suffer not
More grief than ye can weep for. That is well –
That is light grieving! lighter, none befell
Since Adam forfeited the primal lot.
Tears! what are tears? The babe weeps in its cot,
The mother singing, – at her marriage-bell
The bride weeps, – and before the oracle
Of high-faned hills, the poet has forgot
Such moisture on his cheeks. Thank God for grace,
Ye who weep only! If, as some have done,   10
Ye grope tear-blinded in a desert place
And touch but tombs, – look up! those tears will run
Soon in long rivers down the lifted face,
And leave the vision clear for stars and sun.

SUBSTITUTION

When some beloved voice that was to you
Both sound and sweetness, faileth suddenly,
And silence against which you dare not cry,
Aches round you like a strong disease and new –
What hope? what help? what music will undo
That silence to your sense? Not friendship's sigh –
Not reason's subtle count; not melody
Of viols, nor of pipes that Faunus blew.
Not songs of poets, nor of nightingales
Whose hearts leap upward through the cypress-trees   10
To the clear moon! nor yet the spheric laws
Self-chanted, – nor the angels' sweet All hails,
Met in the smile of God: nay, none of these.
Speak THOU, availing Christ! – and fill this pause.

LADY GERALDINE'S COURTSHIP

A ROMANCE OF THE AGE

A poet writes to his friend.
PLACE – *A room in Wycombe Hall.*
TIME – *Late in the evening.*

Dear my friend and fellow student,
    I would lean my spirit o'er you!
Down the purple of this chamber, tears
    should scarcely run at will.
I am humbled who was humble. Friend,
    – I bow my head before you.
You should lead me to my peasants, –
    but their faces are too still.

There's a lady – an earl's daughter, –
    she is proud and she is noble,   10
And she treads the crimson carpet, and
    she breathes the perfumed air,
And a kingly blood sends glances up her
    princely eye to trouble,
And the shadow of a monarch's crown
    is softened in her hair.

She has halls among the woodlands,
    she has castles by the breakers,
She has farms and she has manors, she
    can threaten and command,   20
And the palpitating engines snort in
    steam across her acres,
As they mark upon the blasted heaven
    the measure of the land.

There are none of England's daughters
    who can show a prouder presence;
Upon princely suitors praying, she has
    looked in her disdain.
She was sprung of English nobles,
    I was born of English peasants;   30
What was *I* that I should love her –
    save for competence to pain?

I was only a poor poet, made for singing
    at her casement,
As the finches or the thrushes, while
    she thought of other things.
Oh, she walked so high above me, she
    appeared to my abasement,
In her lovely silken murmur, like an
    angel clad in wings!   40

Many vassals bow before her as her
    carriage sweeps their doorways;
She has blest their little children, – as a
    priest or queen were she.
Far too tender, or too cruel far, her
    smile upon the poor was,
For I thought it was the same smile
    which she used to smile on *me*.

She has voters in the Commons, she has
    lovers in the palace;   50
And of all the fair court-ladies, few have
    jewels half as fine;
Oft the prince has named her beauty
    'twixt the red wine and the chalice.
Oh, and what was *I* to love her? my
    beloved, my Geraldine!

Yet I could not choose but love her.
    I was born to poet-uses,
To love all things set above me, all of
    good and all of fair: 60
Nymphs of mountain, not of valley, we
    are wont to call the Muses
And in nympholeptic climbing, poets
    pass from mount to star.

And because I was a poet, and because
    the public praised me,
With a critical deduction for the modern
    writer's fault,
I could sit at rich men's tables, – though
    the courtesies that raised me,   70
Still suggested clear between us the
    pale spectrum of the salt.

And they praised me in her presence;
    – 'Will your book appear this summer?'
Then returning to each other – 'Yes,
    our plans are for the moors.'
Then with whisper dropped behind me
    – 'There he is! the latest comer!
Oh, she only likes his verses! what is
    over, she endures.   80

'Quite low-born! self-educated! some-
    what gifted though by nature, –
And we make a point of asking him, –
    of being very kind.
You may speak, he does not hear you!
    and besides, he writes no satire, –
All these serpents kept by charmers
    leave the natural sting behind.'

I grew scornfuller, grew colder, as I
      stood up there among them,   90
Till as frost intense will burn you, the
      cold scorning scorched my brow;
When a sudden silver speaking, gravely
      cadenced, over-rung them,
And a sudden silken stirring touched
      my inner nature through.

I looked upward and beheld her. With
      a calm and regnant spirit,
Slowly round she swept her eyelids,
      and said clear before them all –   100
'Have you such superfluous honour, sir,
      that able to confer it
You will come down, Mister Bertram,
      as my guest to Wycombe Hall?'

Here she paused, – she had been paler
      at the first word of her speaking,
But because a silence followed it,
      blushed somewhat, as for shame,
Then, as scorning her own feeling,
      resumed calmly – 'I am seeking   110
More distinction than these gentlemen
      think worthy of my claim.

'Ne'ertheless, you see, I seek it – not
      because I am a woman'
(Here her smile sprang like a fountain,
      and, so, overflowed her mouth),
'But because my woods in Sussex have
      some purple shades at gloaming
Which are worthy of a king in state, or
      poet in his youth.   120

'I invite you, Mister Bertram, to no
      scene for worldly speeches –
Sir, I scarce should dare – but only where
      God asked the thrushes first –
And if *you* will sing beside them, in the
      covert of my beeches,
I will thank you for the woodlands, . . .
      for the human world, at worst.'

Then she smiled around right childly,
      then she gazed around right queenly,   130
And I bowed – I could not answer;
      alternated light and gloom –
While as one who quells the lions, with
      a steady eye serenely,
She, with level fronting eyelids, passed
      out stately from the room.

Oh, the blessèd woods of Sussex, I can
      hear them still around me,
With their leafy tide of greenery still
      rippling up the wind.   140
Oh, the cursèd woods of Sussex! where
      the hunter's arrow found me,
When a fair face and a tender voice had
      made me mad and blind!

In that ancient hall of Wycombe, thronged
      the numerous guests invited,
And the lovely London ladies trod the
      floors with gliding feet;
And their voices low with fashion, not
      with feeling, softly freighted   150
All the air about the windows, with
      elastic laughters sweet.

For at eve, the open windows flung their
      light out on the terrace,
Which the floating orbs of curtains did
      with gradual shadow sweep,
While the swans upon the river, fed at
      morning by the heiress,
Trembled downward through their
      snowy wings at music in their sleep.   160

And there evermore was music, both of
      instrument and singing,
Till the finches of the shrubberies grew
      restless in the dark;
But the cedars stood up motionless,
      each in a moonlight ringing,
And the deer, half in the glimmer,
      strewed the hollows of the park.

And though sometimes she would bind me
      with her silver-corded speeches   170
To commix my words and laughter with
      the converse and the jest,
Oft I sate apart, and gazing on the river
      through the beeches,
Heard, as pure the swans swam down
      it, her pure voice o'erfloat the rest.

In the morning, horn of huntsman, hoof
      of steed, and laugh of rider,
Spread out cheery from the court-yard
      till we lost them in the hills,   180
While herself and other ladies, and her
      suitors left beside her,
Went a-wandering up the gardens
      through the laurels and abeles.

Thus, her foot upon the new-mown grass,
    bareheaded, with the flowing
Of the virginal white vesture gathered
    closely to her throat, –
And the golden ringlets in her neck
    just quickened by her going,   190
And appearing to breathe sun for air,
    and doubting if to float, –

With a branch of dewy maple, which
    her right hand held above her,
And which trembled a green shadow in
    betwixt her and the skies,
As she turned her face in going, thus,
    she drew me on to love her,
And to worship the divineness of the
    smile hid in her eyes.   200

For her eyes alone smile constantly:
    her lips have serious sweetness,
And her front is calm – the dimple rarely
    ripples on the cheek;
But her deep blue eyes smile constantly,
    as if they in discreetness
Kept the secret of a happy dream she
    did not care to speak.

Thus she drew me the first morning,
    out across into the garden,   210
And I walked among her noble friends
    and could not keep behind.
Spake she unto all and unto me –
    'Behold, I am the warden
Of the song-birds in these lindens,
    which are cages to their mind.

'But within this swarded circle, into
    which the lime-walk brings us,
Whence the beeches, rounded greenly,
    stand away in reverent fear,   220
I will let no music enter, saving what
    the fountain sings us,
Which the lilies round the basin may
    seem pure enough to hear.

'The live air that waves the lilies waves
    the slender jet of water
Like a holy thought sent feebly up from
    soul of fasting saint:
Whereby lies a marble Silence, sleeping!
    (Lough the sculptor wrought her)   230
So asleep she is forgetting to say Hush!
    – a fancy quaint.

'Mark how heavy white her eyelids!
    not a dream between them lingers,
And the left hand's index droppeth from
    the lips upon the cheek;
While the right hand, – with the symbol
    rose held slack within the fingers, –
Has fallen backward in the basin – yet
    this Silence will not speak!   240

'That the essential meaning growing
    may exceed the special symbol,
Is the thought as I conceive it: it applies
    more high and low.
Our true noblemen will often through
    right nobleness grow humble,
And assert an inward honour by
    denying outward show.'

'Nay, your Silence,' said I, 'truly, holds
    her symbol rose but slackly,   250
Yet *she holds it* – or would scarcely be a
    Silence to our ken;
And your nobles wear their ermine on
    the outside, or walk blackly
In the presence of the social law as
    mere ignoble men.

'Let the poets dream such dreaming!
    madam, in these British islands
'Tis the substance that wanes ever, 'tis
    the symbol that exceeds.   260
Soon we shall have nought but symbol!
    and, for statues like this Silence,
Shall accept the rose's image – in another
    case, the weed's.'

'Not so quickly,' she retorted, – 'I confess,
    where'er you go, you
Find for things, names – shows for
    actions, and pure gold for honour clear;
But when all is run to symbol in the
    Social, I will throw you   270
The world's book which now reads dryly
    and sit down with Silence here.'

Half in playfulness she spoke, I thought,
    and half in indignation;
Friends who listened, laughed her words
    off, while her lovers deemed her fair:
A fair woman, flushed with feeling, in
    her noble-lighted station
Near the statue's white reposing – and
    both bathed in sunny air! –   280

With the trees round, not so distant but
    you heard their vernal murmur,
And beheld in light and shadow the
    leaves in and outward move,
And the little fountain leaping toward
    the sun-heart to be warmer,
Then recoiling in a tremble from the
    too much light above.

'Tis a picture for remembrance. And
    thus, morning after morning,   290
Did I follow as she drew me by the
    spirit to her feet.
Why, her greyhound followed also!
    dogs – we both were dogs for scorning –
To be sent back when she pleased it and
    her path lay through the wheat.

And thus, morning after morning, spite
    of vows and spite of sorrow,
Did I follow at her drawing, while the
    week-days passed along,   300
Just to feed the swans this noontide, or
    to see the fawns to-morrow,
Or to teach the hill-side echo some
    sweet Tuscan in a song.

Aye, for sometimes on the hill-side, while
    we sate down in the gowans,
With the forest green behind us, and
    its shadow cast before,
And the river running under, and across
    it from the rowans   310
A brown partridge whirring near us,
    till we felt the air it bore, –

There, obedient to her praying, did I
    read aloud the poems
Made to Tuscan flutes, or instruments
    more various of our own;
Read the pastoral parts of Spenser – or
    the subtle interflowings
Found in Petrarch's sonnets – here's the
    book – the leaf is folded down!   320

Or at times a modern volume, – Wordsworth's
    solemn-thoughted idyl,
Howitt's ballad-verse, or Tennyson's
    enchanted reverie, –
Or from Browning some 'Pomegranate,'
    which, if cut deep down the middle,
Shows a heart within blood-tinctured,
    of a veined humanity.

Or at times I read there, hoarsely, some
    new poem of my making: 330
Poets ever fail in reading their own
    verses to their worth, –
For the echo in you breaks upon the
    words which you are speaking,
And the chariot-wheels jar in the gate
    through which you drive them forth.

After, when we were grown tired of
    books, the silence round us flinging
A slow arm of sweet compression, felt
    with beatings at the breast,   340
She would break out, on a sudden, in
    a gush of woodland singing,
Like a child's emotion in a god – a naiad
    tired of rest.

Oh, to see or hear her singing! scarce
    I know which is divinest –
For her looks sing too – she modulates
    her gestures on the tune;
And her mouth stirs with the song, like
    song; and when the notes are finest,   350
'Tis the eyes that shoot out vocal light
    and seem to swell them on.

Then we talked – oh, how we talked! her
    voice, so cadenced in the talking,
Made another singing – of the soul!
    a music without bars;
While the leafy sounds of woodlands,
    humming round where we were walking,
Brought interposition worthy-sweet, –
    as skies about the stars.   360

And she spake such good thoughts
    natural, as if she always thought them;
She had sympathies so rapid, open, free
    as bird on branch,
Just as ready to fly east as west, which-
    ever way besought them,
In the birchen-wood a chirrup, or a
    cock-crow in the grange.

In her utmost lightness there is truth –
    and often she speaks lightly,   370
Has a grace in being gay, which even
    mournful souls approve,
For the root of some grave earnest
    thought is understruck so rightly
As to justify the foliage and the waving
    flowers above.

And she talked on – *we* talked, rather!
    upon all things, substance, shadow,
Of the sheep that browsed the grasses,
    of the reapers in the corn,   380
Of the little children from the schools,
    seen winding through the meadow –
Of the poor rich world beyond them, still
    kept poorer by its scorn.

So, of men, and so, of letters – books are
    men of higher stature,
And the only men that speak aloud for
    future times to hear;
So, of mankind in the abstract, which
    grows slowly into nature,   390
Yet will lift the cry of 'progress,' as it
    trod from sphere to sphere.

And her custom was to praise me when
    I said, – 'The Age culls simples,
With a broad clown's back turned
    broadly to the glory of the stars.
We are gods by our own reck'ning, and
    may well shut up the temples,
And wield on, amid the incense-steam,
    the thunder of our cars.   400

'For we throw out acclamations of self-
    thanking, self-admiring,
With, at every mile run faster, – "O the
    wondrous wondrous age,"
Little thinking if we work our SOULS as
    nobly as our iron,
Or if angels will commend us at the goal
    of pilgrimage.

'Why, what *is* this patient entrance
    into nature's deep resources,   410
But the child's most gradual learning to
    walk upright without bane?
When we drive out, from the cloud of
    steam, majestical white horses,
Are we greater than the first men who
    led black ones by the mane?

'If we trod the deeps of ocean, if we
    struck the stars in rising,
If we wrapped the globe intensely with
    one hot electric breath,   420
'Twere but power within our tether, no
    new spirit-power comprising,
And in life we were not greater men,
    nor bolder men in death.'

She was patient with my talking; and
    I loved her, loved her, certes,
As I loved all heavenly objects, with
    uplifted eyes and hands!
As I loved pure inspirations, loved the
    graces, loved the virtues,   430
In a Love content with writing his own
    name on desert sands.

Or at least I thought so, purely! – thought
    no idiot Hope was raising
Any crown to crown Love's silence –
    silent Love that sate alone.
Out, alas! the stag is like me – he, that
    tries to go on grazing
With the great deep gun-wound in his
    neck, then reels with sudden moan.   440

It was thus I reeled. I told you that her
      hand had many suitors;
But she smiles them down imperially,
      as Venus did the waves,
And with such a gracious coldness, that
      they cannot press their futures
On the present of her courtesy, which
      yieldingly enslaves.

And this morning, as I sate alone within
      the inner chamber,   450
With the great saloon beyond it, lost in
      pleasant thought serene,
For I had been reading Camoëns – that
      poem you remember,
Which his lady's eyes are praised in, as
      the sweetest ever seen.

And the book lay open, and my thought
      flew from it, taking from it
A vibration and impulsion to an end
      beyond its own,   460
As the branch of a green osier, when a
      child would overcome it,
Springs up freely from his clasping and
      goes swinging in the sun.

As I mused I heard a murmur, – it grew
      deep as it grew longer –
Speakers using earnest language –
      'Lady Geraldine, you *would*!'
And I heard a voice that pleaded ever
      on, in accents stronger   470
As a sense of reason gave it power to
      make its rhetoric good.

Well I knew that voice – it was an earl's,
    of soul that matched his station,
Soul completed into lordship – might and
    right read on his brow;
Very finely courteous – far too proud to
    doubt his domination
Of the common people, he atones for
    grandeur by a bow.   480

High straight forehead, nose of eagle,
    cold blue eyes, of less expression
Than resistance, coldly casting off the
    looks of other men,
As steel, arrows, – unelastic lips, which
    seem to taste possession,
And be cautious lest the common air
    should injure or distrain.

For the rest, accomplished, upright, –
    aye, and standing by his order   490
With a bearing not ungraceful; fond of
    art and letters too;
Just a good man made a proud man, – as
    the sandy rocks that border
A wild coast, by circumstances, in a
    regnant ebb and flow.

Thus, I knew that voice – I heard it, and
    I could not help the hearkening.
In the room I stood up blindly, and my
    burning heart within   500
Seemed to seethe and fuse my senses, till
    they ran on all sides darkening,
And scorched, weighed, like melted metal
    round my feet that stood therein.

And that voice, I heard it pleading, for
      love's sake, for wealth, position,
For the sake of liberal uses, and great
      actions to be done –
And she interrupted gently, 'Nay, my
      lord, the old tradition   510
Of your Normans, by some worthier hand
      than mine is, should be won.'

'Ah, that white hand!' he said quickly, –
      and in his he either drew it
Or attempted – for with gravity and
      instance she replied,
'Nay, indeed, my lord, this talk is vain,
      and we had best eschew it,
And pass on, like friends, to other points
      less easy to decide.'   520

What he said again, I know not. It is
      likely that his trouble
Worked his pride up to the surface, for
      she answered in slow scorn,
'And your lordship judges rightly.
      Whom I marry, shall be noble,
Aye, and wealthy. I shall never blush
      to think how he was born.'

There, I maddened! her words stung me.
      Life swept through me into fever,   530
And my soul sprang up astonished,
      sprang, full-statured in an hour.
Know you what it is when anguish, with
      apocalyptic NEVER,
To a Pythian height dilates you, – and
      despair sublimes to power?

From my brain, the soul-wings budded, –
    waved a flame about my body,
Whence conventions coiled to ashes,
    I felt self-drawn out, as man,   540
From amalgamate false natures, and I
    saw the skies grow ruddy
With the deepening feet of angels, and
    I knew what spirits can.

I was mad – inspired – say either!
    (anguish worketh inspiration)
Was a man, or beast – perhaps so, for
    the tiger roars, when speared;
And I walked on, step by step, along
    the level of my passion –   550
Oh my soul! and passed the doorway
    to her face, and never feared.

He had left her, peradventure, when my
    footstep proved my coming –
But for *her* – she half arose, then sate –
    grew scarlet and grew pale.
Oh, she trembled! – 'tis so always with
    a worldly man or woman
In the presence of true spirits – what else
    can they do but quail?   560

Oh, she fluttered like a tame bird, in
    among its forest-brothers
Far too strong for it; then drooping,
    bowed her face upon her hands –
And I spake out wildly, fiercely, brutal
    truths of her and others:
I, she planted in the desert, swathed her,
    windlike, with my sands.

I plucked up her social fictions, bloody-
    rooted though leaf-verdant, –   570
Trod them down with words of shaming,
    – all the purple and the gold,
All the 'landed stakes' and lordships,
    all, that spirits pure and ardent
Are cast out of love and honour because
    chancing not to hold.

'For myself I do not argue,' said I,
    'though I love you, madam,
But for better souls that nearer to the
    height of yours have trod;   580
And this age shows, to my thinking, still
    more infidels to Adam,
Than directly, by profession, simple in-
    fidels to God.

'Yet, O God,' I said, 'O grave,' I said,
    'O mother's heart and bosom,
With whom first and last are equal,
    saint and corpse and little child!
We are fools to your deductions, in these
    figments of heart-closing;   590
We are traitors to your causes, in these
    sympathies defiled.

'Learn more reverence, madam, not for
    rank or wealth – *that* needs no learning,
That comes quickly – quick as sin does,
    aye, and culminates to sin;
But for Adam's seed, MAN! Trust me,
    'tis a clay above your scorning,
With God's image stamped upon it, and
    God's kindling breath within.   600

'What right have you, madam, gazing in
          your palace mirror daily,
Getting so by heart your beauty which
          all others must adore,
While you draw the golden ringlets down
          your fingers, to vow gaily
You will wed no man that's only good to
          God, and nothing more?

'Why, what right have you, made fair
          by that same God – the sweetest woman   610
Of all women He has fashioned – with
          your lovely spirit-face,
Which would seem too near to vanish if
          its smile were not so human,
And your voice of holy sweetness, turning
          common words to grace,

'What right *can* you have, God's other
          works to scorn, despise, revile them
In the gross, as mere men, broadly – not
          as *noble* men, forsooth, –   620
As mere Parias of the outer world, for-
          bidden to assoil them
In the hope of living, dying, near that
          sweetness of your mouth?

'Have you any answer, madam? If my
          spirit were less earthly,
If its instrument were gifted with a better
          silver string,
I would kneel down where I stand, and
          say – Behold me! I am worthy   630
Of thy loving, for I love thee! I am
          worthy as a king.

'As it is – your ermined pride, I swear,
      shall feel this stain upon her,
That *I*, poor, weak, tost with passion,
      scorned by me and you again,
Love you, madam – dare to love you – to
      my grief and your dishonour,
To my endless desolation, and your
      impotent disdain!'   640

More mad words like these – mere madness!
      friend, I need not write them fuller,
For I hear my hot soul dropping on the
      lines in showers of tears.
Oh, a woman! friend, a woman! why,
      a beast had scarce been duller
Than roar bestial loud complaints against
      the shining of the spheres.

But at last there came a pause. I stood
      all vibrating with thunder   650
Which my soul had used. The silence
      drew her face up like a call.
Could you guess what word she uttered?
      She looked up, as if in wonder,
With tears beaded on her lashes, and
      said 'Bertram!' – it was all.

If she had cursed me, and she might have
      – or if even, with queenly bearing
Which at need is used by women, she
      had risen up and said,   660
'Sir, you are my guest, and therefore I
      have given you a full hearing,
Now, beseech you, choose a name exact-
      ing somewhat less, instead,' –

I had borne it! – but that 'Bertram' –
      why it lies there on the paper
A mere word, without her accent, – and
      you cannot judge the weight
Of the calm which crushed my passion:
      I seemed drowning in a vapour, –   670
And her gentleness destroyed me whom
      her scorn made desolate.

So, struck backward and exhausted by
      that inward flow of passion
Which had rushed on, sparing nothing,
      into forms of abstract truth,
By a logic agonizing through unseemly
      demonstration,
And by youth's own anguish turning
      grimly grey the hairs of youth, –   680

By the sense accursed and instant, that
      if even I spake wisely
I spake basely – using truth, if what I
      spake, indeed was true,
To avenge wrong on a woman – *her*, who
      sate there weighing nicely
A poor manhood's worth, found guilty of
      such deeds as I could do! –

By such wrong and woe exhausted –
      what I suffered and occasioned, –   690
As a wild horse through a city runs with
      lightning in his eyes,
And then dashing at a church's cold and
      passive wall, impassioned,
Strikes the death into his burning brain,
      and blindly drops and dies –

So I fell, struck down before her! do
  you blame me, friend, for weakness?
'Twas my strength of passion slew me!
  – fell before her like a stone. 700
Fast the dreadful world rolled from me,
  on its roaring wheels of blackness –
When the light came, I was lying in this
  chamber, and alone.

Oh, of course, she charged her lacqueys
  to bear out the sickly burden,
And to cast it from her scornful sight –
  but not *beyond* the gate;
She is too kind to be cruel, and too
  haughty not to pardon 710
Such a man as I – 'twere something to
  be level to her hate.

But for me – you now are conscious
  why, my friend, I write this letter,
How my life is read all backward, and
  the charm of life undone:
I shall leave her house at dawn; I would
  to-night, if I were better –
And I charge my soul to hold my body
  strengthened for the sun. 720

When the sun has dyed the oriel, I depart,
  with no last gazes,
No weak moanings (one word only, left
  in writing for her hands),
Out of reach of all derision, and some
  unavailing praises,
To make front against this anguish in the
  far and foreign lands.

Blame me not. I would not squander
    life in grief – I am abstemious: 730
I but nurse my spirit's falcon, that its
    wing may soar again.
There's no room for tears of weakness in
    the blind eyes of a Phemius!
Into work the poet kneads them, – and
    he does not die *till then*.

CONCLUSION

Bertram finished the last pages, while
    along the silence ever
Still in hot and heavy splashes, fell the
    tears on every leaf: 740
Having ended he leans backward in his
    chair, with lips that quiver
From the deep unspoken, aye, and deep
    unwritten thoughts of grief.

Soh! how still the lady standeth! 'tis a
    dream – a dream of mercies!
'Twixt the purple lattice-curtains, how
    she standeth still and pale!
'Tis a vision, sure, of mercies, sent to
    soften his self-curses –   750
Sent to sweep a patient quiet o'er the
    tossing of his wail.

'Eyes,' he said, 'now throbbing through
    me! are ye eyes that did undo me?
Shining eyes, like antique jewels set in
    Parian statue-stone!
Underneath that calm white forehead, are
    ye ever burning torrid
O'er the desolate sand-desert of my heart
    and life undone?'   760

With a murmurous stir uncertain, in the
    air, the purple curtain
Swelleth in and swelleth out around her
    motionless pale brows,
While the gliding of the river sends a
    rippling noise for ever
Through the open casement whitened by
    the moonlight's slant repose.

Said he – 'Vision of a lady! stand there
    silent, stand there steady!   770
Now I see it plainly, plainly; now I
    cannot hope or doubt –
There, the brows of mild repression –
    there, the lips of silent passion,
Curvèd like an archer's bow to send the
    bitter arrows out.'

Ever, evermore the while in a slow
    silence she kept smiling,
And approached him slowly, slowly, in
    a gliding measured pace;   780
With her two white hands extended, as
    if praying one offended,
And a look of supplication, gazing earnest
    in his face.

Said he – 'Wake me by no gesture, –
    sound of breath, or stir of vesture!
Let the blessèd apparition melt not yet
    to its divine!
No approaching – hush, no breathing! or
    my heart must swoon to death in   790
The too utter life thou bringest – O thou
    dream of Geraldine!'

Ever, evermore the while in a slow
    silence she kept smiling –
But the tears ran over lightly from her
    eyes, and tenderly;
'Dost thou, Bertram, truly love me?
    Is no woman far above me
Found more worthy of thy poet-heart
    than such a one as *I*?'   800

Said he – 'I would dream so ever, like
    the flowing of that river,
Flowing ever in a shadow greenly onward
    to the sea!
So, thou vision of all sweetness – princely
    to a full completeness, –
Would my heart and life flow onward –
    deathward – through this dream of THEE!'

Ever, evermore the while in a slow
    silence she kept smiling,   810
While the silver tears ran faster down
    the blushing of her cheeks;
Then with both her hands enfolding both
    of his, she softly told him,
'Bertram, if I say I love thee, . . . 'tis
    the vision only speaks.'

Softened, quickened to adore her, on his
    knee he fell before her –
And she whispered low in triumph, 'It
    shall be as I have sworn!   820
Very rich he is in virtues, – very noble –
    noble, certes;
And I shall not blush in knowing that
    men call him lowly born.'

THE LOST BOWER

I

In the pleasant orchard closes,
'God bless all our gains,' say we;
But 'May God bless all our losses,'
Better suits with our degree.
Listen, gentle – ay, and simple! listen, children on the knee!

II

Green the land is where my daily
Steps in jocund childhood played,
Dimpled close with hill and valley,
Dappled very close with shade;
Summer-snow of apple-blossoms running up from glade to
     glade.   10

III

There is one hill I see nearer,
In my vision of the rest;
And a little wood seems clearer
As it climbeth from the west,
Sideway from the tree-locked valley, to the airy upland crest.

IV

Small the wood is, green with hazels,
And, completing the ascent,
Where the wind blows and sun dazzles
Thrills in leafy tremblement,
Like a heart that after climbing beateth quickly through
     content.   20

V

Not a step the wood advances
O'er the open hill-tops bound;
There, in green arrest, the branches
See their image on the ground:
You may walk beneath them smiling, glad with sight and
      glad with sound.

VI

For you harken on your right hand,
How the birds do leap and call
In the greenwood, out of sight and
Out of reach and fear of all;
And the squirrels crack the filberts through their cheerful
      madrigal.   30

VII

On your left, the sheep are cropping
The slant grass and daisies pale,
And five apple-trees stand dropping
Separate shadows toward the vale
Over which, in choral silence, the hills look you their 'All
      hail!'

VIII

Far out, kindled by each other,
Shining hills on hills arise,
Close as brother leans to brother
When they press beneath the eyes
Of some father praying blessings from the gifts of
      paradise.   40

IX

> While beyond, above them mounted,
> And above their woods alsò,
> Malvern hills, for mountains counted
> Not unduly, loom a-row –
> Keepers of Piers Plowman's visions through the sunshine and
> the snow.

X

> Yet in childhood, little prized I
> That fair walk and far survey;
> 'Twas a straight walk unadvised by
> The least mischief worth a nay;
> Up and down – as dull as grammar on the eve of holiday.   50

XI

> But the wood, all close and clenching
> Bough in bough and root in root, –
> No more sky (for over-branching)
> At your head than at your foot, –
> Oh, the wood drew me within it by a glamour past dispute!

XII

> Few and broken paths showed through it,
> Where the sheep had tried to run, –
> Forced with snowy wool to strew it
> Round the thickets, where anon
> They, with silly thorn-pricked noses, bleated back into the
> sun.   60

XIII

But my childish heart beat stronger
Than those thickets dared to grow:
I could pierce them! I could longer
Travel on, methought, than so:
Sheep for sheep-paths! braver children climb and creep where
      they would go.

XIV

And the poets wander, (said I,)
Over places all as rude:
Bold Rinaldo's lovely lady
Sate to meet him in a wood:
Rosalinda, like a fountain, laughed out pure with solitude. 70

XV

And if Chaucer had not travelled
Through a forest by a well,
He had never dreamt nor marvelled
At those ladies fair and fell
Who lived smiling without loving in their island-citadel.

XVI

Thus I thought of the old singers
And took courage from their song,
Till my little struggling fingers
Tore asunder gyve and thong
Of the brambles which entrapped me, and the barrier
      branches strong. 80

XVII

On a day, such pastime keeping,
With a fawn's heart debonair,
Under-crawling, overleaping
Thorns that prick and boughs that bear,
I stood suddenly astonied – I was gladdened unaware.

XVIII

From the place I stood in, floated
Back the covert dim and close,
And the open ground was coated
Carpet-smooth with grass and moss,
And the blue-bell's purple presence signed it worthily
      across.   90

XIX

Here a linden-tree stood, bright'ning
All adown its silver rind;
For as some trees draw the lightning,
So this tree, unto my mind,
Drew to earth the blessed sunshine from the sky where it was
      shrined.

XX

Tall the linden-tree and near it
An old hawthorn also grew;
And wood-ivy like a spirit
Hovered dimly round the two,
Shaping thence that bower of beauty which I sing of thus to
      you.   100

XXI

'Twas a bower for garden fitter
Than for any woodland wide:
Though a fresh and dewy glitter
Struck it through from side to side,
Shaped and shaven was the freshness, as by garden-cunning
      plied.

XXII

Oh, a lady might have come there,
Hooded fairly like her hawk,
With a book or lute in summer,
And a hope of sweeter talk, –
Listening less to her own music than for footsteps on the
    walk.   110

XXIII

But that bower appeared a marvel
In the wildness of the place;
With such seeming art and travail,
Finely fixed and fitted was
Leaf to leaf, the dark-green ivy, to the summit from the base.

XXIV

And the ivy veined and glossy
Was enwrought with eglantine;
And the wild hop fibred closely,
And the large-leaved columbine,
Arch of door and window-mullion, did right sylvanly
    entwine.   120

XXV

Rose-trees either side the door were
Growing lithe and growing tall,
Each one set, a summer warder
For the keeping of the hall, –
With a red rose and a white rose, leaning, nodding at the
    wall.

XXVI

As I entered, mosses hushing
Stole all noises from my foot;
And a green elastic cushion,
Clasped within the linden's root,
Took me in a chair of silence very rare and absolute.   130

XXVII

All the floor was paved with glory,
Greenly, silently inlaid
(Through quick motions made before me)
With fair counterparts in shade
Of the fair serrated ivy-leaves which slanted overhead.

XXVIII

'Is such pavement in a palace?'
So I questioned in my thought:
The sun, shining through the chalice
Of the red rose hung without,
Threw within a red libation, like an answer to my doubt.   140

XXIX

At the same time, on the linen
Of my childish lap there fell
Two white may-leaves, downward winning
Through the ceiling's miracle,
From a blossom, like an angel, out of sight yet blessing well.

XXX

Down to floor and up to ceiling
Quick I turned my childish face,
With an innocent appealing
For the secret of the place
To the trees, which surely knew it in partaking of the
          grace.   150

XXXI

Where's no foot of human creature
How could reach a human hand?
And if this be work of nature,
Why has nature turned so bland,
Breaking off from other wild-work? It was hard to
understand.

XXXII

Was she weary of rough-doing,
Of the bramble and the thorn?
Did she pause in tender rueing
Here of all her sylvan scorn?
Or in mock of art's deceiving was the sudden mildness
worn?   160

XXXIII

Or could this same bower (I fancied)
Be the work of Dryad strong,
Who, surviving all that chancëd
In the world's old pagan wrong,
Lay hid, feeding in the woodland on the last true poet's
song?

XXXIV

Or was this the house of fairies,
Left, because of the rough ways,
Unassoiled by Ave Marys
Which the passing pilgrim prays,
And beyond St Catherine's chiming on the blessed Sabbath
days?   170

XXXV

So, young muser, I sate listening
To my fancy's wildest word.
On a sudden, through the glistening
Leaves around, a little stirred,
Came a sound, a sense of music which was rather felt than
      heard.

XXXVI

Softly, finely, it enwound me;
From the world it shut me in, –
Like a fountain falling round me,
Which with silver waters thin
Clips a little water Naiad sitting smilingly within.   180

XXXVII

Whence the music came, who knoweth?
I know nothing: but indeed
Pan or Faunus never bloweth
So much sweetness from a reed
Which has sucked the milk of waters at the oldest riverhead.

XXXVIII

Never lark the sun can waken
With such sweetness! when the lark,
The high planets overtaking
In the half-evanished Dark,
Casts his singing to their singing, like an arrow to the
      mark.   190

XXXIX

Never nightingale so singeth:
Oh, she leans on thorny tree
And her poet-song she flingeth
Over pain to victory!
Yet she never sings such music, – or she sings it not to me.

XL

Never blackbirds, never thrushes
Nor small finches sing so sweet,
When the sun strikes through the bushes
To their crimson clinging feet,
And their pretty eyes look sideways to the summer heavens
     complete.   200

XLI

If it *were* a bird, it seemëd
Most like Chaucer's, which, in sooth,
He of green and azure dreamèd,
While it sate in spirit-ruth
On that bier of a crowned lady, singing nigh her silent
     mouth.

XLII

If it *were* a bird? – ah, sceptic,
Give me 'yea' or give me 'nay' –
Though my soul were nympholeptic
As I heard that virëlay,
You may stoop your pride to pardon, for my sin is far
     away!   210

XLIII

I rose up in exaltation
And an inward trembling heat,
And (it seemed) in geste of passion
Dropped the music to my feet
Like a garment rustling downwards – such a silence followed
     it!

XLIV

Heart and head beat through the quiet
Full and heavily, though slower:
In the song, I think, and by it,
Mystic Presences of power
Had up-snatched me to the Timeless, then returned me to the
      Hour.   220

XLV

In a child-abstraction lifted,
Straightway from the bower I past,
Foot and soul being dimly drifted
Through the greenwood, till, at last,
In the hill-top's open sunshine I all consciously was cast.

XLVI

Face to face with the true mountains
I stood silently and still,
Drawing strength from fancy's dauntings,
From the air about the hill
And from Nature's open mercies and most debonair
      goodwill.   230

XLVII

Oh, the golden-hearted daisies
Witnessed there, before my youth,
To the truth of things, with praises
Of the beauty of the truth;
And I woke to Nature's real, laughing joyfully for both.

XLVIII

And I said within me, laughing,
'I have found a bower to-day,
A green lusus, fashioned half in
Chance and half in Nature's play;
And a little bird sings nigh it, I will nevermore missay.   240

XLIX

'Henceforth, *I* will be the fairy
Of this bower not built by one;
I will go there, sad or merry,
With each morning's benison,
And the bird shall be my harper in the dream-hall I have
     won.'

L

So I said. But the next morning,
(– Child, look up into my face –
'Ware, oh sceptic, of your scorning!
This is truth in its pure grace!)
The next morning all had vanished, or my wandering missed
     the place.   250

LI

Bring an oath most sylvan-holy,
And upon it swear me true –
By the wind-bells swinging slowly
Their mute curfews in the dew,
By the advent of the snow-drop, by the rosemary and rue, –

LII

I affirm by all or any,
Let the cause be charm or chance,
That my wandering searches many
Missed the bower of my romance –
That I nevermore upon it turned my mortal countenance. 260

LIII

I affirm that, since I lost it,
Never bower has seemed so fair;
Never garden-creeper crossed it
With so deft and brave an air,
Never bird sung in the summer, as I saw and heard them
there.

LIV

Day by day, with new desire,
Toward my wood I ran in faith,
Under leaf and over brier,
Through the thickets, out of breath;
Like the prince who rescued Beauty from the sleep as long as
death.   270

LV

But his sword of mettle clashëd,
And his arm smote strong, I ween,
And her dreaming spirit flashëd
Through her body's fair white screen,
And the light thereof might guide him up the cedar alleys
green:

LVI

But for me I saw no splendour –
All my sword was my child-heart;
And the wood refused surrender
Of that bower it held apart,
Safe as Œdipus's grave-place 'mid Colone's olives swart.   280

LVII

As Aladdin sought the basements
His fair palace rose upon,
And the four-and-twenty casements
Which gave answers to the sun;
So, in wilderment of gazing, I looked up and I looked down.

LVIII

Years have vanished since, as wholly
As the little bower did then;
And you call it tender folly
That such thoughts should come again?
Ah, I cannot change this sighing for your smiling, brother
     men!   290

LIX

For this loss it did prefigure
Other loss of better good,
When my soul, in spirit vigour
And in ripened womanhood,
Fell from visions of more beauty than an arbour in a wood.

LX

I have lost – oh, many a pleasure,
Many a hope and many a power –
Studious health and merry leisure,
The first dew on the first flower!
But the first of all my losses was the losing of the bower.   300

LXI

I have lost the dream of Doing,
And the other dream of Done,
The first spring in the pursuing,
The first pride in the Begun, –
First recoil from incompletion, in the face of what is won –

LXII

Exaltations in the far light
Where some cottage only is;
Mild dejections in the starlight,
Which the sadder-hearted miss;
And the child-cheek blushing scarlet for the very shame of
       bliss.   310

LXIII

I have lost the sound child-sleeping
Which the thunder could not break;
Something too of the strong leaping
Of the staglike heart awake,
Which the pale is low for keeping in the road it ought to
       take.

LXIV

Some respect to social fictions
Has been also lost by me;
And some generous genuflexions,
Which my spirit offered free
To the pleasant old conventions of our false humanity.   320

LXV

All my losses did I tell you,
Ye perchance would look away, –
Ye would answer me, 'Farewell! you
Make sad company to-day,
And your tears are falling faster than the bitter words you
       say.'

LXVI

For God placed me like a dial
In the open ground with power,
And my heart had for its trial
All the sun and all the shower:
And I suffered many losses, – and my first was of the
      bower. 330

LXVII

Laugh you? If that loss of mine be
Of no heavy-seeming weight –
When the cone falls from the pine-tree,
The young children laugh thereat;
Yet the wind that struck it, riseth, and the tempest shall be
      great.

LXVIII

One who knew me in my childhood
In the glamour and the game,
Looking on me long and mild, would
Never know me for the same.
Come, unchanging recollections, where those changes
      overcame! 340

LXIX

By this couch I weakly lie on,
While I count my memories, –
Through the fingers which, still sighing,
I press closely on mine eyes, –
Clear as once beneath the sunshine, I behold the bower arise.

LXX

Springs the linden-tree as greenly,
Stroked with light adown its rind;
And the ivy-leaves serenely
Each in either intertwined;
And the rose-trees at the doorway, they have neither grown
        nor pined.   350

LXXI

From those overblown faint roses
Not a leaf appeareth shed,
And that little bud discloses
Not a thorn's-breadth more of red
For the winters and the summers which have passed me
        overhead.

LXXII

And that music overfloweth,
Sudden sweet, the sylvan eaves:
Thrush or nightingale – who knoweth?
Fay or Faunus – who believes?
But my heart still trembles in me to the trembling of the
        leaves.   360

LXXIII

Is the bower lost, then? who sayeth
That the bower indeed is lost?
Hark! my spirit in it prayeth
Through the sunshine and the frost, –
And the prayer preserves it greenly, to the last and uttermost.

LXXIV

Till another open for me
　　In God's Eden-land unknown,
　　　　With an angel at the doorway,
　　　　White with gazing at His throne;
And a saint's voice in the palm-trees, singing – 'All is lost . . .
　　　　and won!'   370

RIME OF THE DUCHESS MAY

I

To the belfry, one by one, went the
　　ringers from the sun,
　　　　Toll slowly.
And the oldest ringer said, 'Ours is
　　music for the Dead,
　　　　When the rebecks are all done.'

II

Six abeles i' the churchyard grow on the
　　northside in a row,
　　　　Toll slowly.
And the shadows of their tops rock across   10
　　the little slopes
　　　　Of the grassy graves below.

III

On the south side and the west, a small
　　river runs in haste,
　　　　Toll slowly.
And between the river flowing and the
　　fair green trees a-growing
　　　　Do the dead lie at their rest.

IV

On the east I sate that day, up against
     a willow grey.   20
         Toll slowly.
Through the rain of willow-branches, I
     could see the low hill-ranges,
     And the river on its way.

V

There I sate beneath the tree, and the
     bell tolled solemnly,
         Toll slowly.
While the trees' and river's voices flowed
     between the solemn noises, –
     Yet death seemed more loud to me.   30

VI

There, I read this ancient rime, while
     the bell did all the time
         Toll slowly.
And the solemn knell fell in with the tale
     of life and sin,
     Like a rhythmic fate sublime.

THE RIME

I

Broad the forests stood (I read) on the
     hills of Linteged –
         Toll slowly.
And three hundred years had stood mute   40
     adown each hoary wood,
     Like a full heart having prayed.

II

And the little birds sang east, and the
  little birds sang west,
    Toll slowly.
And but little thought was theirs of the
  silent antique years,
    In the building of their nest.

III

Down the sun dropt large and red, on
  the towers of Linteged, –
    Toll slowly.
Lance and spear upon the height,
  bristling strange in fiery light,
    While the castle stood in shade.

50

IV

There, the castle stood up black, with
  the red sun at its back, –
    Toll slowly.
Like a sullen smouldering pyre, with a
  top that flickers fire
    When the wind is on its track.

60

V

And five hundred archers tall did besiege
  the castle wall,
    Toll slowly.
And the castle, seethed in blood, fourteen
  days and nights had stood,
    And to-night was near its fall.

VI

Yet thereunto, blind to doom, three
    months since, a bride did come, –
      Toll slowly.
One who proudly trod the floors, and   70
    softly whispered in the doors,
      'May good angels bless our home.'

VII

Oh, a bride of queenly eyes, with a front
    of constancies!
      Toll slowly.
Oh, a bride of cordial mouth, – where the
    untired smile of youth
      Did light outward its own sighs.

VIII

'Twas a Duke's fair orphan-girl, and her
    uncle's ward, the Earl;   80
      Toll slowly.
Who betrothed her twelve years old, for
    the sake of dowry gold,
      To his son Lord Leigh, the churl.

IX

But what time she had made good all her
    years of womanhood,
      Toll slowly.
Unto both those lords of Leigh, spake
    she out right sovranly,
      'My will runneth as my blood.'   90

X

'And while this same blood makes red
    this same right hand's veins,' she said, –
        Toll slowly.
''Tis my will as lady free, not to wed
    a lord of Leigh,
      But Sir Guy of Linteged.'

XI

The old Earl he smilèd smooth, then he
    sighed for wilful youth, –
        Toll slowly.
'Good my niece, that hand withal looketh
    somewhat soft and small
      For so large a will, in sooth.'   100

XII

She, too, smiled by that same sign, – but
    her smile was cold and fine, –
        Toll slowly.
'Little hand clasps muckle gold, or it
    were not worth the hold
      Of thy son, good uncle mine!'

XIII

Then the young lord jerked his breath,
    and sware thickly in his teeth, –   110
        Toll slowly.
'He would wed his own betrothed, an
    she loved him an she loathed,
      Let the life come or the death.'

XIV

Up she rose with scornful eyes, as her
    father's child might rise, –
        Toll slowly.
'Thy hound's blood, my lord of Leigh,
    stains thy knightly heel,' quoth she,
      'And he moans not where he lies.   120

XV

'But a woman's will dies hard, in the
    hall or on the sward!' –
        Toll slowly.
'By that grave, my lords, which made me
    orphaned girl and dowered lady,
      I deny you wife and ward.'

XVI

Unto each she bowed her head, and
    swept past with lofty tread.
        Toll slowly.
Ere the midnight-bell had ceased,   130
    in the chapel had the priest
      Blessed her, bride of Linteged.

XVII

Fast and fain the bridal train along the
    night-storm rode amain.
        Toll slowly.
Hard the steeds of lord and serf struck
    their hoofs out on the turf,
      In the pauses of the rain.

XVIII

Fast and fain the kinsmen's train along
  the storm pursued amain –   140
   Toll slowly.
Steed on steed-track, dashing off –
  thickening, doubling, hoof on hoof,
  In the pauses of the rain.

XIX

And the bridegroom led the flight on his
  red-roan steed of might,
   Toll slowly.
And the bride lay on his arm, still, as if
  she feared no harm,
  Smiling out into the night.   150

XX

'Dost thou fear?' he said at last. – 'Nay,'
  she answered him in haste, –
   Toll slowly.
'Not such death as we could find – only
  life with one behind –
  Ride on fast as fear – ride fast!'

XXI

Up the mountain wheeled the steed –
  girth to ground, and fetlocks spread, –
   Toll slowly.
Headlong bounds, and rocking flanks, –   160
  down he staggered, down the banks,
  To the towers of Linteged.

XXII

High and low the serfs looked out, red
　　the flambeaus tossed about, –
　　　　Toll slowly.
In the courtyard rose the cry – 'Live the
　　Duchess and Sir Guy!'
　　But she never heard them shout.

XXIII

On the steed she dropt her cheek, kissed
　　his mane and kissed his neck. –
　　　　Toll slowly.
'I had happier died by thee, than lived
　　on, a Lady Leigh,'
　　Were the first words she did speak.

XXIV

But a three months' joyaunce lay 'twixt
　　that moment and to-day,
　　　　Toll slowly.
When five hundred archers tall stand
　　beside the castle wall,
　　To recapture Duchess May.

XXV

And the castle standeth black, with the
　　red sun at its back, –
　　　　Toll slowly.
And a fortnight's siege is done – and,
　　except the duchess, none
　　Can misdoubt the coming wrack.

170

180

XXVI

Then the captain, young Lord Leigh, with
    his eyes so grey of blee,
      Toll slowly.
And thin lips that scarcely sheath the cold   190
    white gnashing of his teeth,
      Gnashed in smiling, absently,

XXVII

Cried aloud, 'So goes the day, bridegroom
    fair of Duchess May!' –
      Toll slowly.
'Look thy last upon that sun! if thou
    seest to-morrow's one,
      'Twill be through a foot of clay.

XXVIII

'Ha, fair bride! dost hear no sound, save
    that moaning of the hound?' –   200
      Toll slowly.
'Thou and I have parted troth, – yet
    I keep my vengeance-oath,
      And the other may come round.

XXIX

'Ha! thy will is brave to dare, and thy
    new love past compare,' –
      Toll slowly.
'Yet thine old love's faulchion brave is
    as strong a thing to have
      As the will of lady fair.   210

XXX

'Peck on blindly, netted dove! – If a
        wife's name thee behove,'
            Toll slowly.
'Thou shalt wear the same to-morrow,
        ere the grave has hid the sorrow
    Of thy last ill-mated love.

XXXI

'O'er his fixed and silent mouth, thou
        and I will call back troth.'
            Toll slowly.
'He shall altar be and priest, – and he   220
        will not cry at least
    "I forbid you – I am loath!"'

XXXII

'I will wring thy fingers pale in the
        gauntlet of my mail.'
            Toll slowly.
'"Little hand and muckle gold" close
        shall lie within my hold,
    As the sword did, to prevail.'

XXXIII

Oh, the little birds sang east, and the
        little birds sang west,   230
            Toll slowly.
Oh, and laughed the Duchess May, and
        her soul did put away
    All his boasting, for a jest.

XXXIV

In her chamber did she sit, laughing low
    to think of it, –
       Toll slowly.
'Tower is strong and will is free – thou
    canst boast, my lord of Leigh,
    But thou boastest little wit.'   240

XXXV

In her tire-glass gazèd she, and she
    blushed right womanly.
       Toll slowly.
She blushed half from her disdain – half,
    her beauty was so plain,
    – 'Oath for oath, my lord of Leigh!'

XXXVI

Straight she called her maidens in –
    'Since ye gave me blame herein,'
       Toll slowly.
'That a bridal such as mine should lack
    gauds to make it fine,
    Come and shrive me from that sin.   250

XXXVII

'It is three months gone to-day since
    I gave mine hand away.'
       Toll slowly.
'Bring the gold and bring the gem, we
    will keep bride-state in them,
    While we keep the foe at bay.

XXXVIII

'On your arms I loose mine hair! – comb
    it smooth and crown it fair.'   260
      Toll slowly.
'I would look in purple pall from this
    lattice down the wall,
      And throw scorn to one that's there!'

XXXIX

Oh, the little birds sang east, and the
    little birds sang west.
      Toll slowly.
On the tower the castle's lord leant in
    silence on his sword,
      With an anguish in his breast.   270

XL

With a spirit-laden weight, did he lean
    down passionate.
      Toll slowly.
They have almost sapped the wall, – they
    will enter therewithal,
      With no knocking at the gate.

XLI

Then the sword he leant upon, shivered,
    snapped upon the stone, –
      Toll slowly.
'Sword,' he thought, with inward laugh,   280
    'ill thou servest for a staff
      When thy nobler use is done!

XLII

'Sword, thy nobler use is done! – tower
is lost, and shame begun!' –
Toll slowly.
'If we met them in the breach, hilt to
hilt or speech to speech,
We should die there, each for one.

XLIII

'If we met them at the wall, we should
singly, vainly fall,' –
Toll slowly.
'But if *I* die here alone, – then I die,
who am but one,
And die nobly for them all.

XLIV

'Five true friends lie for my sake, in the
moat and in the brake,' –
Toll slowly.
'Thirteen warriors lie at rest, with a
black wound in the breast,
And not one of these will wake.

XLV

'So no more of this shall be! – heart-blood
weighs too heavily,' –
Toll slowly.
'And I could not sleep in grave, with the
faithful and the brave
Heaped around and over me.

XLVI

'Since young Clare a mother hath, and
      young Ralph a plighted faith,' –
            Toll slowly.
'Since my pale young sister's cheeks   310
      blush like rose when Ronald speaks,
      Albeit never a word she saith –

XLVII

'These shall never die for me – life-blood
      falls too heavily:'
            Toll slowly.
'And if *I* die here apart, – o'er my dead
      and silent heart
      They shall pass out safe and free.

XLVIII

'When the foe hath heard it said –
      "Death holds Guy of Linteged,"'   320
            Toll slowly.
'That new corse new peace shall bring,
      and a blessèd, blessèd thing
      Shall the stone be at its head.

XLIX

'Then my friends shall pass out free, and
      shall bear my memory,' –
            Toll slowly.
'Then my foes shall sleek their pride,
      soothing fair my widowed bride,
      Whose sole sin was love of me.   330

L

'With their words all smooth and sweet,
    they will front her and entreat,'
      Toll slowly.
'And their purple pall will spread under-
    neath her fainting head
    While her tears drop over it.

LI

'She will weep her woman's tears, she
    will pray her woman's prayers,' –
      Toll slowly.
'But her heart is young in pain, and her   340
    hopes will spring again
    By the suntime of her years.

LII

'Ah, sweet May! ah, sweetest grief! –
    once I vowed thee my belief,'
      Toll slowly.
'That thy name expressed thy sweetness,
    – May of poets, in completeness!
    Now my May-day seemeth brief.'

LIII

All these silent thoughts did swim o'er
    his eyes grown strange and dim, –   350
      Toll slowly.
Till his true men in the place, wished
    they stood there face to face
    With the foe instead of him.

LIV

'One last oath, my friends that wear
    faithful hearts to do and dare!' –
       Toll slowly.
'Tower must fall, and bride be lost! –
    swear me service worth the cost!'
    – Bold they stood around to swear.   360

LV

'Each man clasp my hand and swear, by
    the deed we failed in there,'
       Toll slowly.
'Not for vengeance, not for right, will
    ye strike one blow to-night!'
    – Pale they stood around to swear.

LVI

'One last boon, young Ralph and Clare!
    faithful hearts to do and dare!' –
       Toll slowly.
'Bring that steed up from his stall, which   370
    she kissed before you all!
    Guide him up the turret-stair.

LVII

'Ye shall harness him aright, and lead
    upward to this height.'
       Toll slowly.
'Once in love and twice in war hath he
    borne me strong and far:
    He shall bear me far to-night.'

LVIII

Then his men looked to and fro, when
    they heard him speaking so.   380
      Toll slowly.
– "Las! the noble heart,' they thought, –
    'he in sooth is grief-distraught:
      Would we stood here with the foe!'

LIX

But a fire flashed from his eye, 'twixt
    their thought and their reply, –
      Toll slowly.
'Have ye so much time to waste? We
    who ride here, must ride fast,
      As we wish our foes to fly.'   390

LX

They have fetched the steed with care,
    in the harness he did wear,
      Toll slowly.
Past the court, and through the doors,
    across the rushes of the floors,
      But they goad him up the stair.

LXI

Then from out her bower chambère, did
    the Duchess May repair.
      Toll slowly.
'Tell me now what is your need,' said   400
    the lady, 'of this steed,
      That ye goad him up the stair?'

LXII

Calm she stood; unbodkined through, fell
    her dark hair to her shoe, –
       Toll slowly.
And the smile upon her face, ere she
    left the tiring-glass,
      Had not time enough to go.

LXIII

'Get thee back, sweet Duchess May!
    hope is gone like yesterday,' –   410
       Toll slowly.
'One half-hour completes the breach;
    and thy lord grows wild of speech!
      Get thee in, sweet lady, and pray.

LXIV

'In the east tower, high'st of all, loud
    he cries for steed from stall.'
       Toll slowly.
'He would ride as far,' quoth he, 'as
    for love and victory,
      Though he rides the castle-wall.'   420

LXV

'And we fetch the steed from stall, up
    where never a hoof did fall.' –
       Toll slowly.
'Wifely prayer meets deathly need!
    may the sweet Heavens hear thee plead
      If he rides the castle-wall.'

LXVI

Low she dropt her head, and lower, till
    her hair coiled on the floor, –
       Toll slowly.
And tear after tear you heard fall dis-   430
    tinct as any word
      Which you might be listening for.

LXVII

'Get thee in, thou soft ladye! – here is
    never a place for thee!' –
       Toll slowly.
'Braid thine hair and clasp thy gown,
    that thy beauty in its moan
      May find grace with Leigh of Leigh.'

LXVIII

She stood up in bitter case, with a pale
    yet steady face,   440
       Toll slowly.
Like a statue thunderstruck, which,
    though quivering, seems to look
      Right against the thunder-place.

LXIX

And her foot trod in, with pride, her
    own tears i' the stone beside. –
       Toll slowly.
'Go to, faithful friends, go to! – judge
    no more what ladies do, –
      No, nor how their lords may ride!'   450

LXX

Then the good steed's rein she took, and
    his neck did kiss and stroke:
       Toll slowly.
Soft he neighed to answer her, and then
    followed up the stair,
      For the love of her sweet look.

LXXI

Oh, and steeply, steeply wound up the
    narrow stair around!
       Toll slowly.
Oh, and closely, closely speeding, step
    by step beside her treading,   460
      Did he follow, meek as hound.

LXXII

On the east tower, high'st of all, – there,
    where never a hoof did fall, –
       Toll slowly.
Out they swept, a vision steady, – noble
    steed and lovely lady,
      Calm as if in bower or stall.

LXXIII

Down she knelt at her lord's knee, and
    she looked up silently, –   470
       Toll slowly.
And he kissed her twice and thrice, for
    that look within her eyes
      Which he could not bear to see.

LXXIV

Quoth he, 'Get thee from this strife, –
    and the sweet saints bless thy life!' –
      Toll slowly.
'In this hour, I stand in need of my
    noble red-roan steed,
      But no more of my noble wife.'   480

LXXV

Quoth she, 'Meekly have I done all thy
    biddings under sun;'
      Toll slowly.
'But by all my womanhood, which is
    proved so, true and good,
      I will never do this one.

LXXVI

'Now by womanhood's degree, and by
    wifehood's verity,'
      Toll slowly.
'In this hour if thou hast need of thy   490
    noble red-roan steed,
      Thou hast also need of *me*.

LXXVII

'By this golden ring ye see on this
    lifted hand, pardiè,'
      Toll slowly.
'If, this hour, on castle-wall, can be
    room for steed from stall,
      Shall be also room for *me*.

LXXVIII

'So the sweet saints with me be' (did
    she utter solemnly)   500
        Toll slowly.
'If a man, this eventide, on this castle
    wall will ride,
      He shall ride the same with *me.*'

LXXIX

Oh, he sprang up in the selle, and he
    laughed out bitter-well, –
        Toll slowly.
'Wouldst thou ride among the leaves,
    as we used on other eves,
      To hear chime a vesper-bell?'   510

LXXX

She clang closer to his knee – 'Aye, be-
    neath the cypress-tree!' –
        Toll slowly.
'Mock me not, for otherwhere than along
    the greenwood fair
      Have I ridden fast with thee.

LXXXI

'Fast I rode with new-made vows, from
    my angry kinsman's house.'   520
        Toll slowly.
'What, and would you men should reck
    that I dared more for love's sake
      As a bride than as a spouse?

LXXXII

'What, and would you it should fall, as
    a proverb, before all,'
      Toll slowly.
'That a bride may keep your side while
    through castle-gate you ride,
      Yet eschew the castle-wall?'

LXXXIII

Ho! the breach yawns into ruin, and
    roars up against her suing,   530
      Toll slowly.
With the inarticulate din, and the
    dreadful falling in –
      Shrieks of doing and undoing!

LXXXIV

Twice he wrung her hands in twain,
    but the small hands closed again.
      Toll slowly.
Back he reined the steed – back, back!
    but she trailed along his track
      With a frantic clasp and strain.   540

LXXXV

Evermore the foemen pour through the
    crash of window and door, –
      Toll slowly.
And the shouts of Leigh and Leigh, and
    the shrieks of 'kill!' and 'flee!'
      Strike up clear amid the roar.

LXXXVI

Thrice he wrung her hands in twain, –
    but they closed and clung again, –
      Toll slowly.
Wild she clung, as one, withstood,   550
    clasps a Christ upon the rood,
    In a spasm of deathly pain.

LXXXVII

She clung wild and she clung mute,
    with her shuddering lips half-shut.
      Toll slowly.
Her head fallen as half in swound, –
    hair and knee swept on the ground,
    She clung wild to stirrup and foot.

LXXXVIII

Back he reined his steed back-thrown
    on the slippery coping-stone:
      Toll slowly.   560
Back the iron hoofs did grind on the
    battlement behind
    Whence a hundred feet went down.

LXXXXIX

And his heel did press and goad on the
    quivering flank bestrode, –
      Toll slowly.
'Friends and brothers, save my wife! –
    Pardon, sweet, in change for life, –
    But I ride alone to God.'   570

XC

Straight as if the Holy name had up-
    breathed her like a flame,
      Toll slowly.
She upsprang, she rose upright, – in his
    selle she sate in sight,
      By her love she overcame.

XCI

And her head was on his breast, where
    she smiled as one at rest, –
      Toll slowly.
'Ring,' she cried, 'O vesper-bell, in the
    beechwood's old chapelle!
      But the passing-bell rings best.'

580

XCII

They have caught out at the rein, which
    Sir Guy threw loose – in vain, –
      Toll slowly.
For the horse in stark despair, with his
    front hoofs poised in air,
      On the last verge rears amain.

XCIII

Now he hangs, he rocks between, and
    his nostrils curdle in! –
      Toll slowly.
Now he shivers head and hoof – and the
    flakes of foam fall off,
      And his face grows fierce and thin!

590

XCIV

And a look of human woe from his
          staring eyes did go,
                    Toll slowly.
And a sharp cry uttered he, in a foretold
          agony
          Of the headlong death below, –   600

XCV

And, 'Ring, ring, thou passing-bell,'
          still she cried, 'i' the old chapelle!' –
                    Toll slowly.
Then back-toppling, crashing back –
          a dead weight flung out to wrack,
          Horse and riders overfell.

I

Oh, the little birds sang east, and the
          little birds sang west,
                    Toll slowly.
And I read this ancient Rime, in the
          churchyard, while the chime   610
          Slowly tolled for one at rest.

II

The abeles moved in the sun, and the
          river smooth did run,
                    Toll slowly.
And the ancient Rime rang strange,
          with its passion and its change,
          Here, where all done lay undone.

III

And beneath a willow tree, I a little
    grave did see,   620
      Toll slowly.
Where was graved, – HERE UNDEFILED,
    LIETH MAUD, A THREE-YEAR CHILD,
    EIGHTEEN HUNDRED, FORTY-THREE.

IV

Then, O spirits, did I say, ye who rode
    so fast that day, –
      Toll slowly.
Did star-wheels and angel wings, with
    their holy winnowings,
    Keep beside you all the way?   630

V

Though in passion ye would dash, with
    a blind and heavy crash,
      Toll slowly.
Up against the thick-bossed shield of
    God's judgement in the field, –
    Though your heart and brain were rash, –

VI

Now, your will is all unwilled – now,
    your pulses are all stilled!
      Toll slowly.
Now, ye lie as meek and mild (whereso   640
    laid) as Maud the child,
    Whose small grave was lately filled.

VII

Beating heart and burning brow, ye are
     very patient now,
        Toll slowly.
And the children might be bold to pluck
     the kingcups from your mould
     Ere a month had let them grow.

VIII

And you let the goldfinch sing in the alder
     near in spring,   650
        Toll slowly.
Let her build her nest and sit all the
     three weeks out on it,
     Murmuring not at anything.

IX

In your patience ye are strong; cold
     and heat ye take not wrong.
        Toll slowly.
When the trumpet of the angel blows
     eternity's evangel,
     Time will seem to you not long.   660

X

Oh, the little birds sang east, and the
     little birds sang west,
        Toll slowly.
And I said in underbreath, – All our life
     is mixed with death,
     And who knoweth which is best?

XI

Oh, the little birds sang east, and the
    little birds sang west,
      Toll slowly.
And I smiled to think God's greatness
    flowed around our incompleteness, –
    Round our restlessness, His rest.

670

BERTHA IN THE LANE

I

Put the broidery-frame away,
    For my sewing is all done:
The last thread is used to-day,
    And I need not join it on.
Though the clock stands at the noon
I am weary. I have sewn,
Sweet, for thee, a wedding gown.

II

Sister, help me to the bed,
    And stand near me, Dearest-sweet.
Do not shrink nor be afraid,
    Blushing with a sudden heat!
No one standeth in the street? –
By God's love I go to meet,
Love I thee with love complete.

10

III

Lean thy face down; drop it in
   These two hands, that I may hold
'Twixt their palms thy cheek and chin,
   Stroking back the curls of gold:
'Tis a fair, fair face, in sooth –
Larger eyes and redder mouth   20
Than mine were in my first youth.

IV

Thou art younger by seven years –
   Ah! – so bashful at my gaze,
That the lashes, hung with tears,
   Grow too heavy to upraise?
I would wound thee by no touch
Which thy shyness feels as such:
Dost though mind me, Dear, so much?

V

Have I not been nigh a mother
   To thy sweetness – tell me, Dear?   30
Have we not loved one another
   Tenderly, from year to year,
Since our dying mother mild
Said with accents undefiled,
'Child, be mother to this child!'

VI

Mother, mother, up in heaven,
   Stand up on the jasper sea,
And be witness I have given
   All the gifts required of me, –
Hope that blessed me, bliss that crowned,   40
Love that left me with a wound,
Life itself that turneth round!

VII

Mother, mother, thou art kind,
   Thou art standing in the room,
In a molten glory shrined
   That rays off into the gloom!
But thy smile is bright and bleak
Like cold waves – I cannot speak,
I sob in it, and grow weak.

VIII

Ghostly mother, keep aloof   50
   One hour longer from my soul,
For I still am thinking of
   Earth's warm-beating joy and dole!
On my finger is a ring
Which I still see glittering
When the night hides everything.

IX

Little sister, thou art pale!
   Ah, I have a wandering brain –
But I lose that fever-bale,
   And my thoughts grow calm again.   60
Lean down closer – closer still!
I have words thine ear to fill, –
And would kiss thee at my will.

X

Dear, I heard thee in the spring,
   Thee and Robert – through the trees, –
When we all went gathering
   Boughs of May-bloom for the bees.
Do not start so! think instead
How the sunshine overhead
Seemed to trickle through the shade.   70

XI

What a day it was, that day!
  Hills and vales did openly
Seem to heave and throb away
  At the sight of the great sky;
And the silence, as it stood
In the glory's golden flood,
Audibly did bud, and bud.

XII

Through the winding hedgerows green,
  How we wandered, I and you, –
With the bowery tops shut in,   80
  And the gates that showed the view!
How we talked there! thrushes soft
Sang our praises out, or oft
Bleatings took them, from the croft:

XIII

Till the pleasure grown too strong
  Left me muter evermore,
And, the winding road being long,
  I walked out of sight, before,
And so, wrapt in musings fond,
Issued (past the wayside pond)   90
On the meadow-lands beyond.

XIV

I sate down beneath the beech
  Which leans over to the lane,
And the far sound of your speech
  Did not promise any pain;
And I blessed you full and free,
With a smile stooped tenderly
O'er the May-flowers on my knee.

XV

But the sound grew into word
    As the speakers drew more near –   100
Sweet, forgive me that I heard
    What you wished me not to hear.
Do not weep so – do not shake –
Oh, – I heard thee, Bertha, make
Good true answers for my sake.

XVI

Yes, and HE too! let him stand
    In thy thoughts untouched by blame.
Could he help it, if my hand
    He had claimed with hasty claim?
That was wrong perhaps – but then   110
Such things be – and will, again.
Women cannot judge for men.

XVII

Had he seen thee when he swore
    He would love but me alone?
Thou wast absent, sent before
    To our kin in Sidmouth town.
When we saw thee who art best
Past compare, and loveliest,
He but judged thee as the rest.

XVIII

Could we blame him with grave words,   120
    Thou and I, Dear, if we might?
Thy brown eyes have looks like birds
    Flying straightway to the light:
Mine are older. – Hush! – look out –
Up the street! Is none without?
How the poplar swings about!

XIX

And that hour – beneath the beech,
   When I listened in a dream,
And he said in his deep speech
   That he owed me all *esteem*, –   130
Each word swam in on my brain
With a dim, dilating pain,
Till it burst with that last strain.

XX

I fell flooded with a dark,
   In the silence of a swoon.
When I rose, still cold and stark,
   There was night, – I saw the moon:
And the stars, each in its place,
And the May-blooms on the grass,
Seemed to wonder what I was.   140

XXI

And I walked as if apart
   From myself, when I could stand –
And I pitied my own heart,
   As if I held it in my hand,
Somewhat coldly, – with a sense
Of fulfilled benevolence,
And a 'Poor thing' negligence.

XXII

And I answered coldly too,
   When you met me at the door;
And I only *heard* the dew   150
   Dripping from me to the floor;
And the flowers I bade you see,
Were too withered for the bee, –
As my life, henceforth, for me.

XXIII

Do not weep so – Dear – heart-warm!
    All was best as it befell.
If I say he did me harm,
    I speak wild, – I am not well.
All his words were kind and good –
He esteemed me. Only, blood   160
Runs so faint in womanhood!

XXIV

Then I always was too grave, –
    Liked the saddest ballad sung, –
With that look, besides, we have
    In our faces, who die young.
I had died, Dear, all the same;
Life's long, joyous, jostling game
Is too loud for my meek shame.

XXV

We are so unlike each other,
    Thou and I, that none could guess   170
We were children of one mother,
    But for mutual tenderness.
Thou art rose-lined from the cold,
And meant verily to hold
Life's pure pleasures manifold.

XXVI

I am pale as crocus grows
    Close behind a rose-tree's root;
Whosoe'er would reach the rose,
    Treads the crocus underfoot.
I, like May-bloom on thorn-tree,   180
Thou, like merry summer-bee!
Fit that I be plucked for thee!

XXVII

Yet who plucks me? – no one mourns,
  I have lived my season out,
And now die of my own thorns
  Which I could not live without.
Sweet, be merry! How the light
Comes and goes! If it be night
Keep the candles in my sight.

XXVIII

Are there footsteps at the door?   190
  Look out quickly. Yea, or nay?
Some one might be waiting for
  Some last word that I might say.
Nay? So best! – so angels would
Stand off clear from deathly road,
Not to cross the sight of God.

XXIX

Colder grow my hands and feet.
  When I wear the shroud I made,
Let the folds lie straight and neat,
  And the rosemary be spread,   200
That if any friend should come,
(To see *thee*, Sweet!) all the room
May be lifted out of gloom.

XXX

And, dear Bertha, let me keep
  On my hand this little ring,
Which at nights, when others sleep,
  I can still see glittering.
Let me wear it out of sight,
In the grave, – where it will light
All the dark up, day and night.   210

XXXI

On that grave drop not a tear!
  Else, though fathom-deep the place,
Through the woollen shroud I wear
  I shall feel it on my face.
Rather smile there, blessëd one,
Thinking of me in the sun,
Or forget me – smiling on!

XXXII

Art thou near me? nearer? so!
  Kiss me close upon the eyes,
That the earthly light may go
  Sweetly, as it used to rise,
When I watched the morning-grey
Strike, betwixt the hills, the way
He was sure to come that day.

XXXIII

So, – no more vain words be said!
  The hosannas nearer roll.
Mother, smile now on thy Dead,
  I am death-strong in my soul.
Mystic Dove alit on cross,
Guide the poor bird of the snows
Through the snow-wind above loss!

XXXIV

Jesus, Victim, comprehending
  Love's divine self-abnegation,
Cleanse my love in its self-spending,
  And absorb the poor libation!
Wind my thread of life up higher.
Up, through angels' hands of fire!
I aspire while I expire.

CATARINA TO CAMOËNS

DYING IN HIS ABSENCE ABROAD,
AND REFERRING TO THE POEM IN WHICH
HE RECORDED THE SWEETNESS OF
HER EYES

I

On the door you will not enter,
  I have gazed too long – adieu!
Hope withdraws her peradventure –
  Death is near me, – and not *you*.
      Come, O lover,
      Close and cover
These poor eyes, you called, I ween,
'Sweetest eyes, were ever seen.'

II

When I heard you sing that burden
  In my vernal days and bowers,   10
Other praises disregarding,
  I but hearkened that of yours –
      Only saying
      In heart-playing,
'Blessed eyes mine eyes have been,
If the sweetest, HIS have seen!'

III

But all changes. At this vesper,
  Cold the sun shines down the door.
If you stood there, would you whisper
  'Love, I love you,' as before, –   20
      Death pervading
      Now, and shading
Eyes you sang of, that yestreen,
As the sweetest ever seen?

IV

Yes, I think, were you beside them,
   Near the bed I die upon, –
Though their beauty you denied them,
   As you stood there, looking down,
      You would truly
       Call them duly,   30
For the love's sake found therein, –
'Sweetest eyes, were ever seen.'

V

And if *you* looked down upon them,
   And if *they* looked up to *you*,
All the light which has foregone them
   Would be gathered back anew.
      They would truly
      Be as duly
Love-transformed to beauty's sheen, –
'Sweetest eyes, were ever seen.'   40

VI

But, ah me! you only see me,
   In your thoughts of loving man,
Smiling soft perhaps and dreamy
   Through the wavings of my fan, –
      And unweeting
      Go repeating,
In your reverie serene,
'Sweetest eyes, were ever seen.'

VII

While my spirit leans and reaches
   From my body still and pale,   50
Fain to hear what tender speech is
   In your love to help my bale –
         O my poet,
         Come and show it!
Come, of latest love, to glean
'Sweetest eyes, were ever seen.'

VIII

O my poet, O my prophet,
   When you praised their sweetness so,
Did you think, in singing of it,
   That it might be near to go?   60
         Had you fancies
         From their glances,
That the grave would quickly screen
'Sweetest eyes, were ever seen'?

IX

No reply! the fountain's warble
   In the court-yard sounds alone.
As the water to the marble
   So my heart falls with a moan
         From love-sighing
         To this dying.   70
Death forerunneth Love to win
'Sweetest eyes, were ever seen.'

X

Will you come? When I'm departed
    Where all sweetnesses are hid;
Where thy voice, my tender-hearted,
    Will not lift up either lid.
        Cry, O lover,
        Love is over!
Cry beneath the cypress green –
'Sweetest eyes, were ever seen.'   80

XI

When the angelus is ringing,
    Near the convent will you walk,
And recall the choral singing
    Which brought angels down our talk?
        Spirit-shriven
        I viewed Heaven,
Till you smiled – 'Is earth unclean,
Sweetest eyes, were ever seen?'

XII

When beneath the palace-lattice,
    You ride slow as you have done,   90
And you see a face there – that is
    Not the old familiar one, –
        Will you oftly
        Murmur softly,
'Here, ye watched me morn and e'en,
Sweetest eyes, were ever seen'?

XIII

When the palace-ladies, sitting
   Round your gittern, shall have said,
'Poet, sing those verses written
   For the lady who is dead,'   100
      Will you tremble,
      Yet dissemble, –
Or sing hoarse, with tears between,
'Sweetest eyes, were ever seen'?

XIV

'Sweetest eyes!' how sweet in flowings
   The repeated cadence is!
Though you sang a hundred poems,
   Still the best one would be this.
      I can hear it
      'Twixt my spirit   110
And the earth-noise intervene –
'Sweetest eyes, were ever seen!'

XV

But the priest waits for the praying,
   And the choir are on their knees,
And the soul must pass away in
   Strains more solemn high than these.
      Miserere
      For the weary!
Oh, no longer for Catrine,
'Sweetest eyes, were ever seen!'   120

XVI

Keep my ribbon, take and keep it
    (I have loosed it from my hair),
Feeling, while you overweep it,
    Not alone in your despair,
            Since with saintly
            Watch unfaintly
Out of heaven shall o'er you lean
'Sweetest eyes, were ever seen.'

XVII

But – but *now* – yet unremovèd
    Up to Heaven, they glisten fast.   130
You may cast away, Belovèd,
    In your future all my past.
            Such old phrases
            May be praises
For some fairer bosom-queen –
'Sweetest eyes, were ever seen!'

XVIII

Eyes of mine, what are ye doing?
    Faithless, faithless, – praised amiss
If a tear be of your showing,
    Dropt for any hope of HIS!   140
            Death has boldness
            Besides coldness,
If unworthy tears demean
'Sweetest eyes, were ever seen.'

XIX

I will look out to his future;
  I will bless it till it shine.
Should he ever be a suitor
  Unto sweeter eyes than mine,
    Sunshine gild them,
    Angels shield them,
Whatsoever eyes terrene
Be the sweetest HIS have seen!   150

THE ROMANCE OF THE SWAN'S NEST

I

Little Ellie sits alone
'Mid the beeches of a meadow
  By a stream-side on the grass,
  And the trees are showering down
Doubles of their leaves in shadow
  On her shining hair and face.

II

She has thrown her bonnet by,
And her feet she has been dipping
  In the shallow water's flow;
  Now she holds them nakedly   10
In her hands, all sleek and dripping,
  While she rocketh to and fro.

III

Little Ellie sits alone,
And the smile she softly uses
  Fills the silence like a speech,
  While she thinks what shall be done, –
And the sweetest pleasure chooses
  For her future within reach.

IV

Little Ellie in her smile
Chooses – 'I will have a lover,   20
   Riding on a steed of steeds!
   He shall love me without guile,
And to *him* I will discover
   The swan's nest among the reeds.

V

'And the steed shall be red-roan,
And the lover shall be noble,
   With an eye that takes the breath;
   And the lute he plays upon
Shall strike ladies into trouble,
   As his sword strikes men to death.   30

VI

'And the steed it shall be shod
All in silver, housed in azure,
   And the mane shall swim the wind;
   And the hoofs along the sod
Shall flash onward and keep measure,
   Till the shepherds look behind.

VII

'But my lover will not prize
All the glory that he rides in,
   When he gazes in my face:
   He will say, "O Love, thine eyes   40
Build the shrine my soul abides in,
   And I kneel here for thy grace!"

VIII

'Then, aye, then he shall kneel low,
With the red-roan steed anear him
    Which shall seem to understand, –
    Till I answer, "Rise and go!
For the world must love and fear him
    Whom I gift with heart and hand."

IX

'Then he will arise so pale,
I shall feel my own lips tremble   50
    With a *yes* I must not say,
    Nathless maiden-brave, "Farewell,"
I will utter, and dissemble –
    "Light to-morrow with to-day!"

X

'Then he'll ride among the hills
To the wide world past the river,
    There to put away all wrong;
    To make straight distorted wills,
And to empty the broad quiver
    Which the wicked bear along.   60

XI

'Three times shall a young foot-page
Swim the stream and climb the mountain
    And kneel down beside my feet –
    "Lo, my master sends this gage,
Lady, for thy pity's counting!
    What wilt thou exchange for it?"

XII

'And the first time, I will send
A white rosebud for a guerdon,
  And the second time, a glove;
  But the third time – I may bend   70
From my pride, and answer – "Pardon,
  If he comes to take my love."

XIII

'Then the young foot-page will run,
Then my lover will ride faster,
  Till he kneeleth at my knee:
  "I am a duke's eldest son!
Thousand serfs do call me master, –
  But, O Love, I love but *thee*!"

XIV

'He will kiss me on the mouth
Then, and lead me as a lover   80
  Through the crowds that praise his deeds:
  And, when soul-tied by one troth,
Unto *him* I will discover
  That swan's nest among the reeds.'

XV

Little Ellie, with her smile
Not yet ended, rose up gaily,
  Tied the bonnet, donned the shoe,
  And went homeward round a mile,
Just to see, as she did daily,
  What more eggs were with the two.   90

XVI

Pushing through the elm-tree copse,
Winding up the stream, light-hearted,
   Where the osier pathway leads –
Past the boughs she stoops – and stops.
Lo, the wild swan had deserted,
   And a rat had gnawed the reeds.

XVII

Ellie went home sad and slow.
If she found the lover ever,
   With his red-roan steed of steeds,
   Sooth I know not! but I know
She could never show him – never,
   That swan's nest among the reeds!

100

THE CRY OF THE HUMAN

I

'There is no God,' the foolish saith,
   But none 'There is no sorrow,'
And nature oft the cry of faith
   In bitter need will borrow:
Eyes, which the preacher could not school,
   By wayside graves are raisèd,
And lips say 'God be pitiful,'
   Who ne'er said 'God be praisèd.'
              Be pitiful, O God!

II

The tempest stretches from the steep   10
  The shadow of its coming,
The beasts grow tame, and near us creep,
  As help were in the human;
Yet, while the cloud-wheels roll and grind,
  We spirits tremble under! –
The hills have echoes, but we find
  No answer for the thunder.
                          Be pitiful, O God!

III

The battle hurtles on the plains,
  Earth feels new scythes upon her;   20
We reap our brothers for the wains,
  And call the harvest – honour;
Draw face to face, front line to line,
  One image all inherit, –
Then kill, curse on, by that same sign,
  Clay, clay, – and spirit, spirit.
                          Be pitiful, O God!

IV

The plague runs festering through the town,
  And never a bell is tolling,
And corpses, jostled 'neath the moon,   30
  Nod to the dead-cart's rolling.
The young child calleth for the cup,
  The strong man brings it weeping;
The mother from her babe looks up,
  And shrieks away its sleeping.
                          Be pitiful, O God!

V

The plague of gold strikes far and near,
    And deep and strong it enters;
This purple chimar which we wear
    Makes madder than the centaur's: 40
Our thoughts grow blank, our words grow strange,
    We cheer the pale gold-diggers –
Each soul is worth so much on 'Change,
    And marked, like sheep, with figures.
                    Be pitiful, O God!

VI

The curse of gold upon the land
    The lack of bread enforces;
The rail-cars snort from strand to strand,
    Like more of Death's white horses!
The rich preach 'rights' and future days,   50
    And hear no angel scoffing, –
The poor die mute – with starving gaze
    On corn-ships in the offing.
                    Be pitiful, O God!

VII

We meet together at the feast,
    To private mirth betake us;
We stare down in the winecup, lest
    Some vacant chair should shake us.
We name delight, and pledge it round –
    'It shall be ours to-morrow!'   60
God's seraphs, do your voices sound
    As sad in naming sorrow?
                    Be pitiful, O God!

VIII

We sit together, with the skies,
   The steadfast skies, above us,
We look into each other's eyes,
   'And how long will you love us?' –
The eyes grow dim with prophecy,
   The voices, low and breathless, –
'Till death us part!' – O words, to be   70
   Our *best*, for love the deathless!
                  Be pitiful, O God!

IX

We tremble by the harmless bed
   Of one loved and departed:
Our tears drop on the lips that said
   Last night, 'Be stronger-hearted!'
O God, – to clasp those fingers close,
   And yet to feel so lonely! –
To see a light upon such brows,
   Which is the daylight only!   80
                  Be pitiful, O God!

X

The happy children come to us,
   And look up in our faces:
They ask us – Was it thus, and thus,
   When we were in their places? –
We cannot speak; – we see anew
   The hills we used to live in,
And feel our mother's smile press through
   The kisses she is giving.
                  Be pitiful, O God!   90

XI

We pray together at the kirk,
   For mercy, mercy, solely:
Hands weary with the evil work,
   We lift them to the Holy.
The corpse is calm below our knee,
   Its spirit, bright before Thee –
Between them, worse than either, we –
   Without the rest of glory!

                    Be pitiful, O God!

XII

We leave the communing of men,   100
   The murmur of the passions,
And live alone, to live again
   With endless generations.
Are we so brave? – The sea and sky
   In silence lift their mirrors,
And, glassed therein, our spirits high
   Recoil from their own terrors.

                    Be pitiful, O God!

XIII

We sit on hills our childhood wist,
   Woods, hamlets, streams, beholding: 110
The sun strikes through the farthest mist,
   The city's spire to golden.
The city's golden spire it was,
   When hope and health were strongest,
But now it is the churchyard grass
   We look upon the longest.

                    Be pitiful, O God!

XIV

And soon all vision waxeth dull –
    Men whisper, 'He is dying':
We cry no more 'Be pitiful!'   120
    We have no strength for crying.
No strength, no need. Then, soul of mine,
    Look up and triumph rather –
Lo, in the depth of God's Divine,
    The Son adjures the Father,
                       BE PITIFUL, O GOD!

THE CRY OF THE CHILDREN

I

Do ye hear the children weeping, O my brothers,
    Ere the sorrow comes with years?
They are leaning their young heads against their mothers,
    And *that* cannot stop their tears.
The young lambs are bleating in the meadows,
    The young birds are chirping in the nest,
The young fawns are playing with the shadows,
    The young flowers are blowing toward the west –
But the young, young children, O my brothers,
    They are weeping bitterly!   10
They are weeping in the playtime of the others,
    In the country of the free.

II

Do you question the young children in the sorrow
     Why their tears are falling so?
The old man may weep for his to-morrow
     Which is lost in Long Ago;
The old tree is leafless in the forest,
  The old year is ending in the frost,
The old wound, if stricken, is the sorest,
  The old hope is hardest to be lost.   20
But the young, young children, O my brothers,
     Do you ask them why they stand
Weeping sore before the bosoms of their mothers,
     In our happy Fatherland?

III

They look up with their pale and sunken faces,
     And their looks are sad to see,
For the man's hoary anguish draws and presses
     Down the cheeks of infancy.
'Your old earth,' they say, 'is very dreary;
  Our young feet,' they say, 'are very weak!   30
Few paces have we taken, yet are weary –
  Our grave-rest is very far to seek.
Ask the aged why they weep, and not the children;
     For the outside earth is cold;
And we young ones stand without, in our bewildering,
     And the graves are for the old.'

IV

'True,' say the children, 'it may happen
    That we die before our time;
Little Alice died last year – her grave is shapen
    Like a snowball, in the rime.   40
We looked into the pit prepared to take her:
  Was no room for any work in the close clay!
From the sleep wherein she lieth none will wake her,
  Crying, "Get up, little Alice! it is day."
If you listen by that grave, in sun and shower,
  With your ear down, little Alice never cries;
Could we see her face, be sure we should not know her,
  For the smile has time for growing in her eyes:
And merry go her moments, lulled and stilled in
    The shroud by the kirk-chime   50
'It is good when it happens,' say the children,
    'That we die before our time.'

V

Alas, alas, the children! they are seeking
    Death in life, as best to have;
They are binding up their hearts away from breaking,
    With a cerement from the grave.
Go out, children, from the mine and from the city,
  Sing out, children, as the little thrushes do;
Pluck you handfuls of the meadow-cowslips pretty,
  Laugh aloud, to feel your fingers let them through!   60
But they answer, 'Are your cowslips of the meadows
    Like our weeds anear the mine?
Leave us quiet in the dark of the coal-shadows,
    From your pleasures fair and fine!

VI

'For oh,' say the children, 'we are weary,
　　And we cannot run or leap;
If we cared for any meadows, it were merely
　　To drop down in them and sleep.
Our knees tremble sorely in the stooping,
　　We fall upon our faces, trying to go;
And, underneath our heavy eyelids drooping,
　　The reddest flower would look as pale as snow;
For, all day, we drag our burden tiring
　　Through the coal-dark, underground –
Or, all day, we drive the wheels of iron
　　In the factories, round and round.

70

VII

'For all day, the wheels are droning, turning;
　　Their wind comes in our faces, –
Till our hearts turn, – our heads with pulses burning,
　　And the walls turn in their places:
Turns the sky in the high window blank and reeling,
　　Turns the long light that drops adown the wall,
Turn the black flies that crawl along the ceiling,
　　All are turning, all the day, and we with all.
And all day, the iron wheels are droning,
　　And sometimes we could pray,
"O ye wheels," (breaking out in a mad moaning)
　　"Stop! be silent for to-day!" '

80

VIII

Aye, be silent! Let them hear each other breathing
    For a moment, mouth to mouth!   90
Let them touch each other's hands, in a fresh wreathing
    Of their tender human youth!
Let them feel that this cold metallic motion
  Is not all the life God fashions or reveals:
Let them prove their living souls against the notion
  That they live in you, or under you, O wheels! –
Still, all day, the iron wheels go onward,
    Grinding life down from its mark;
And the children's souls, which God is calling sunward,
    Spin on blindly in the dark.   100

IX

Now tell the poor young children, O my brothers,
    To look up to Him and pray;
So the blessed One who blesseth all the others,
    Will bless them another day.
They answer, 'Who is God that He should hear us,
  While the rushing of the iron wheels is stirred?
When we sob aloud, the human creatures near us
  Pass by, hearing not, or answer not a word.
And *we* hear not (for the wheels in their resounding)
    Strangers speaking at the door: 110
Is it likely God, with angels singing round him,
    Hears our weeping any more?

X

'Two words, indeed, of praying we remember,
        And at midnight's hour of harm,
"Our Father," looking upward in the chamber,
        We say softly for a charm.
We know no other words except "Our Father,"
    And we think that, in some pause of angels' song,
God may pluck them with the silence sweet to gather,
    And hold both within His right hand which is strong.   120
"Our Father!" If He heard us, He would surely
        (For they call Him good and mild)
Answer, smiling down the steep world very purely,
        "Come and rest with Me, My child."'

XI

'But no!' say the children, weeping faster,
        'He is speechless as a stone:
And they tell us, of His image is the master
        Who commands us to work on.
Go to!' say the children, – 'up in heaven,
    Dark, wheel-like, turning clouds are all we find.   130
Do not mock us; grief has made us unbelieving –
    We look up for God, but tears have made us blind.'
Do you hear the children weeping and disproving,
        O my brothers, what ye preach?
For God's possible is taught by His world's loving,
        And the children doubt of each.

XII

And well may the children weep before you!
      They are weary ere they run;
They have never seen the sunshine, nor the glory
      Which is brighter than the sun.   140
They know the grief of man, without its wisdom;
   They sink in man's despair, without its calm;
Are slaves, without the liberty in Christdom,
   Are martyrs, by the pang without the palm, –
Are worn as if with age, yet unretrievingly
      The harvest of its memories cannot reap, –
Are orphans of the earthly love and heavenly.
      Let them weep! let them weep!

XIII

They look up with their pale and sunken faces,
      And their look is dread to see,   150
For they mind you of their angels in high places,
      With eyes turned on Deity! –
'How long,' they say, 'how long, O cruel nation,
   Will you stand, to move the world, on a child's heart, –
Stifle down with a mailed heel its palpitation,
   And tread onward to your throne amid the mart?
Our blood splashes upward, O gold-heaper,
      And your purple shows your path!
But the child's sob in the silence curses deeper
      Than the strong man in his wrath.'   160

THE POET AND THE BIRD

A FABLE

I

Said a people to a poet – 'Go out from
    among us straightway!
While we are thinking earthly things,
    thou singest of divine.
There's a little fair brown nightingale,
    who, sitting in the gateway,
  Makes fitter music to our ear than any
    song of thine!'

II

The poet went out weeping – the nightin-
    gale ceased chanting,   10
  'Now, wherefore, O thou nightingale,
    is all thy sweetness done?'
– 'I cannot sing my earthly things, the
    heavenly poet wanting,
  Whose highest harmony includes the
    lowest under sun.'

III

The poet went out weeping, – and died
    abroad, bereft there:
  The bird flew to his grave and died
    amid a thousand wails.
And, when I last came by the place,   20
    I swear the music left there
  Was only of the poet's song, and not
    the nightingale's.

From

POEMS
(1850)

A SABBATH MORNING AT SEA

I

The ship went on with solemn face;
   To meet the darkness on the deep,
     The solemn ship went onward.
I bowed down weary in the place,
   For parting tears and present sleep
     Had weighed mine eyelids downward.

II

Thick sleep which shut all dreams from me,
   And kept my inner self apart
     And quiet from emotion,
Then brake away and left me free,   10
   Made conscious of a human heart
     Betwixt the heaven and ocean.

III

The new sight, the new wondrous sight!
   The waters round me, turbulent, –
     The skies impassive o'er me,
Calm, in a moonless, sunless light,
   Half glorified by that intent
     Of holding the day-glory!

IV

Two pale thin clouds did stand upon
   The meeting line of sea and sky,   20
     With aspect still and mystic.
I think they did foresee the sun,
   And rested on their prophecy
     In quietude majestic,

V

Then flushed to radiance where they stood,
  Like statues by the open tomb
    Of shining saints half risen. –
The sun! – he came up to be viewed,
  And sky and sea made mighty room
    To inaugurate the vision.   30

VI

I oft had seen the dawnlight run,
  As red wine, through the hills, and break
    Through many a mist's inurning;
But, here, no earth profaned the sun!
  Heaven, ocean, did alone partake
    The sacrament of morning.

VII

Away with thoughts fantastical!
  I would be humble to my worth,
    Self-guarded as self-doubted:
Though here no earthly shadows fall,   40
  I, joying, grieving without earth,
    May desecrate without it.

VIII

God's sabbath morning sweeps the waves;
  I would not praise the pageant high,
    Yet miss the dedicature.
I, carried toward the sunless graves
  By force of natural things, – should I
    Exult in only nature?

IX

And could I bear to sit alone
  'Mid nature's fixed benignities,   50
    While my warm pulse was moving?
Too dark thou art, O glittering sun,
  Too strait ye are, capacious seas,
    To satisfy the loving!

X

It seems a better lot than so,
  To sit with friends beneath the beech,
    And feel them dear and dearer;
Or follow children as they go
  In pretty pairs, with softened speech,
    As the church-bells ring nearer.   60

XI

Love me, sweet friends, this sabbath day!
  The sea sings round me while ye roll
    Afar the hymn unaltered,
And kneel, where once I knelt to pray,
  And bless me deeper in the soul,
    Because the voice has faltered.

XII

And though this sabbath comes to me
  Without the stolèd minister
    Or chanting congregation,
God's spirit brings communion, HE   70
  Who brooded soft on waters drear,
    Creator on creation.

XIII

Himself, I think, shall draw me higher,
  Where keep the saints with harp and song
  An endless sabbath morning,
And on that sea commixed with fire
  Oft drop their eyelids, raised too long
  To the full Godhead's burning.

HUMAN LIFE'S MYSTERY

I

We sow the glebe, we reap the corn,
  We build the house where we may rest,
And then, at moments, suddenly,
We look up to the great wide sky,
Inquiring wherefore we were born . . .
  For earnest, or for jest?

II

The senses folding thick and dark
  About the stifled soul within,
We guess diviner things beyond,
And yearn to them with yearning fond;
We strike out blindly to a mark
  Believed in, but not seen.

III

We vibrate to the pant and thrill
  Wherewith Eternity has curled
In serpent-twine about God's seat;
While, freshening upward to His feet,
In gradual growth His full-leaved will
  Expands from world to world.

IV

And, in the tumult and excess
　　Of act and passion under sun,　　　　　　20
We sometimes hear – oh, soft and far,
As silver star did touch with star,
The kiss of Peace and Righteousness
　　Through all things that are done.

V

God keeps His holy mysteries
　　Just on the outside of man's dream.
In diapason slow, we think
To hear their pinions rise and sink,
While they float pure beneath His eyes,
　　Like swans adown a stream.　　　　　　30

VI

Abstractions, are they, from the forms
　　Of His great beauty? – exaltations
From His great glory? – strong previsions
Of what we shall be? – intuitions
Of what we are – in calms and storms,
　　Beyond our peace and passions?

VII

Things nameless! which, in passing so,
　　Do stroke us with a subtle grace.
We say, 'Who passes?' – they are dumb.
We cannot see them go or come:　　　　　　40
Their touches fall soft – cold – as snow
　　Upon a blind man's face.

VIII

Yet, touching so, they draw above
  Our common thoughts to Heaven's
        unknown;
Our daily joy and pain, advance
To a divine significance, –
Our human love – O mortal love,
  That light is not its own!

IX

And, sometimes, horror chills our blood
  To be so near such mystic Things,   50
And we wrap round us, for defence,
Our purple manners, moods of sense –
As angels, from the face of God,
  Stand hidden in their wings.

X

And, sometimes, through life's heavy swound
  We grope for them! – with strangled breath
We stretch our hands abroad and try
To reach them in our agony. –
And widen, so, the broad life-wound
  Which soon is large enough for death.   60

QUESTION AND ANSWER

I

Love you seek for, presupposes
  Summer heat and sunny glow.
Tell me, do you find moss-roses
  Budding, blooming in the snow?
Snow might kill the rose-tree's root –
Shake it quickly from your foot,
  Lest it harm you as you go.

II

From the ivy where it dapples
    A grey ruin, stone by stone, –
Do you look for grapes or apples,   10
    Or for sad green leaves alone?
Pluck the leaves off, two or three –
Keep them for morality
    When you shall be safe and gone.

CHANGE UPON CHANGE

I

Five months ago the stream did flow,
    The lilies bloomed within the sedge,
And we were lingering to and fro,
Where none will track thee in this snow,
    Along the stream beside the hedge.
Ah, Sweet, be free to love and go!
    For if I do not hear thy foot,
    The frozen river is as mute,
    The flowers have dried down to the root.
    And why, since these be changed since May,   10
        Shouldst *thou* change less than *they*?

II

And slow, slow as the winter snow
    The tears have drifted to mine eyes;
And my poor cheeks, five months ago
Set blushing at thy praises so,
    Put paleness on for a disguise.
Ah Sweet, be free to praise and go!
    For if my face is turned too pale,
    It was thine oath that first did fail, –
    It was thy love proved false and frail!   20
    And why, since these be changed enow,
        Should *I* change less than *thou*?

A WOMAN'S SHORTCOMINGS

I

She has laughed as softly as if she sighed,
   She has counted six, and over,
Of a purse well filled and a heart well tried –
   Oh, each a worthy lover!
They 'give her time;' for her soul must slip
   Where the world has set the grooving.
She will lie to none with her fair red lip, –
   But love seeks truer loving.

II

She trembles her fan in a sweetness dumb,
   As her thoughts were beyond recalling,   10
With a glance for *one*, and a glance for *some*,
   From her eyelids rising and falling;
Speaks common words with a blushful air,
   Hears bold words, unreproving;
But her silence says – what she never will swear –
   And love seeks better loving.

III

Go, lady, lean to the night-guitar
   And drop a smile to the bringer,
Then smile as sweetly, when he is far,
   At the voice of an in-door singer.   20
Bask tenderly beneath tender eyes;
   Glance lightly, on their removing;
And join new vows to old perjuries –
   But dare not call it loving.

IV

Unless you can think, when the song is done,
   No other is soft in the rhythm;
Unless you can feel, when left by One,
   That all men else go with him;
Unless you can know, when unpraised by his breath,
   That your beauty itself wants proving;   30
Unless you can swear 'For life, for death!' –
   Oh, fear to call it loving!

V

Unless you can muse in a crowd all day
   On the absent face that fixed you;
Unless you can love, as the angels may,
   With the breadth of heaven betwixt you;
Unless you can dream that his faith is fast,
   Through behoving and unbehoving;
Unless you can *die* when the dream is past –
   Oh, never call it loving!   40

THE MASK

I

I have a smiling face, she said,
   I have a jest for all I meet,
I have a garland for my head
   And all its flowers are sweet, –
And so you call me gay, she said.

II

Grief taught to me this smile, she said,
   And Wrong did teach this jesting bold;
These flowers were plucked from garden-bed
   While a death-chime was tolled.
And what now will you say? – she said.   10

III

Behind no prison-grate, she said,
   Which slurs the sunshine half a mile
Live captives so uncomforted
   As souls behind a smile.
God's pity let us pray, she said.

IV

I know my face is bright, she said, –
   Such brightness, dying suns diffuse;
I bear upon my forehead shed
   The sign of what I lose, –
The ending of my day, she said.   20

V

If I dared leave this smile, she said,
   And take a moan upon my mouth,
And tie a cypress round my head,
   And let my tears run smooth, –
It were the happier way, she said.

VI

And since that must not be, she said,
   I fain your bitter world would leave.
How calmly, calmly, smile the Dead,
   Who do not, therefore, grieve!
The yea of Heaven is yea, she said.   30

VII

But in your bitter world, she said,
   Face-joy's a costly mask to wear.
'Tis bought with pangs long nourishèd,
   And rounded to despair.
Grief's earnest makes life's play, she said.

VIII

Ye weep for those who weep? she said –
    Ah fools! I bid you pass them by.
Go, weep for those whose hearts have bled
    What time their eyes were dry.
Whom sadder can I say? she said.   40

A MAN'S REQUIREMENTS

I

Love me, Sweet, with all thou art,
    Feeling, thinking, seeing, –
Love me in the lightest part,
    Love me in full being.

II

Love me with thine open youth
    In its frank surrender;
With the vowing of thy mouth,
    With its silence tender.

III

Love me with thine azure eyes,
    Made for earnest granting,   10
Taking colour from the skies,
    Can Heaven's truth be wanting?

IV

Love me with their lids, that fall
    Snow-like at first meeting;
Love me with thine heart, that all
    Neighbours then see beating.

V

Love me with thine hand stretched out
    Freely – open-minded;
Love me with thy loitering foot, –
    Hearing one behind it.   20

VI

Love me with thy voice, that turns
    Sudden faint above me;
Love me with thy blush that burns
    When I murmur, *Love me!*

VII

Love me with thy thinking soul,
    Break it to love-sighing;
Love me with thy thoughts that roll
    On through living – dying.

VIII

Love me in thy gorgeous airs,
    When the world has crowned thee!   30
Love me, kneeling at thy prayers,
    With the angels round thee.

IX

Love me pure, as musers do,
    Up the woodlands shady;
Love me gaily, fast and true,
    As a winsome lady.

X

Through all hopes that keep us brave,
    Further off or nigher,
Love me for the house and grave, –
    And for something higher.   40

XI

Thus, if thou wilt prove me, Dear,
    Woman's love no fable,
I will love *thee* – half a year –
    As a man is able.

A DENIAL

I

We have met late – it is too late to meet,
    O friend, not more than friend!
Death's forecome shroud is tangled round my feet,
And if I step or stir, I touch the end.
    In this last jeopardy
Can I approach thee, I, who cannot move?
How shall I answer thy request for love?
    Look in my face and see.

II

I love thee not, I dare not love thee! go
    In silence; drop my hand.
If thou seek roses, seek them where they blow
In garden-alleys, not in desert-sand.
    Can life and death agree,
That thou shouldst stoop thy song to my complaint?
I cannot love thee. If the word is faint,
    Look in my face and see.

10

III

I might have loved thee in some former days.
   Oh, then, my spirits had leapt
As now they sink, at hearing thy love-praise.
Before these faded cheeks were overwept,   20
   Had this been asked of me,
To love thee with my whole strong heart and head, –
I should have said still . . . yes, but *smiled* and said,
   'Look in my face and see!'

IV

But now . . . God sees me, God, who took my heart
   And drowned it in life's surge.
In all your wide warm earth I have no part –
A light song overcomes me like a dirge.
   Could Love's great harmony
The saints keep step to when their bonds are loose,   30
Not weigh me down? am *I* a wife to choose?
   Look in my face and see.

V

While I behold, as plain as one who dreams,
   Some woman of full worth,
Whose voice, as cadenced as a silver stream's,
Shall prove the fountain-soul which sends it forth;
   One younger, more thought-free
And fair and gay, than I, thou must forget,
With brighter eyes than these . . . which are not wet . . .
   Look in my face and see!   40

VI

So farewell thou, whom I have known too late
  To let thee come so near.
Be counted happy while men call thee great,
And one belovèd woman feels thee dear! –
  Not I! – that cannot be.
I am lost, I am changed, – I must go farther, where
The change shall take me worse, and no one dare
  Look in my face to see.

VII

Meantime I bless thee. By these thoughts of mine
  I bless thee from all such!
I bless thy lamp to oil, thy cup to wine,   50
Thy hearth to joy, thy hand to an equal touch
  Of loyal troth. For me,
I love thee not, I love thee not! – away!
Here's no more courage in my soul to say
  'Look in my face and see.'

A REED

I

I am no trumpet, but a reed:
No flattering breath shall from me lead
  A silver sound, a hollow sound:
I will not ring, for priest or king,
One blast that in re-echoing
  Would leave a bondsman faster bound.

II

I am no trumpet, but a reed, –
A broken reed, the wind indeed
   Left flat upon a dismal shore;
Yet if a little maid or child   10
Should sigh within it, earnest-mild
   This reed will answer evermore.

III

I am no trumpet, but a reed.
Go, tell the fishers, as they spread
   Their nets along the river's edge,
I will not tear their nets at all,
Nor pierce their hands, if they should fall;
   Then let them leave me in the sedge.

HECTOR IN THE GARDEN

I

Nine years old! The first of any
   Seem the happiest years that come:
   Yet when *I* was nine, I said
   No such word! – I thought instead
That the Greeks had used as many
   In besieging Ilium.

II

Nine green years had scarcely brought me
   To my childhood's haunted spring:
   I had life, like flowers and bees,
   In betwixt the country trees.   10
And the sun the pleasure taught me
   Which he teacheth every thing.

III

If the rain fell, there was sorrow,
  Little head leant on the pane,
  Little finger drawing down it
  The long trailing drops upon it,
And the 'Rain, rain, come to-morrow,'
  Said for charm against the rain.

IV

Such a charm was right Canidian,
  Though you meet it with a jeer!   20
  If I said it long enough,
  Then the rain hummed dimly off,
And the thrush with his pure Lydian
  Was left only to the ear;

V

And the sun and I together
  Went a-rushing out of doors!
  We, our tender spirits, drew
  Over hill and dale in view,
Glimmering hither, glimmering thither,
  In the footsteps of the showers.   30

VI

Underneath the chestnuts dripping,
  Through the grasses wet and fair,
  Straight I sought my garden-ground
  With the laurel on the mound,
And the pear-tree oversweeping
  A side-shadow of green air.

VII

In the garden lay supinely
  A huge giant wrought of spade!
  Arms and legs were stretched at length
  In a passive giant strength, –   40
The fine meadow turf, cut finely,
  Round them laid and interlaid.

VIII

Call him Hector, son of Priam!
  Such his title and degree:
  With my rake I smoothed his brow,
  Both his cheeks I weeded through,
But a rimer such as I am
  Scarce can sing his dignity.

IX

Eyes of gentianellas azure,
  Staring, winking at the skies;   50
  Nose of gillyflowers and box;
  Scented grasses put for locks,
Which a little breeze, at pleasure,
  Set a-waving round his eyes.

X

Brazen helm of daffodillies,
  With a glitter toward the light;
  Purple violets for the mouth,
  Breathing perfumes west and south;
And a sword of flashing lilies,
  Holden ready for the fight.   60

XI

And a breastplate made of daisies,
   Closely fitting, leaf on leaf;
   Periwinkles interlaced
   Drawn for belt about the waist;
While the brown bees, humming praises,
   Shot their arrows round the chief.

XII

And who knows (I sometimes wondered)
   If the disembodied soul
   Of old Hector, once of Troy,
   Might not take a dreary joy   70
Here to enter – if it thundered,
   Rolling up the thunder-roll?

XIII

Rolling this way from Troy-ruin,
   In this body rude and rife
   Just to enter, and take rest
   'Neath the daisies of the breast –
They, with tender roots, renewing
   His heroic heart to life?

XIV

Who could know? I sometimes started
   At a motion or a sound!   80
   Did his mouth speak – naming Troy,
   With an ὀτοτοτοτοῖ?
Did the pulse of the Strong-hearted
   Make the daisies tremble round?

XV

It was hard to answer, often:
   But the birds sang in the tree –
   But the little birds sang bold
   In the pear-tree green and old,
And my terror seemed to soften
   Through the courage of their glee.   90

XVI

Oh, the birds, the tree, the ruddy
   And white blossoms, sleek with rain!
   Oh, my garden, rich with pansies!
   Oh, my childhood's bright romances!
All revive, like Hector's body,
   And I see them stir again!

XVII

And despite life's changes – chances,
   And despite the deathbell's toll,
   They press on me in full seeming!
   Help, some angel! stay this dreaming!   100
As the birds sang in the branches,
   Sing God's patience through my soul!

XVIII

That no dreamer, no neglecter
   Of the present's work unsped,
   I may wake up and be doing,
   Life's heroic ends pursuing,
Though my past is dead as Hector,
   And though Hector is twice dead.

FLUSH OR FAUNUS

You see this dog. It was but yesterday
I mused forgetful of his presence here
Till thought on thought drew downward tear on tear,
When from the pillow where wet-cheeked I lay,
A head as hairy as Faunus thrust its way
Right sudden against my face, – two golden-clear
Great eyes astonished mine, – a drooping ear
Did flap me on either cheek to dry the spray!
I started first as some Arcadian
Amazed by goatly god in twilight grove,   10
But as the bearded vision closelier ran
My tears off, I knew Flush, and rose above
Surprise and sadness, – thanking the true PAN
Who, by low creatures, leads to heights of love.

HIRAM POWERS' GREEK SLAVE

They say Ideal beauty cannot enter
The house of anguish. On the threshold stands
An alien Image with enshackled hands,
Called the Greek Slave! as if the artist meant her
(That passionless perfection which he lent her,
Shadowed not darkened where the sill expands)
To, so, confront man's crimes in different lands
With man's ideal sense. Pierce to the centre,
Art's fiery finger! – and break up ere long
The serfdom of this world! appeal, fair stone,   10
From God's pure heights of beauty against man's wrong!
Catch up in thy divine face, not alone
East griefs but west, – and strike and shame the strong,
By thunders of white silence, overthrown.

THE RUNAWAY SLAVE AT
PILGRIM'S POINT

I

I stand on the mark beside the shore
   Of the first white pilgrim's bended knee,
Where exile turned to ancestor,
   And God was thanked for liberty.
I have run through the night, my skin is as dark,
I bend my knee down on this mark:
   I look on the sky and the sea.

II

O pilgrim-souls, I speak to you!
   I see you come proud and slow
From the land of the spirits pale as dew   10
   And round me and round me ye go.
O pilgrims, I have gasped and run
All night long from the whips of one
   Who in your names works sin and woe!

III

And thus I thought that I would come
   And kneel here where ye knelt before,
And feel your souls around me hum
   In undertone to the ocean's roar;
And lift my black face, my black hand,
Here, in your names, to curse this land   20
   Ye blessed in freedom's, evermore.

IV

I am black, I am black,
    And yet God made me, they say:
But if He did so, smiling back
    He must have cast His work away
Under the feet of His white creatures,
With a look of scorn, that the dusky features
    Might be trodden again to clay.

V

And yet He has made dark things
    To be glad and merry as light:
There's a little dark bird sits and sings,   30
    There's a dark stream ripples out of sight,
And the dark frogs chant in the safe morass,
And the sweetest stars are made to pass
    O'er the face of the darkest night.

VI

But *we* who are dark, we are dark!
    Ah God, we have no stars!
About our souls in care and cark
    Our blackness shuts like prison-bars:
The poor souls crouch so far behind   40
That never a comfort can they find
    By reaching through the prison-bars.

VII

Indeed we live beneath the sky,
    That great smooth Hand of God stretched out
On all His children fatherly,
    To save them from the dread and doubt
Which would be if, from this low place,
All opened straight up to His face
    Into the grand eternity.

VIII

And still God's sunshine and His frost,   50
   They make us hot, they make us cold,
As if we were not black and lost;
   And the beasts and birds, in wood and fold,
Do fear and take us for very men:
Could the whip-poor-will or the cat of the glen
   Look into my eyes and be bold?

IX

I am black, I am black!
   But, once, I laughed in girlish glee,
For one of my colour stood in the track
   Where the drivers drove, and looked at me,   60
And tender and full was the look he gave –
Could a slave look so at another slave –
   I look at the sky and the sea.

X

And from that hour our spirits grew
   As free as if unsold, unbought:
Oh, strong enough, since we were two,
   To conquer the world, we thought.
The drivers drove us day by day;
We did not mind, we went one way,
   And no better a freedom sought.   70

XI

In the sunny ground between the canes,
   He said 'I love you' as he passed;
When the shingle-roof rang sharp with the rains,
   I heard how he vowed it fast:
While others shook he smiled in the hut,
As he carved me a bowl of the cocoa-nut
   Through the roar of the hurricanes.

XII

I sang his name instead of a song,
   Over and over I sang his name,
Upward and downward I drew it along   80
   My various notes, – the same, the same!
I sang it low, that the slave-girls near
Might never guess, from aught they could hear,
   It was only a name – a name.

XIII

I look on the sky and the sea.
   We were two to love, and two to pray:
Yes, two, O God, who cried to Thee,
   Though nothing didst Thou say!
Coldly Thou sat'st behind the sun:
And now I cry who am but one,   90
   Thou wilt not speak to-day.

XIV

We were black, we were black,
   We had no claim to love and bliss,
What marvel if each went to wrack?
   They wrung my cold hands out of his,
They dragged him – where? I crawled to touch
His blood's mark in the dust . . . not much,
   Ye pilgrim-souls, though plain *as this*!

XV

Wrong, followed by a deeper wrong!
   Mere grief's too good for such as I: 100
So the white men brought the shame ere long
   To strangle the sob of my agony.
They would not leave me for my dull
Wet eyes! – it was too merciful
   To let me weep pure tears and die.

XVI

I am black, I am black!
   I wore a child upon my breast,
An amulet that hung too slack,
   And, in my unrest, could not rest:
Thus we went moaning, child and mother,   110
One to another, one to another,
   Until all ended for the best.

XVII

For hark! I will tell you low, low,
   I am black, you see, –
And the babe who lay on my bosom so,
   Was far too white, too white for me;
As white as the ladies who scorned to pray
Beside me at church but yesterday,
   Though my tears had washed a place for my knee.

XVIII

My own, own child! I could not bear   120
   To look in his face, it was so white;
I covered him up with a kerchief there,
   I covered his face in close and tight:
And he moaned and struggled, as well might be,
For the white child wanted his liberty –
   Ha, ha! he wanted the master-right.

XIX

He moaned and beat with his head and feet,
   His little feet that never grew;
He struck them out, as it was meet,
   Against my heart to break it through: 130
I might have sung and made him mild,
But I dared not sing to the white-faced child
   The only song I knew.

XX

I pulled the kerchief very close:
    He could not see the sun, I swear,
More, then, alive, than now he does
    From between the roots of the mango ... where?
I know where. Close! A child and mother
Do wrong to look at one another
    When one is black and one is fair.   140

XXI

Why, in that single glance I had
    Of my child's face, ... I tell you all,
I saw a look that made me mad!
    The *master's* look, that used to fall
On my soul like his lash ... or worse!
And so, to save it from my curse,
    I twisted it round in my shawl.

XXII

And he moaned and trembled from foot to head,
    He shivered from head to foot;
Till after a time, he lay instead   150
    Too suddenly still and mute.
I felt, beside, a stiffening cold:
I dared to lift up just a fold,
    As in lifting a leaf of the mango-fruit.

XXIII

But *my* fruit ... ha, ha! – there, had been
    (I laugh to think on't at this hour!)
Your fine white angels (who have seen
    Nearest the secret of God's power)
And plucked my fruit to make them wine,
And sucked the soul of that child of mine   160
    As the humming-bird sucks the soul of the flower.

XXIV

Ha, ha, the trick of the angels white!
    They freed the white child's spirit so.
I said not a word, but day and night
    I carried the body to and fro,
And it lay on my heart like a stone, as chill.
– The sun may shine out as much as he will:
    I am cold, though it happened a month ago.

XXV

From the white man's house, and the black man's hut,
    I carried the little body on;   170
The forest's arms did round us shut,
    And silence through the trees did run:
They asked no question as I went,
They stood too high for astonishment,
    They could see God sit on His throne.

XXVI

My little body, kerchiefed fast,
    I bore it on through the forest, on;
And when I felt it was tired at last,
    I scooped a hole beneath the moon:
Through the forest-tops the angels far,   180
With a white sharp finger from every star,
    Did point and mock at what was done.

XXVII

Yet when it was all done aright, –
    Earth, 'twixt me and my baby, strewed, –
All, changed to black earth – nothing white, –
    A dark child in the dark! – ensued
Some comfort, and my heart grew young;
I sate down smiling there and sung
    The song I learnt in my maidenhood.

XXVIII

And thus we two were reconciled,   190
    The white child and black mother, thus;
For as I sang it soft and wild,
    The same song, more melodious,
Rose from the grave whereon I sate:
It was the dead child singing that,
    To join the souls of both of us.

XXIX

I look on the sea and the sky.
    Where the pilgrims' ships first anchored lay
The free sun rideth gloriously,
    But the pilgrim-ghosts have slid away   200
Through the earliest streaks of the morn:
My face is black, but it glares with a scorn
    Which they dare not meet by day.

XXX

Ha! – in their stead, their hunter sons!
    Ha, ha! they are on me – they hunt in a ring!
Keep off! I brave you all at once,
    I throw off your eyes like snakes that sting!
You have killed the black eagle at nest, I think:
Did you ever stand still in your triumph, and shrink
    From the stroke of her wounded wing?   210

XXXI

(Man, drop that stone you dared to lift! –)
    I wish you who stand there five abreast,
Each, for his own wife's joy and gift,
    A little corpse as safely at rest
As mine in the mangoes! Yes, but *she*
May keep live babies on her knee,
    And sing the song she likes the best.

XXXII

I am not mad: I am black.
   I see you staring in my face –
I know you staring, shrinking back,   220
   Ye are born of the Washington-race,
And this land is the free America,
And this mark on my wrist – (I prove what I say)
   Ropes tied me up here to the flogging-place.

XXXIII

You think I shrieked then? Not a sound!
   I hung, as a gourd hangs in the sun;
I only cursed them all around
   As softly as I might have done
My very own child: from these sands
Up to the mountains, lift your hands,   230
   O slaves, and end what I begun!

XXXIV

Whips, curses; these must answer those!
   For in this Union you have set
Two kinds of men in adverse rows,
   Each loathing each; and all forget
The seven wounds in Christ's body fair,
While He sees gaping everywhere
   Our countless wounds that pay no debt.

XXXV

Our wounds are different. Your white men
   Are, after all, not gods indeed,   240
Nor able to make Christs again
   Do good with bleeding. *We* who bleed
(Stand off!) we help not in our loss!
We are too heavy for our cross,
   And fall and crush you and your seed.

XXXVI

I fall, I swoon! I look at the sky.
   The clouds are breaking on my brain;
I am floated along, as if I should die
   Of liberty's exquisite pain.
In the name of the white child waiting for me   250
In the death-dark where we may kiss and agree,
White men, I leave you all curse-free
   In my broken heart's disdain!

CONFESSIONS

I

Face to face in my chamber, my silent
         chamber, I saw her:
God and she and I only, . . . there, I sate
         down to draw her
Soul through the clefts of confession . . .
         Speak, I am holding thee fast,
As the angels of resurrection shall do it
         at the last.
         'My cup is blood-red
         With my sin,' she said,   10
   'And I pour it out to the bitter lees,
As if the angels of judgement stood over
         me strong at the last,
      Or as thou wert as these!'

II

When God smote His hands together,
   and struck out thy soul as a spark
Into the organized glory of things, from
   deeps of the dark, –
Say, didst thou shine, didst thou burn,
   didst thou honour the power in the form, 20
As the star does at night, or the fire-fly,
   or even the little ground-worm?
   'I have sinned,' she said,
   'For my seed-light shed
 Has smouldered away from His first decrees!
The cypress praiseth the fire-fly, the
   ground-leaf praiseth the worm, –
  I am viler than these!'

III

When God on that sin had pity, and
   did not trample thee straight 30
With His wild rains beating and drench-
   ing thy light found inadequate;
When He only sent thee the north-
   winds, a little searching and chill,
To quicken thy flame . . . didst thou kindle
   and flash to the heights of His will?
   'I have sinned,' she said,
   'Unquickened, unspread
 My fire dropt down, and I wept on my knees!
I only said of His winds of the north as 40
   I shrank from their chill, . . .
  What delight is in these?'

IV

When God on that sin had pity, and did
              not meet it as such,
But tempered the wind to thy uses, and
              softened the world to thy touch,
At least thou wast moved in thy soul,
              though unable to prove it afar,
Thou couldst carry thy light like a jewel,
              not giving it out like a star?   50
         'I have sinned,' she said,
         'And not merited
   The gift He gives, by the grace He sees!
The mine-cave praiseth the jewel, the
              hillside praiseth the star;
      I am viler than these.'

V

Then I cried aloud in my passion, . . .
              Unthankful and impotent creature,
To throw up thy scorn unto God through
              the rents in thy beggarly nature!   60
If He, the all-giving and loving, is
              served so unduly, what then
Hast thou done to the weak and the false,
              and the changing, . . . thy fellows of men?
         'I have *loved*,' she said,
         (Words bowing her head
   As the wind the wet acacia-trees!)
'I saw God sitting above me, – but I . . .
              I sate among men,
      And I have loved these.'   70

VI

Again with a lifted voice, like a choral
                    trumpet that takes
The lowest note of a viol that trembles,
                    and triumphing breaks
On the air with it solemn and clear, –
                    'Behold! I have sinned not in this!
Where I loved, I have loved much and
                    well, – I have verily loved not amiss.
          Let the living,' she said,
                    'Inquire of the Dead,   80
     In the house of the pale-fronted Images:
My own true dead will answer for me,
                    that I have not loved amiss
          In my love for all these.

VII

'The least touch of their hands in the
                    morning, I keep it by day and by night;
Their least step on the stair, at the door,
                    still throbs through me, if ever so light;
Their least gift, which they left to my
                    childhood, far off, in the long-ago years,   90
Is now turned from a toy to a relic, and
                    seen through the crystals of tears.
          Dig the snow,' she said,
                    'For my churchyard bed,
     Yet I, as I sleep, shall not fear to freeze.
If one only of these my beloveds, shall
                    love me with heart-warm tears,
          As I have loved these!

VIII

'If I angered any among them, from
        thenceforth my own life was sore;   100
If I fell by chance from their presence,
        I clung to their memory more.
Their tender I often felt holy, their
        bitter I sometimes called sweet;
And whenever their heart has refused
        me, I fell down straight at their feet.
        I have loved,' she said, –
        'Man is weak, God is dread,
  Yet the weak man dies with his spirit at ease,
Having poured such an unguent of love   110
        but once on the Saviour's feet,
    As I lavished for these.'

IX

'Go,' I cried, 'thou hast chosen the
        Human, and left the Divine!
Then, at least, have the Human shared
        with thee their wild berry-wine?
Have they loved back thy love, and
        when strangers approached thee with blame,
Have they covered thy fault with their
        kisses, and loved thee the same?'   120
        But she shrunk and said,
        'God, over my head,
  Must sweep in the wrath of his judgement-seas,
If *He* shall deal with me sinning, but
        only indeed the same
    And no gentler than these.'

SONNETS FROM THE PORTUGUESE

I

I thought once how Theocritus had sung
Of the sweet years, the dear and wished-for years,
Who each one in a gracious hand appears
To bear a gift for mortals, old or young:
And, as I mused it in his antique tongue,
I saw, in gradual vision through my tears,
The sweet, sad years, the melancholy years,
Those of my own life, who by turns had flung
A shadow across me. Straightway I was 'ware,
So weeping, how a mystic Shape did move   10
Behind me, and drew me backward by the hair;
And a voice said in mastery, while I strove, –
'Guess now who holds thee?' – 'Death,' I said. But, there,
The silver answer rang, – 'Not Death, but Love.'

II

But only three in all God's universe
Have heard this word thou hast said, – Himself, beside
Thee speaking, and me listening! and replied
One of us . . . *that* was God, . . . and laid the curse
So darkly on my eyelids, as to amerce
My sight from seeing thee, – that if I had died,
The death-weights, placed there, would have signified
Less absolute exclusion. 'Nay' is worse
From God than from all others, O my friend!
Men could not part us with their worldly jars,   10
Nor the seas change us, nor the tempests bend;
Our hands would touch for all the mountain-bars. –
And, heaven being rolled between us at the end,
We should but vow the faster for the stars.

III

Unlike are we, unlike, O princely Heart!
Unlike our uses and our destinies.
Our ministering two angels look surprise
On one another, as they strike athwart
Their wings in passing. Thou, bethink thee, art
A guest for queens to social pageantries,
With gages from a hundred brighter eyes
Than tears even can make mine, to play thy part
Of chief musician. What hast *thou* to do
With looking from the lattice-lights at me,   10
A poor, tired, wandering singer, . . . singing through
The dark, and leaning up a cypress tree?
The chrism is on thine head, – on mine, the dew, –
And Death must dig the level where these agree.

IV

Thou hast thy calling to some palace-floor,
Most gracious singer of high poems! where
The dancers will break footing, from the care
Of watching up thy pregnant lips for more.
And dost thou lift this house's latch too poor
For hand of thine? and canst thou think and bear
To let thy music drop here unaware
In folds of golden fulness at my door?
Look up and see the casement broken in,
The bats and owlets builders in the roof!   10
My cricket chirps against thy mandolin.
Hush, call no echo up in further proof
Of desolation! there's a voice within
That weeps . . . as thou must sing . . . alone, aloof.

V

I lift my heavy heart up solemnly,
As once Electra her sepulchral urn,
And, looking in thine eyes, I overturn
The ashes at thy feet. Behold and see
What a great heap of grief lay hid in me,
And how the red wild sparkles dimly burn
Through the ashen greyness. If thy foot in scorn
Could tread them out to darkness utterly,
It might be well perhaps. But if instead
Thou wait beside me for the wind to blow   10
The grey dust up, . . . those laurels on thine head,
O my Belovèd, will not shield thee so,
That none of all the fires shall scorch and shred
The hair beneath. Stand further off then! go.

VI

Go from me. Yet I feel that I shall stand
Henceforward in thy shadow. Nevermore
Alone upon the threshold of my door
Of individual life, I shall command
The uses of my soul, nor lift my hand
Serenely in the sunshine as before,
Without the sense of that which I forbore –
Thy touch upon the palm. The widest land
Doom takes to part us, leaves thy heart in mine
With pulses that beat double. What I do   10
And what I dream include thee, as the wine
Must taste of its own grapes. And when I sue
God for myself, He hears that name of thine,
And sees within my eyes the tears of two.

VII

The face of all the world is changed, I think,
Since first I heard the footsteps of thy soul
Move still, oh, still, beside me, as they stole
Betwixt me and the dreadful outer brink
Of obvious death, where I, who thought to sink,
Was caught up into love, and taught the whole
Of life in a new rhythm. The cup of dole
God gave for baptism, I am fain to drink,
And praise its sweetness, Sweet, with thee anear.
The names of country, heaven, are changed away   10
For where thou art or shalt be, there or here;
And this . . . this lute and song . . . loved yesterday
(The singing angels know) are only dear
Because thy name moves right in what they say.

VIII

What can I give thee back, O liberal
And princely giver, who hast brought the gold
And purple of thine heart, unstained, untold,
And laid them on the outside of the wall
For such as I to take or leave withal,
In unexpected largesse? am I cold,
Ungrateful, that for these most manifold
High gifts, I render nothing back at all?
Not so; not cold, – but very poor instead.
Ask God who knows. For frequent tears have run   10
The colours from my life, and left so dead
And pale a stuff, it were not fitly done
To give the same as pillow to thy head.
Go farther! let it serve to trample on.

IX

Can it be right to give what I can give?
To let thee sit beneath the fall of tears
As salt as mine, and hear the sighing years
Re-sighing on my lips renunciative
Through those infrequent smiles which fail to live
For all thy adjurations? O my fears,
That this can scarce be right! We are not peers,
So to be lovers; and I own, and grieve,
That givers of such gifts as mine are, must
Be counted with the ungenerous. Out, alas!   10
I will not soil thy purple with my dust,
Nor breathe my poison on thy Venice-glass,
Nor give thee any love – which were unjust.
Beloved, I only love thee! let it pass.

X

Yet, love, mere love, is beautiful indeed
And worthy of acceptation. Fire is bright,
Let temple burn, or flax. An equal light
Leaps in the flame from cedar-plank or weed.
And love is fire. And when I say at need
I love thee . . . mark! . . . *I love thee* – in thy sight
I stand transfigured, glorified aright,
With conscience of the new rays that proceed
Out of my face toward thine. There's nothing low
In love, when love the lowest: meanest creatures   10
Who love God, God accepts while loving so.
And what I *feel*, across the inferior features
Of what I *am*, doth flash itself, and show
How that great work of Love enhances Nature's.

XI

And therefore if to love can be desert,
I am not all unworthy. Cheeks as pale
As these you see, and trembling knees that fail
To bear the burden of a heavy heart. –
This weary minstrel-life that once was girt
To climb Aornus, and can scarce avail
To pipe now 'gainst the valley nightingale
A melancholy music, – why advert
To these things? O Beloved, it is plain
I am not of thy worth nor for thy place!   10
And yet, because I love thee, I obtain
From that same love this vindicating grace,
To live on still in love, and yet in vain, . . .
To bless thee, yet renounce thee to thy face.

XII

Indeed this very love which is my boast,
And which, when rising up from breast to brow,
Doth crown me with a ruby large enow
To draw men's eyes and prove the inner cost, . . .
This love even, all my worth, to the uttermost,
I should not love withal, unless that thou
Hadst set me an example, shown me how,
When first thine earnest eyes with mine were crossed
And love called love. And thus, I cannot speak
Of love even, as a good thing of my own.   10
Thy soul hath snatched up mine all faint and weak
And placed it by thee on a golden throne, –
And that I love (O soul, we must be meek!)
Is by thee only, whom I love alone.

XIII

And wilt thou have me fashion into speech
The love I bear thee, finding words enough,
And hold the torch out, while the winds are rough
Between our faces, to cast light on each? –
I drop it at thy feet. I cannot teach
My hand to hold my spirit so far off
From myself . . . me . . . that I should bring thee proof
In words, of love hid in me out of reach.
Nay, let the silence of my womanhood
Commend my woman-love to thy belief, –
Seeing that I stand unwon, however wooed,
And rend the garment of my life, in brief,
By a most dauntless, voiceless fortitude,
Lest one touch of this heart convey its grief.

XIV

If thou must love me, let it be for nought
Except for love's sake only. Do not say
'I love her for her smile . . . her look . . . her way
Of speaking gently, . . . for a trick of thought
That falls in well with mine, and certes brought
A sense of pleasant ease on such a day' –
For these things in themselves, Belovèd, may
Be changed, or change for thee, – and love, so wrought
May be unwrought so. Neither love me for
Thine own dear pity's wiping my cheeks dry, –
A creature might forget to weep, who bore
Thy comfort long, and lose thy love thereby!
But love me for love's sake, that evermore
Thou may'st love on, through love's eternity.

XV

Accuse me not, beseech thee, that I wear
Too calm and sad a face in front of thine;
For we two look two ways, and cannot shine
With the same sunlight on our brow and hair.
On me thou lookest with no doubting care,
As on a bee shut in a crystalline, –
Since sorrow hath shut me safe in love's divine,
And to spread wing and fly in the outer air
Were most impossible failure, if I strove
To fail so. But I look on thee – on thee –   10
Beholding, besides love, the end of love,
Hearing oblivion beyond memory!
As one who sits and gazes from above,
Over the rivers to the bitter sea.

XVI

And yet, because thou overcomest so,
Because thou art more noble and like a king,
Thou canst prevail against my fears and fling
Thy purple round me, till my heart shall grow
Too close against thine heart henceforth to know
How it shook when alone. Why, conquering
May prove as lordly and complete a thing
In lifting upward, as in crushing low!
And as a vanquished soldier yields his sword
To one who lifts him from the bloody earth, –   10
Even so, Belovëd, I at last record,
Here ends my strife. If *thou* invite me forth,
I rise above abasement at the word.
Make thy love larger to enlarge my worth.

XVII

My poet, thou canst touch on all the notes
God set between His After and Before,
And strike up and strike off the general roar
Of the rushing worlds a melody that floats
In a serene air purely. Antidotes
Of medicated music, answering for
Mankind's forlornest uses, thou canst pour
From thence into their ears. God's will devotes
Thine to such ends, and mine to wait on thine.
How, Dearest, wilt thou have me for most use?   10
A hope, to sing by gladly? . . . or a fine
Sad memory, with thy songs to interfuse?
A shade, in which to sing . . . of palm or pine?
A grave, on which to rest from singing? . . . Choose.

XVIII

I never gave a lock of hair away
To a man, Dearest, except this to thee,
Which now upon my fingers thoughtfully
I ring out to the full brown length and say
'Take it.' My day of youth went yesterday;
My hair no longer bounds to my foot's glee,
Nor plant I it from rose- or myrtle-tree,
As girls do, any more. It only may
Now shade on two pale cheeks the mark of tears,
Taught drooping from the head that hangs aside   10
Through sorrow's trick. I thought the funeral-shears
Would take this first, but Love is justified, –
Take it thou, . . . finding pure, from all those years,
The kiss my mother left here when she died.

XIX

The soul's Rialto hath its merchandise;
I barter curl for curl upon that mart,
And from my poet's forehead to my heart
Receive this lock which outweighs argosies, –
As purply black, as erst to Pindar's eyes
The dim purpureal tresses gloomed athwart
The nine white Muse-brows. For this counterpart, . . .
The bay-crown's shade, Belovèd, I surmise,
Still lingers on thy curl, it is so black!
Thus, with a fillet of smooth-kissing breath,   10
I tie the shadows safe from gliding back,
And lay the gift where nothing hindereth,
Here on my heart, as on thy brow, to lack
No natural heat till mine grows cold in death.

XX

Belovèd, my Belovèd, when I think
That thou wast in the world a year ago,
What time I sat alone here in the snow
And saw no footprint, heard the silence sink
No moment at thy voice, . . . but, link by link,
Went counting all my chains as if that so
They never could fall off at any blow
Struck by thy possible hand . . . why, thus I drink
Of life's great cup of wonder! Wonderful,
Never to feel thee thrill the day or night   10
With personal act or speech, – nor even cull
Some prescience of thee with the blossoms white
Thou sawest growing! Atheists are as dull,
Who cannot guess God's presence out of sight.

XXI

Say over again, and yet once over again,
That thou dost love me. Though the word repeated
Should seem 'a cuckoo-song,' as thou dost treat it.
Remember, never to the hill or plain,
Valley and wood, without her cuckoo-strain
Comes the fresh Spring in all her green completed.
Belovèd, I, amid the darkness greeted
By a doubtful spirit-voice, in that doubt's pain
Cry, . . . 'Speak once more . . . thou lovest!' Who can fear
Too many stars, though each in heaven shall roll, –   10
Too many flowers, though each shall crown the year?
Say thou dost love me, love me, love me – toll
The silver iterance! – only minding, Dear,
To love me also in silence with thy soul.

XXII

When our two souls stand up erect and strong,
Face to face, silent, drawing nigh and nigher,
Until the lengthening wings break into fire
At either curvèd point, – what bitter wrong
Can the earth do to us, that we should not long
Be here contented? Think. In mounting higher,
The angels would press on us and aspire
To drop some golden orb of perfect song
Into our deep, dear silence. Let us stay
Rather on earth, Belovèd, – where the unfit   10
Contrarious moods of men recoil away
And isolate pure spirits, and permit
A place to stand and love in for a day,
With darkness and the death-hour rounding it.

XXIII

Is it indeed so? If I lay here dead,
Wouldst thou miss any life in losing mine?
And would the sun for thee more coldly shine
Because of grave-damps falling round my head?
I marvelled, my Belovèd, when I read
Thy thought so in the letter. I am thine –
But . . . *so* much to thee? Can I pour thy wine
While my hands tremble? Then my soul, instead
Of dreams of death, resumes life's lower range.
Then, love me, Love! look on me . . . breathe on me!   10
As brighter ladies do not count it strange,
For love, to give up acres and degree,
I yield the grave for thy sake, and exchange
My near sweet view of heaven, for earth with thee!

XXIV

Let the world's sharpness like a clasping knife
Shut in upon itself and do no harm
In this close hand of Love, now soft and warm,
And let us hear no sound of human strife
After the click of the shutting. Life to life –
I lean upon thee, Dear, without alarm,
And feel as safe as guarded by a charm
Against the stab of worldlings, who if rife
Are weak to injure. Very whitely still
The lilies of our lives may reassure   10
Their blossoms from their roots, accessible
Alone to heavenly dews that drop not fewer:
Growing straight, out of man's reach, on the hill.
God only, who made us rich, can make us poor.

XXV

A heavy heart, Belovèd, have I borne
From year to year until I saw thy face,
And sorrow after sorrow took the place
Of all those natural joys as lightly worn
As the stringed pearls, . . . each lifted in its turn
By a beating heart at dance-time. Hopes apace
Were changed to long despairs, till God's own grace
Could scarcely lift above the world forlorn
My heavy heart. Then *thou* didst bid me bring
And let it drop adown thy calmly great   10
Deep being! Fast it sinketh, as a thing
Which its own nature does precipitate,
While thine doth close above it, mediating
Betwixt the stars and the unaccomplished fate.

XXVI

I lived with visions for my company
Instead of men and women, years ago,
And found them gentle mates, nor thought to know
A sweeter music than they played to me.
But soon their trailing purple was not free
Of this world's dust, – their lutes did silent grow,
And I myself grew faint and blind below
Their vanishing eyes. Then THOU didst come . . . to be,
Belovèd, what they seemed. Their shining fronts,
Their songs, their splendours, (better, yet the same,   10
As river-water hallowed into fonts)
Met in thee, and from out thee overcame
My soul with satisfaction of all wants –
Because God's gifts put man's best dreams to shame.

XXVII

My own Belovèd, who hast lifted me
From this drear flat of earth where I was thrown,
And, in betwixt the languid ringlets, blown
A life-breath, till the forehead hopefully
Shines out again, as all the angels see,
Before thy saving kiss! My own, my own,
Who camest to me when the world was gone,
And I who looked for only God, found *thee*!
I find thee; I am safe, and strong, and glad.
As one who stands in dewless asphodel,   10
Looks backward on the tedious time he had
In the upper life, – so I, with bosom-swell,
Make witness, here, between the good and bad,
That Love, as strong as death, retrieves as well.

XXVIII

My letters! all dead paper, . . . mute and white!
And yet they seem alive and quivering
Against my tremulous hands which loose the string
And let them drop down on my knee to-night.
This said, . . . he wished to have me in his sight
Once, as a friend: this fixed a day in spring
To come and touch my hand . . . a simple thing,
Yet I wept for it! – this, . . . the paper's light . . .
Said, *Dear I love thee*; and I sank and quailed
As if God's future thundered on my past.   10
This said, *I am thine* – and so its ink has paled
With lying at my heart that beat too fast.
And this . . . O Love, thy words have ill availed
If, what this said, I dared repeat at last!

XXIX

I think of thee! – my thoughts do twine and bud
About thee, as wild vines, about a tree,
Put out broad leaves, and soon there's nought to see
Except the straggling green which hides the wood.
Yet, O my palm-tree, be it understood
I will not have my thoughts instead of thee
Who art dearer, better! Rather, instantly
Renew thy presence. As a strong tree should,
Rustle thy boughs and set thy trunk all bare,
And let these bands of greenery which insphere thee,   10
Drop heavily down, . . . burst, shattered, everywhere!
Because, in this deep joy to see and hear thee
And breathe within thy shadow a new air,
I do not think of thee – I am too near thee.

XXX

I see thine image through my tears to-night,
And yet to-day I saw thee smiling. How
Refer the cause? – Belovèd, is it thou
Or I, who makes me sad? The acolyte
Amid the chanted joy and thankful rite
May so fall flat, with pale insensate brow,
On the altar-stair. I hear thy voice and vow,
Perplexed, uncertain, since thou art out of sight,
As he, in his swooning ears, the choir's amen.
Belovèd, dost thou love? or did I see all   10
The glory as I dreamed, and fainted when
Too vehement light dilated my ideal,
For my soul's eyes? Will that light come again,
As now these tears come . . . falling hot and real?

XXXI

Thou comest! all is said without a word.
I sit beneath thy looks, as children do
In the noon-sun, with souls that tremble through
Their happy eyelids from an unaverred
Yet prodigal inward joy. Behold, I erred
In that last doubt! and yet I cannot rue
The sin most, but the occasion . . . that we two
Should for a moment stand unministered
By a mutal presence. Ah, keep near and close,
Thou dove-like help! and, when my fears would rise,   10
With thy broad heart serenely interpose.
Brood down with thy divine sufficiencies
These thoughts which tremble when bereft of those,
Like callow birds left desert to the skies.

XXXII

The first time that the sun rose on thine oath
To love me, I looked forward to the moon
To slacken all those bonds which seemed too soon
And quickly tied to make a lasting troth.
Quick-loving hearts, I thought, may quickly loathe;
And, looking on myself, I seemed not one
For such man's love! – more like an out-of-tune
Worn viol, a good singer would be wroth
To spoil his song with, and which, snatched in haste,
Is laid down at the first ill-sounding note.   10
I did not wrong myself so, but I placed
A wrong on *thee*. For perfect strains may float
'Neath master-hands, from instruments defaced, –
And great souls, at one stroke, may do and dote.

XXXIII

Yes, call me by my pet-name! let me hear
The name I used to run at, when a child,
From innocent play, and leave the cowslips piled,
To glance up in some face that proved me dear
With the look of its eyes. I miss the clear
Fond voices which, being drawn and reconciled
Into the music of Heaven's undefiled,
Call me no longer. Silence on the bier,
While I call God . . . call God! – So let thy mouth
Be heir to those who are now exanimate.   10
Gather the north flowers to complete the south,
And catch the early love up in the late.
Yes, call me by that name, – and I, in truth,
With the same heart, will answer and not wait.

XXXIV

With the same heart, I said, I'll answer thee
As those, when thou shalt call me by my name –
Lo, the vain promise! is the same, the same,
Perplexed and ruffled by life's strategy?
When called before, I told how hastily
I dropped my flowers or brake off from a game,
To run and answer with the smile that came
At play last moment, and went on with me
Through my obedience. When I answer now,
I drop a grave thought, break from solitude;   10
Yet still my heart goes to thee . . . ponder how . . .
Not as to a single good, but all my good!
Lay thy hand on it, best one, and allow
That no child's foot could run fast as this blood.

XXXV

If I leave all for thee, wilt thou exchange
And be all to me? Shall I never miss
Home-talk and blessing and the common kiss
That comes to each in turn, nor count it strange,
When I look up, to drop on a new range
Of walls and floors, . . . another home than this?
Nay, wilt thou fill that place by me which is
Filled by dead eyes too tender to know change?
That's hardest. If to conquer love, has tried,
To conquer grief, tries more . . . as all things prove,   10
For grief indeed is love and grief beside.
Alas, I have grieved so I am hard to love.
Yet love me – wilt thou? Open thine heart wide,
And fold within, the wet wings of thy dove.

XXXVI

When we met first and loved, I did not build
Upon the event with marble. Could it mean
To last, a love set pendulous between
Sorrow and sorrow? Nay, I rather thrilled,
Distrusting every light that seemed to gild
The onward path, and feared to overlean
A finger even. And, though I have grown serene
And strong since then, I think that God has willed
A still renewable fear . . . O love, O troth . .
Lest these enclaspèd hands should never hold,   10
This mutual kiss drop down between us both
As an unowned thing, once the lips being cold.
And Love, be false! if *he*, to keep one oath,
Must lose one joy, by his life's star foretold.

XXXVII

Pardon, oh, pardon, that my soul should make
Of all that strong divineness which I know
For thine and thee, an image only so
Formed of the sand, and fit to shift and break.
It is that distant years which did not take
Thy sovranty, recoiling with a blow,
Have forced my swimming brain to undergo
Their doubt and dread, and blindly to forsake
Thy purity of likeness and distort
Thy worthiest love to a worthless counterfeit.   10
As if a shipwrecked Pagan, safe in port,
His guardian sea-god to commemorate,
Should set a sculptured porpoise, gills a-snort
And vibrant tail, within the temple-gate.

XXXVIII

First time he kissed me, he but only kissed
The fingers of this hand wherewith I write;
And ever since, it grew more clean and white, . . .
Slow to world-greetings, quick with its 'Oh, list,'
When the angels speak. A ring of amethyst
I could not wear here, plainer to my sight,
Than that first kiss. The second passed in height
The first, and sought the forehead, and half missed,
Half falling on the hair. O beyond meed!
That was the chrism of love, which love's own crown   10
With sanctifying sweetness, did precede.
The third upon my lips was folded down
In perfect, purple state; since when, indeed,
I have been proud and said, 'My love, my own.'

XXXIX

Because thou hast the power and own'st the grace
To look through and behind this mask of me,
(Against which, years have beat thus blanchingly
With their rains,) and behold my soul's true face,
The dim and weary witness of life's race! —
Because thou hast the faith and love to see,
Through that same soul's distracting lethargy,
The patient angel waiting for a place
In the new heavens! — because nor sin nor woe,
Nor God's infliction, nor death's neighbourhood,   10
Nor all which others viewing, turn to go, . . .
Nor all which makes me tired of all, self-viewed, . . .
Nothing repels thee, . . . Dearest, teach me so
To pour out gratitude, as thou dost, good.

XL

Oh, yes! they love through all this world of ours!
I will not gainsay love, called love forsooth.
I have heard love talked in my early youth,
And since, not so long back but that the flowers
Then gathered, smell still. Mussulmans and Giaours
Throw kerchiefs at a smile, and have no ruth
For any weeping. Polypheme's white tooth
Slips on the nut if, after frequent showers,
The shell is over-smooth, — and not so much
Will turn the thing called love, aside to hate   10
Or else to oblivion. But thou art not such
A lover, my Belovèd! thou canst wait
Through sorrow and sickness, to bring souls to touch
And think it soon when others cry 'Too late.'

XLI

I thank all who have loved me in their hearts,
With thanks and love from mine. Deep thanks to all
Who paused a little near the prison-wall
To hear my music in its louder parts
Ere they went onward, each one to the mart's
Or temple's occupation, beyond call.
But thou, who, in my voice's sink and fall
When the sob took it, thy divinest Art's
Own instrument didst drop down at thy foot
To harken what I said between my tears, . . .   10
Instruct me how to thank thee! – Oh, to shoot
My soul's full meaning into future years,
That *they* should lend it utterance, and salute
Love that endures, from Life that disappears!

XLII

'*My future will not copy fair my past*' –
I wrote that once; and thinking at my side
My ministering life-angel justified
The word by his appealing look upcast
To the white throne of God, I turned at last,
And there, instead, saw thee, not unallied
To angels in thy soul! Then I, long tried
By natural ills, received the comfort fast,
While budding, at thy sight, my pilgrim's staff
Gave out green leaves with morning dews impearled.   10
I seek no copy now of life's first half:
Leave here the pages with long musing curled,
And write me new my future's epigraph,
New angel mine, unhoped for in the world!

XLIII

How do I love thee? Let me count the ways.
I love thee to the depth and breadth and height
My soul can reach, when feeling out of sight
For the ends of Being and ideal Grace.
I love thee to the level of everyday's
Most quiet need, by sun and candlelight.
I love thee freely, as men strive for Right;
I love thee purely, as they turn from Praise.
I love thee with the passion put to use
In my old griefs, and with my childhood's faith.   10
I love thee with a love I seemed to lose
With my lost saints, – I love thee with the breath,
Smiles, tears, of all my life! – and, if God choose,
I shall but love thee better after death.

XLIV

Belovèd, thou hast brought me many flowers
Plucked in the garden, all the summer through
And winter, and it seemed as if they grew
In this close room, nor missed the sun and showers.
So, in the like name of that love of ours,
Take back these thoughts which here unfolded too,
And which on warm and cold days I withdrew
From my heart's ground. Indeed, those beds and bowers
Be overgrown with bitter weeds and rue,
And wait thy weeding; yet here's eglantine,   10
Here's ivy! – take them, as I used to do
Thy flowers, and keep them where they shall not pine.
Instruct thine eyes to keep their colours true,
And tell thy soul, their roots are left in mine.

CASA GUIDI WINDOWS
PART ONE
(1851)

CASA GUIDI WINDOWS

PART ONE

I heard last night a little child go singing
   'Neath Casa Guidi windows, by the church,
O bella libertà, O bella! stringing
   The same words still on notes he went in search
So high for, you concluded the upspringing
   Of such a nimble bird to sky from perch
Must leave the whole bush in a tremble green,
    And that the heart of Italy must beat,
While such a voice had leave to rise serene
    'Twixt church and palace of a Florence street!   10
A little child, too, who not long had been
    By mother's finger steadied on his feet,
And still *O bella libertà* he sang.

Then I thought, musing, of the innumerous
   Sweet songs which still for Italy outrang
From older singers' lips, who sang not thus
   Exultingly and purely, yet, with pang
Fast sheathed in music, touched the heart of us
   So finely, that the pity scarcely pained.
I thought how Filicaja led on others,   20
   Bewailers for their Italy enchained,
And how they called her childless among mothers,
   Widow of empires, aye, and scarce refrained
Cursing her beauty to her face, as brothers
   Might a shamed sister's, – 'Had she been less fair
She were less wretched,' – how, evoking so
   From congregated wrong and heaped despair
Of men and women writhing under blow,
   Harrowed and hideous in a filthy lair,
Some personating Image, wherein woe   30
   Was wrapt in beauty from offending much,
They called it Cybele, or Niobe,
   Or laid it corpse-like on a bier for such,
Where all the world might drop for Italy
   Those cadenced tears which burn not where they touch, –

'Juliet of nations, canst thou die as we?
    And was the violet crown that crowned thy head
So over-large, though new buds made it rough,
    It slipped down and across thine eyelids dead,
O sweet, fair Juliet?' Of such songs enough,   40
    Too many of such complaints! behold, instead,
Void at Verona, Juliet's marble trough.

    As void as that is, are all images
Men set between themselves and actual wrong,
    To catch the weight of pity, meet the stress
Of conscience, – since 'tis easier to gaze long
    On mournful masks, and sad effigies,
Than on real, live, weak creatures crushed by strong.

    For me who stand in Italy to-day,
Where worthier poets stood and sang before,   50
    I kiss their footsteps, yet their words gainsay.
I can but muse in hope upon this shore
    Of golden Arno as it shoots away
Through Florence' heart beneath her bridges four!
    Bent bridges, seeming to strain off like bows,
And tremble while the arrowy undertide
    Shoots on and cleaves the marble as it goes,
And strikes up palace-walls on either side,
    And froths the cornice out in glittering rows,
With doors and windows quaintly multiplied,   60
    And terrace-sweeps, and gazers upon all,
By whom if flower or kerchief were thrown out
    From any lattice there, the same would fall
Into the river underneath no doubt,
    It runs so close and fast 'twixt wall and wall.
How beautiful! the mountains from without
    In silence listen for the word said next.
What word will men say, – here where Giotto planted
    His campanile, like an unperplexed
Fine question Heaven-ward, touching the things granted   70
    A noble people who, being greatly vexed
In act, in aspiration keep undaunted?
    What word will God say? Michel's Night and Day
And Dawn and Twilight wait in marble scorn,
    Like dogs upon a dunghill, couched on clay

From whence the Medicean stamp's outworn,
   The final putting off of all such sway
By all such hands, and freeing of the unborn
   In Florence and the great world outside Florence.
Three hundred years his patient statues wait   80
   In that small chapel of the dim St Lawrence.
Day's eyes are breaking bold and passionate
   Over his shoulder, and will flash abhorrence
On darkness and with level looks meet fate,
   When once loose from that marble film of theirs;
The Night has wild dreams in her sleep, the Dawn
   Is haggard as the sleepless, Twilight wears
A sort of horror; as the veil withdrawn
   'Twixt the artist's soul and works had left them heirs
Of speechless thoughts which would not quail nor fawn,   90
   Of angers and contempts, of hope and love;
For not without a meaning did he place
   The princely Urbino on the seat above
With everlasting shadow on his face,
   While the slow dawns and twilights disapprove
The ashes of his long-extinguished race,
   Which never more shall clog the feet of men.
I do believe, divinest Angelo,
   That winter-hour, in Via Larga, when
They bade thee build a statue up in snow,   100
   And straight that marvel of thine art again
Dissolved beneath the sun's Italian glow,
   Thine eyes, dilated with the plastic passion,
Thawing too, in drops of wounded manhood, since,
   To mock alike thine art and indignation,
Laughed at the palace-window the new prince, –
   ('Aha! this genius needs for exaltation,
When all's said, and howe'er the proud may wince,
   A little marble from our princely mines!')
I do believe that hour thou laughedst too,   110
   For the whole sad world and for thy Florentines,
After those few tears – which were only few!
   That as, beneath the sun, the grand white lines
Of thy snow-statue trembled and withdrew, –
   The head, erect as Jove's, being palsied first,
The eyelids flattened, the full brow turned blank, –

The right hand, raised but now as if it cursed,
Dropt, a mere snowball, (till the people sank
   Their voices, though a louder laughter burst
From the royal window) thou couldst proudly thank   120
   God and the prince for promise and presage,
And laugh the laugh back, I think verily,
   Thine eyes being purged by tears of righteous rage
To read a wrong into a prophecy,
   And measure a true great man's heritage
Against a mere great duke's posterity.
   I think thy soul said then, 'I do not need
A princedom and its quarries, after all;
   For if I write, paint, carve a word, indeed,
On book or board or dust, on floor or wall,   130
   The same is kept of God, who taketh heed
That not a letter of the meaning fall
   Or ere it touch and teach His world's deep heart,
Outlasting, therefore, all your lordships, sir!
   So keep your stone, beseech you, for your part,
To cover up your grave-place and refer
   The proper titles; I live by my art.
The thought I threw into this snow shall stir
   This gazing people when their gaze is done;
And the tradition of your act and mine,   140
   When all the snow is melted in the sun,
Shall gather up, for unborn men, a sign
   Of what is the true princedom, – aye, and none
Shall laugh that day, except the drunk with wine.'

Amen, great Angelo! the day's at hand.
If many laugh not on it, shall we weep?
   Much more we must not, let us understand.
Through rhymers sonneteering in their sleep,
   And archaists mumbling dry bones up the land,
And sketchers lauding ruined towns a-heap, –   150
   Through all that drowsy hum of voices smooth,
The hopeful bird mounts carolling from brake,
   The hopeful child, with leaps to catch his growth,
Sings open-eyed for liberty's sweet sake!
   And I, a singer also, from my youth,
Prefer to sing with these who are awake,

With birds, with babes, with men who will not fear
The baptism of the holy morning dew,
    (And many of such wakers now are here,
Complete in their anointed manhood, who   160
    Will greatly dare and greatlier persevere,)
Than join those old thin voices with my new,
    And sigh for Italy with some safe sigh
Cooped up in music 'twixt an oh and ah, –
    Nay, hand in hand with that young child, will I
Go singing rather, 'Bella libertà,'
    Than, with those poets, croon the dead or cry
'Se tu men bella fossi, Italia!'

'Less wretched if less fair.' Perhaps a truth
Is so far plain in this – that Italy,   170
    Long trammelled with the purple of her youth
Against her age's ripe activity,
    Sits still upon her tombs, without death's ruth,
But also without life's brave energy.
    'Now tell us what is Italy?' men ask:
And others answer, 'Virgil, Cicero,
    Catullus, Cæsar.' What beside? to task
The memory closer – 'Why, Boccaccio,
    Dante, Petrarca,' – and if still the flask
Appears to yield its wine by drops too slow, –   180
    'Angelo, Raffael, Pergolese,' – all
Whose strong hearts beat through stone, or charged again
    The paints with fire of souls electrical,
Or broke up heaven for music. What more then?
    Why, then, no more. The chaplet's last beads fall
In naming the last saintship within ken,
    And, after that, none prayeth in the land.
Alas, this Italy has too long swept
    Heroic ashes up for hour-glass sand;
Of her own past, impassioned nympholept!   190
    Consenting to be nailed here by the hand
To the very bay-tree under which she stepped
    A queen of old, and plucked a leafy branch.
And, licensing the world too long indeed
    To use her broad phylacteries to staunch
And stop her bloody lips, she takes no heed

How one clear word would draw an avalanche
Of living sons around her, to succeed
    The vanished generations. Can she count
These oil-eaters, with large, live, mobile mouths   200
    Agape for maccaroni, in the amount
Of consecrated heroes of her south's
    Bright rosary? The pitcher at the fount,
The gift of gods, being broken, she much loathes
    To let the ground-leaves of the place confer
A natural bowl. So henceforth she would seem
    No nation, but the poet's pensioner,
With alms from every land of song and dream,
    While aye her pipers sadly pipe of her,
Until their proper breaths, in that extreme   210
    Of sighing, split the reed on which they played!
Of which, no more. But never say 'no more'
    To Italy's life! Her memories undismayed
Still argue 'evermore,' – her graves implore
    Her future to be strong and not afraid;
Her very statues send their looks before.

We do not serve the dead – the past is past!
God lives, and lifts his glorious mornings up
    Before the eyes of men, awake at last,
Who put away the meats they used to sup,   220
    And down upon the dust of earth outcast
The dregs remaining of the ancient cup,
    Then turn to wakeful prayer and worthy act.
The dead, upon their awful 'vantage ground,
    The sun not in their faces, – shall abstract
No more our strength: we will not be discrowned
    As guardians of their crowns; nor deign transact
A barter of the present, for a sound
    Of good, so counted in the foregone days.
O Dead, ye shall no longer cling to us   230
    With rigid hands of desiccating praise,
And drag us backward by the garment thus,
    To stand and laud you in long-drawn virelays!
We will not henceforth be oblivious
    Of our own lives, because ye lived before,
Nor of our acts, because ye acted well.

We thank you that ye first unlatched the door,
But will not make it inaccessible
    By thankings on the threshold any more.
We hurry onward to extinguish hell   240
    With our fresh souls, our younger hope, and God's
Maturity of purpose. Soon shall we
    Die also! and, that then our periods
Of life may round themselves to memory,
    As smoothly as on our graves the burial-sods,
We now must look to it to excel as ye,
    And bear our age as far, unlimited
By the last mind-mark! so, to be invoked
    By future generations, as their Dead.

'Tis true that when the dust of death has choked   250
    A great man's voice, the common words he said
Turn oracles, – the common thoughts he yoked
    Like horses, draw like griffins! – this is true
And acceptable. I, too, should desire,
    When men make record, with the flowers they strew,
'Savonarola's soul went out in fire
    Upon our Grand-duke's piazza, and burned through
A moment first, or ere he did expire,
    The veil betwixt the right and wrong, and showed
How near God sate and judged the judges there, – '   260
    Upon the self-same pavement overstrewed,
To cast my violets with as reverent care,
    And prove that all the winters which have snowed
Cannot snow out the scent from stones and air,
    Of a sincere man's virtues. This was he,
Savonarola, who, while Peter sank
    With his whole boat-load, called courageously
'Wake Christ, wake Christ!' – Who, having tried the tank
    Of old church-waters used for baptistry
Ere Luther came to spill them, swore they stank!   270
    Who also by a princely deathbed cried,
'Loose Florence, or God will not loose thy soul!'
    Then fell back the Magnificent and died
Beneath the star-look, shooting from the cowl,
    Which turned to wormwood bitterness the wide
Deep sea of his ambitions. It were foul

To grudge Savonarola and the rest
Their violets! rather pay them quick and fresh!
    The emphasis of death makes manifest
The eloquence of action in our flesh;   280
    And men who, living, were but dimly guessed,
When once free from their life's entangled mesh,
    Show their full length in graves, or oft indeed
Exaggerate their stature, in the flat,
    To noble admirations which exceed
Most nobly, yet will calculate in that
    But accurately. We, who are the seed
Of buried creatures, if we turned and spat
    Upon our antecedents, we were vile.
Bring violets rather! If these had not walked   290
    Their furlong, could we hope to walk our mile?
Therefore bring violets. Yet if we, self-baulked,
    Stand still, a-strewing violets all the while,
These moved in vain, of whom we have vainly talked.
    So rise up henceforth with a cheerful smile,
And having strewn the violets, reap the corn,
    And having reaped and garnered, bring the plough
And draw new furrows 'neath the healthy morn,
    And plant the great Hereafter in this Now.

Of old 'twas so. How step by step was worn,   300
    As each man gained on each, securely! – how
Each by his own strength sought his own ideal, –
    The ultimate Perfection leaning bright
From out the sun and stars, to bless the leal
    And earnest search of all for Fair and Right,
Through doubtful forms, by earth accounted real!
    Because old Jubal blew into delight
The souls of men, with clear-piped melodies,
    If youthful Asaph were content at most
To draw from Jubal's grave, with listening eyes,   310
    Traditionary music's floating ghost
Into the grass-grown silence, were it wise?
    And was't not wiser, Jubal's breath being lost,
That Miriam clashed her cymbals to surprise
    The sun between her white arms flung apart,
With new, glad, golden sounds? that David's strings

O'erflowed his hand with music from his heart?
So harmony grows full from many springs,
    And happy accident turns holy art.

You enter, in your Florence wanderings,   320
    The church of St Maria Novella. Pass
The left stair, where at plague-time Macchiavel
    Saw One with set fair face as in a glass,
Dressed out against the fear of death and hell,
    Rustling her silks in pauses of the mass,
To keep the thought off how her husband fell,
    When she left home, stark dead across her feet, –
The stair leads up to what the Orgagnas save
    Of Dante's dæmons; you, in passing it,
Ascend the right stair from the farther nave,   330
    To muse in a small chapel scarcely lit
By Cimabue's Virgin. Bright and brave,
    That picture was accounted, mark, of old.
A king stood bare before its sovran grace,
    A reverent people shouted to behold
The picture, not the king, and even the place
    Containing such a miracle, grew bold,
Named the Glad Borgo from that beauteous face, –
    Which thrilled the artist, after work, to think
His own ideal Mary-smile should stand   340
    So very near him, – he, within the brink
Of all that glory, let in by his hand
    With too divine a rashness! Yet none shrink
Who come to gaze here now – albeit 'twas planned
    Sublimely in the thought's simplicity.
The Lady, throned in empyreal state,
    Minds only the young babe upon her knee,
While sidelong angels bear the royal weight,
    Prostrated meekly, smiling tenderly
Oblivion of their wings; the Child thereat   350
    Stretching its hand like God. If any should,
Because of some stiff draperies and loose joints,
    Gaze scorn down from the heights of Raffaelhood,
On Cimabue's picture, – Heaven anoints
    The head of no such critic, and his blood
The poet's curse strikes full on and appoints

To ague and cold spasms for evermore.
A noble picture! worthy of the shout
    Wherewith along the streets the people bore
Its cherub faces, which the sun threw out   360
    Until they stooped and entered the church door! –
Yet rightly was young Giotto talked about,
    Whom Cimabue found among the sheep,
And knew, as gods know gods, and carried home
    To paint the things he had painted, with a deep
And fuller insight, and so overcome
    His chapel-lady with a heavenlier sweep
Of light. For thus we mount into the sum
    Of great things known or acted. I hold, too,
That Cimabue smiled upon the lad,   370
    At the first stroke which passed what he could do, –
Or else his Virgin's smile had never had
    Such sweetness in 't. All great men who foreknew
Their heirs in art, for art's sake have been glad,
    And bent their old white heads as if uncrowned,
Fanatics of their pure ideals still
    Far more than of their triumphs, which were found
With some less vehement struggle of the will.
    If old Margheritone trembled, swooned,
And died despairing at the open sill   380
    Of other men's achievements, (who achieved,
By loving art beyond the master!) he
    Was old Margheritone, and conceived
Never, at first youth and most ecstasy,
    A Virgin like that dream of one, which heaved
The death-sigh from his heart. If wistfully
    Margheritone sickened at the smell
Of Cimabue's laurel, let him go! –
    For Cimabue stood up very well
In spite of Giotto's – and Angelico,   390
    The artist-saint, kept smiling in his cell
The smile with which he welcomed the sweet slow
    Inbreak of angels, (whitening through the dim
That he might paint them!) while the sudden sense
    Of Raffael's future was revealed to him
By force of his own fair works' competence.
    The same blue waters where the dolphins swim

Suggest the tritons. Through the blue Immense,
　　Strike out, all swimmers! cling not in the way
Of one another, so to sink; but learn　　　　　　　　400
　　The strong man's impulse, catch the fresh'ning spray
He throws up in his motions, and discern
　　By his clear, westering eye, the time of day.
Thou, God, hast set us worthy gifts to earn,
　　Besides thy heaven and Thee! and when I say
There's room here for the weakest man alive
　　To live and die, – there's room too, I repeat,
For all the strongest to live well, and strive
　　Their own way, by their individual heat, –
Like some new bee-swarm leaving the old hive,　　410
　　Despite the wax which tempts so violet-sweet.
Then let the living live, the dead retain
　　Their grave-cold flowers! – though honour's best supplied,
By bringing actions, to prove theirs not vain.

Cold graves, we say? It shall be testified
That living men who burn in heart and brain,
　　Without the dead were colder. If we tried
To sink the past beneath our feet, be sure
　　The future would not stand. Precipitate
This old roof from the shrine – and, insecure,　　420
　　The nesting swallows fly off, mate from mate.
How scant the gardens, if the graves were fewer!
　　The tall green poplars grew no longer straight,
Whose tops not looked to Troy. Would any fight
　　For Athens, and not swear by Marathon?
Who dared build temples, without tombs in sight?
　　Or live, without some dead man's benison?
Or seek truth, hope for good, and strive for right,
　　If, looking up, he saw not in the sun
Some angel of the martyrs all day long　　　　　430
　　Standing and waiting? Your last rhythm will need
Your earliest key-note. Could I sing this song,
　　If my dead masters had not taken heed
To help the heavens and earth to make me strong,
　　As the wind ever will find out some reed,
And touch it to such issues as belong
　　To such a frail thing? None may grudge the dead,

Libations from full cups. Unless we choose
    To look back to the hills behind us spread,
The plains before us, sadden and confuse;   440
    If orphaned, we are disinherited.

I would but turn these lachrymals to use,
    And pour fresh oil in from the olive grove,
To furnish them as new lamps. Shall I say
    What made my heart beat with exulting love,
A few weeks back? –
                    . . . The day was such a day
    As Florence owes the sun. The sky above,
Its weight upon the mountains seemed to lay,
    And palpitate in glory, like a dove
Who has flown too fast, full-hearted! – take away   450
    The image! for the heart of man beat higher
That day in Florence, flooding all her streets
    And piazzas with a tumult and desire.
The people, with accumulated heats,
    And faces turned one way, as if one fire
Both drew and flushed them, left their ancient beats,
    And went up toward the palace-Pitti wall,
To thank their Grand-duke, who, not quite of course,
    Had graciously permitted, at their call,
The citizens to use their civic force   460
    To guard their civic homes. So, one and all,
The Tuscan cities streamed up to the source
    Of this new good, at Florence, taking it
As good so far, presageful of more good, –
    The first torch of Italian freedom, lit
To toss in the next tiger's face who should
    Approach too near them in a greedy fit, –
The first pulse of an even flow of blood,
    To prove the level of Italian veins
Toward rights perceived and granted. How we gazed   470
    From Casa Guidi windows, while, in trains
Of orderly procession – banners raised,
    And intermittent burst of martial strains
Which died upon the shout, as if amazed
    By gladness beyond music – they passed on!
The Magistracy, with insignia, passed, –

And all the people shouted in the sun,
And all the thousand windows which had cast
A ripple of silks, in blue and scarlet, down,
(As if the houses overflowed at last), 480
Seemed growing larger with fair heads and eyes.
The Lawyers passed, – and still arose the shout,
And hands broke from the windows to surprise
Those grave calm brows with bay-tree leaves thrown out.

The Priesthood passed, – the friars with worldly-wise
Keen sidelong glances from their beards about
The street to see who shouted! many a monk
Who takes a long rope in the waist, was there!
Whereat the popular exultation drunk
With indrawn 'vivas' the whole sunny air, 490
While, through the murmuring windows, rose and sunk
A cloud of kerchiefed hands, – 'The church makes fair
Her welcome in the new Pope's name.' Ensued
The black sign of the 'Martyrs!' (name no name,
But count the graves in silence.) Next, were viewed
The Artists; next, the Trades; and after came
The People, – flag and sign, and rights as good, –
And very loud the shout was for that same
Motto, 'Il popolo.' IL POPOLO, –
The word means dukedom, empire, majesty, 500
And kings in such an hour might read it so.
And next, with banners, each in his degree,
Deputed representatives a-row
Of every separate state of Tuscany.
Siena's she-wolf, bristling on the fold
Of the first flag, preceded Pisa's hare,
And Massa's lion floated calm in gold,
Pienza's following with his silver stare.
Arezzo's steed pranced clear from bridle-hold, –
And well might shout our Florence, greeting there 510
These, and more brethren. Last, the world had sent
The various children of her teeming flanks –
Greeks, English, French – as if to a parliament
Of lovers of her Italy in ranks,
Each bearing its land's symbol reverent.
At which the stones seemed breaking into thanks
And rattling up the sky, such sounds in proof

Arose; the very house-walls seemed to bend;
 The very windows, up from door to roof,
Flashed out a rapture of bright heads, to mend   520
 With passionate looks, the gesture's whirling off
A hurricane of leaves. Three hours did end
 While all these passed; and ever in the crowd,
Rude men, unconscious of the tears that kept
 Their beards moist, shouted; some few laughed aloud,
And none asked any why they laughed and wept.
 Friends kissed each other's cheeks, and foes long vowed
More warmly did it, – two-months' babies leapt
 Right upward in their mother's arms, whose black,
Wide, glittering eyes looked elsewhere; lovers pressed 530
 Each before either, neither glancing back;
And peasant maidens, smoothly 'tired and tressed,
 Forgot to finger on their throats the slack
Great pearl-strings; while old blind men would not rest,
 But pattered with their staves and slid their shoes
Along the stones, and smiled as if they saw.
 O heaven, I think that day had noble use
Among God's days. So near stood Right and Law,
 Both mutually forborne! Law would not bruise,
Nor Right deny, and each in reverent awe 540
 Honoured the other. And if, ne'ertheless,
That good day's sun delivered to the vines
 No charta, and the liberal Duke's excess
Did scarce exceed a Guelf's or Ghibelline's
 In any special actual righteousness
Of what that day he granted, still the signs
 Are good and full of promise, we must say,
When multitudes approach their kings with prayers
 And kings concede their people's right to pray,
Both in one sunshine. Griefs are not despairs, 550
 So uttered, nor can royal claims dismay
When men from humble homes and ducal chairs,
 Hate wrong together. It was well to view
Those banners ruffled in a ruler's face
 Inscribed, 'Live freedom, union, and all true
Brave patriots who are aided by God's grace!'
 Nor was it ill, when Leopoldo drew
His little children to the window-place

He stood in at the Pitti, to suggest
   They too should govern as the people willed.   560
    What a cry rose then! some, who saw the best,
Declared his eyes filled up and overfilled
   With good warm human tears which unrepressed
Ran down. I like his face; the forehead's build
   Has no capacious genius, yet perhaps
Sufficient comprehension, – mild and sad,
   And careful nobly, – not with care that wraps
Self-loving hearts, to stifle and make mad,
   But careful with the care that shuns a lapse
Of faith and duty, studious not to add   570
   A burden in the gathering of a gain.
And so, God save the Duke, I say with those
   Who that day shouted it, and while dukes reign,
May all wear in the visible overflows
   Of spirit, such a look of careful pain!
For God must love it better than repose.

And all the people who went up to let
   Their hearts out to that Duke, as has been told –
Where guess ye that the living people met,
   Kept tryst, formed ranks, chose leaders, first unrolled   580
Their banners?
              In the Loggia? where is set
   Cellini's godlike Perseus, bronze – or gold –
(How name the metal, when the statue flings
   Its soul so in your eyes?) with brow and sword
Superbly calm, as all opposing things,
   Slain with the Gorgon, were no more abhorred
Since ended?
           No, the people sought no wings
   From Perseus in the Loggia, nor implored
An inspiration in the place beside,
   From that dim bust of Brutus, jagged and grand,   590
Where Buonarroti passionately tried
   From out the close-clenched marble to demand
The head of Rome's sublimest homicide, –
   Then dropt the quivering mallet from his hand,
Despairing he could find no model-stuff
   Of Brutus, in all Florence, where he found

The gods and gladiators thick enough.
　　Nor there! the people chose still holier ground!
The people, who are simple, blind, and rough,
　　Know their own angels, after looking round.   600
Whom chose they then? where met they?

　　　　　　　　　　　　　　　On the stone
　　Called Dante's, – a plain flat stone, scarce discerned
From others in the pavement, – whereupon
　　He used to bring his quiet chair out, turned
To Brunelleschi's church, and pour alone
　　The lava of his spirit when it burned.
It is not cold to-day. O passionate
　　Poor Dante, who, a banished Florentine,
Didst sit austere at banquets of the great,
　　And muse upon this far-off stone of thine,   610
And think how oft some passer used to wait
　　A moment, in the golden day's decline,
With 'Good night, dearest Dante!' – well, good night!
　　I muse now, Dante, and think, verily,
Though chapelled in the byeway, out of sight,
　　Ravenna's bones would thrill with ecstasy,
Could'st know thy favourite stone's elected right
　　As tryst-place for thy Tuscans to foresee
Their earliest chartas from. Good night, good morn,
　　Henceforward, Dante! now my soul is sure   620
That thine is better comforted of scorn,
　　And looks down earthward in completer cure,
Than when, in Santa Croce church forlorn
　　Of any corpse, the architect and hewer
Did pile the empty marbles as thy tomb.
　　For now thou art no longer exiled, now
Best honoured! – we salute thee who art come
　　Back to the old stone with a softer brow
Than Giotto drew upon the wall, for some
　　Good lovers of our age to track and plough   630
Their way to, through time's ordures stratified,
　　And startle broad awake into the dull
Bargello chamber! now, thou'rt milder eyed, –
　　Now Beatrix may leap up glad to cull
Thy first smile, even in heaven and at her side,

Like that which, nine years old, looked beautiful
At May-game. What do I say? I only meant
   That tender Dante loved his Florence well,
While Florence, now, to love him is content;
   And, mark ye, that the piercingest sweet smell   640
Of love's dear incense by the living sent
   To find the dead, is not accessible
To lazy livers! no narcotic, – not
   Swung in a censer to a sleepy tune, –
But trod out in the morning air, by hot
   Quick spirits, who tread firm to ends foreshown,
And use the name of greatness unforgot,
   To meditate what greatness may be done.

For Dante sits in heaven, and ye stand here,
   And more remains for doing, all must feel,   650
Than trysting on his stone from year to year
   To shift processions, civic toe to heel,
The town's thanks to the Pitti. Are ye freer
   For what was felt that day? a chariot-wheel
May spin fast, yet the chariot never roll.
   But if that day suggested something good,
And bettered, with one purpose, soul by soul, –
   Better means freer. A land's brotherhood
Is most puissant: men, upon the whole,
   Are what they can be, – nations, what they would.   660

Will, therefore, to be strong, thou Italy!
   Will to be noble! Austrian Metternich
Can fix no yoke unless the neck agree;
   And thine is like the lion's when the thick
Dews shudder from it, and no man would be
   The stroker of his mane, much less would prick
His nostril with a reed. When nations roar
   Like lions, who shall tame them, and defraud
Of the due pasture by the river-shore?
   Roar, therefore! shake your dew-laps dry abroad.   670
The amphitheatre with open door
   Leads back upon the benchers, who applaud
The last spear-thruster.

                              Yet the Heavens forbid
That we should call on passion to confront
The brutal with the brutal, and, amid
    This ripening world, suggest a lion's-hunt
And lion's-vengeance for the wrongs men did
    And do now, though the spears are getting blunt.
We only call, because the sight and proof
    Of lion-strength hurts nothing; and to show   680
A lion-heart, and measure paw with hoof,
    Helps something, even, and will instruct a foe
As well as the onslaught, how to stand aloof!
    Or else the world gets past the mere brute blow
Or given or taken. Children use the fist
    Until they are of age to use the brain;
And so we needed Cæsars to assist
    Man's justice, and Napoleons to explain
God's counsel, when a point was nearly missed,
    Until our generations should attain   690
Christ's stature nearer. Not that we, alas,
    Attain already; but a single inch
Will raise to look down on the swordsman's pass,
    As knightly Roland on the coward's flinch:
And, after chloroform and ether-gas,
    We find out slowly what the bee and finch
Have ready found, through Nature's lamp in each,
    How to our races we may justify
Our individual claims, and, as we reach
    Our own grapes, bend the top vines to supply   700
The children's uses, – how to fill a breach
    With olive branches, – how to quench a lie
With truth, and smite a foe upon the cheek
    With Christ's most conquering kiss. Why, these are things
Worth a great nation's finding, to prove weak
    The 'glorious arms' of military kings.
And so with wide embrace, my England, seek
    To stifle the bad heat and flickerings
Of this world's false and nearly expended fire!
    Draw palpitating arrows to the wood,   710
And twang abroad thy high hopes, and thy higher
    Resolves, from that most virtuous altitude!
Till nations shall unconsciously aspire

By looking up to thee, and learn that good
And glory are not different. Announce law
  By freedom; exalt chivalry by peace;
Instruct how clear calm eyes can overawe,
  And how pure hands, stretched simply to release
A bond-slave, will not need a sword to draw
  To be held dreadful. O my England, crease   720
Thy purple with no alien agonies!
  No struggles toward encroachment, no vile war!
Disband thy captains, change thy victories,
  Be henceforth prosperous as the angels are,
Helping, not humbling.

                     Drums and battle cries
  Go out in music of the morning star –
And soon we shall have thinkers in the place
  Of fighters, each found able as a man
To strike electric influence through a race,
  Unstayed by city-wall and barbican.   730
The poet shall look grander in the face
  Than even of old, (when he of Greece began
To sing 'that Achillean wrath which slew
  So many heroes,') – seeing he shall treat
The deeds of souls heroic toward the true –
  The oracles of life – previsions sweet
And awful, like divine swans gliding through
  White arms of Ledas, which will leave the heat
Of their escaping godship to endue
  The human medium with a heavenly flush.   740

Meanwhile, in this same Italy we want
  Not popular passion, to arise and crush,
But popular conscience, which may covenant
  For what it knows. Concede without a blush,
To grant the 'civic guard' is not to grant
  The civic spirit, living and awake.
Those lappets on your shoulders, citizens,
  Your eyes strain after sideways till they ache,
(While still, in admirations and amens,
  The crowd comes up on festa-days, to take   750
The great sight in) – are not intelligence,

Not courage even – alas, if not the sign
Of something very noble, they are nought;
  For every day ye dress your sallow kine
With fringes down their cheeks, though unbesought
  They loll their heavy heads and drag the wine,
And bear the wooden yoke as they were taught
  The first day. What ye want is light – indeed
Not sunlight – (ye may well look up surprised
  To those unfathomable heavens that feed   760
Your purple hills!) – but God's light organised
  In some high soul, crowned capable to lead
The conscious people, conscious and advised, –
  For if we lift a people like mere clay,
It falls the same. We want thee, O unfound
  And sovran teacher! – if thy beard be grey
Or black, we bid thee rise up from the ground
  And speak the word God giveth thee to say,
Inspiring into all this people round,
  Instead of passion, thought, which pioneers   770
All generous passion, purifies from sin,
  And strikes the hour for. Rise up teacher! here's
A crowd to make a nation! – best begin
  By making each a man, till all be peers
Of earth's true patriots and pure martyrs in
  Knowing and daring. Best unbar the doors
Which Peter's heirs keep locked so overclose
  They only let the mice across the floors,
While every churchman dangles, as he goes,
  The great key at his girdle, and abhors   780
In Christ's name, meekly. Open wide the house,
  Concede the entrance with Christ's liberal mind,
And set the tables with His wine and bread.
  What! 'commune in both kinds?' In every kind –
Wine, wafer, love, hope, truth, unlimited,
  Nothing kept back. For when a man is blind
To starlight, will he see the rose is red?
  A bondsman shivering at a Jesuit's foot –
'Væ! meâ culpâ!' is not like to stand
  A freedman at a despot's, and dispute   790
His titles by the balance in his hand,
  Weighing them 'suo jure.' Tend the root

If careful of the branches, and expand
   The inner souls of men before you strive
For civic heroes.

                But the teacher, where?
   From all these crowded faces, all alive,
Eyes, of their own lids flashing themselves bare,
   And brows that with a mobile life contrive
A deeper shadow, – may we in no wise dare
   To put a finger out, and touch a man,   800
And cry 'this is the leader?' What, all these! –
   Broad heads, black eyes, – yet not a soul that ran
From God down with a message? all, to please
   The donna waving measures with her fan,
And not the judgment-angel on his knees,
   (The trumpet just an inch off from his lips)
Who when he breathes next, will put out the sun?

   Yet mankind's self were foundered in eclipse,
If lacking doers, with great works to be done;
   And lo, the startled earth already dips   810
Back into light – a better day's begun –
   And soon this leader, teacher, will stand plain,
And build the golden pipes and synthesize
   This people-organ for a holy strain.
We hold this hope, and still in all these eyes,
   Go sounding for the deep look which shall drain
Suffused thought into channelled enterprise.
   Where is the teacher? What now may he do,
Who shall do greatly? Doth he gird his waist
   With a monk's rope, like Luther? or pursue   820
The goat, like Tell? or dry his nets in haste,
   Like Masaniello when the sky was blue?
Keep house, like other peasants, with inlaced,
   Bare, brawny arms about a favourite child,
And meditative looks beyond the door,
   (But not to mark the kidling's teeth have filed
The green shoots of his vine which last year bore
   Full twenty bunches,) or, on triple-piled
Throne-velvets sit at ease, to bless the poor,
   Like other pontiffs, in the Poorest's name?   830

The old tiara keeps itself aslope
　　Upon his steady brows, which, all the same,
Bend mildly to permit the people's hope?

　　Whatever hand shall grasp this oriflamme,
Whatever man (last peasant or first pope
　　Seeking to free his country!) shall appear,
Teach, lead, strike fire into the masses, fill
　　These empty bladders with fine air, insphere
These wills into a unity of will,
　　And make of Italy a nation – dear   840
And blessed be that man! the Heavens shall kill
　　No leaf the earth lets grow for him, and Death
Shall cast him back upon the lap of Life
　　To live more surely, in a clarion-breath
Of hero-music. Brutus, with the knife,
　　Rienzi, with the fasces, throb beneath
Rome's stones, – and more, – who threw away joy's fife
　　Like Pallas, that the beauty of their souls
Might ever shine untroubled and entire.
　　But if it can be true that he who rolls   850
The Church's thunders, will reserve her fire
　　For only light, – from eucharistic bowls
Will pour new life for nations that expire,
　　And rend the scarlet of his papal vest
To gird the weak loins of his countrymen –
　　I hold that he surpasses all the rest
Of Romans, heroes, patriots, – and that when
　　He sat down on the throne, he dispossessed
The first graves of some glory. See again,
　　This country-saving is a glorious thing,   860
And if a common man achieved it? well.
　　Say, a rich man did? excellent. A king?
That grows sublime. A priest? improbable.
　　A pope? Ah, there we stop, and cannot bring
Our faith up to the leap, with history's bell
　　So heavy round the neck of it – albeit
We fain would grant the possibility,
　　For *thy* sake, Pio nono!

                                    Stretch thy feet
In that case – I will kiss them reverently
     As any pilgrim to the papal seat!   870
And, such proved possible, thy throne to me
     Shall seem as holy a place as Pellico's
Venetian dungeon, or as Spielberg's grate,
     At which the Lombard woman hung the rose
Of her sweet soul, by its own dewy weight,
     To feel the dungeon round her sunshine close,
And pining so, died early, yet too late
     For what she suffered. Yea, I will not choose
Betwixt thy throne, Pope Pius, and the spot
     Marked red for ever, spite of rains and dews,   880
Where two fell riddled by the Austrian's shot,
     The brothers Bandiera, who accuse,
With one same mother-voice and face (that what
     They speak may be invincible) the sins
Of earth's tormentors before God the just,
     Until the unconscious thunder-bolt begins
To loosen in His grasp.

                                    And yet we must
     Beware, and mark the natural kiths and kins
Of circumstance and office, and distrust
     The rich man reasoning in a poor man's hut,   890
The poet who neglects pure truth to prove
     Statistic fact, the child who leaves a rut
For a smoother road, the priest who vows his glove
     Exhales no grace, the prince who walks a-foot,
The woman who has sworn she will not love,
     And this Ninth Pius in Seventh Gregory's chair,
With Andrea Doria's forehead!

                                    Count what goes
     To making up a pope, before he wear
That triple crown. We pass the world-wide throes
     Which went to make the popedom, – the despair   900
Of free men, good men, wise men; the dread shows
     Of women's faces, by the faggot's flash,
Tossed out, to the minutest stir and throb
     O' the white lips, the least tremble of a lash,

To glut the red stare of a licensed mob;
   The short mad cries down oubliettes, and plash
So horribly far off; priests, trained to rob,
   And kings that, like encouraged nightmares, sate
On nations' hearts most heavily distressed
   With monstrous sights and apophthegms of fate! –   910
We pass these things, – because 'the times' are prest
   With necessary charges of the weight
Of all this sin, and 'Calvin, for the rest,
   Made bold to burn Servetus – Ah, men err!' –
And, so do *churches!* which is all we mean
   To bring to proof in any register
Of theological fat kine and lean –
   So drive them back into the pens! refer
Old sins (with pourpoint, 'quotha' and 'I ween,')
   Entirely to the old times, the old times;   920
Nor ever ask why this preponderant,
   Infallible, pure Church could set her chimes
Most loudly then, just then, – most jubilant,
   Precisely then – when mankind stood in crimes
Full heart-deep, and Heaven's judgments were not scant.
   Inquire still less, what signifies a church
Of perfect inspiration and pure laws,
   Who burns the first man with a brimstone-torch,
And grinds the second, bone by bone, because
   The times, forsooth, are used to rack and scorch!   930
What *is* a holy Church, unless she awes
   The times down from their sins? Did Christ select
Such amiable times, to come and teach
   Love to, and mercy? The whole world were wrecked,
If every mere great man, who lives to reach
   A little leaf of popular respect,
Attained not simply by some special breach
   In the age's customs, by some precedence
In thought and act, which, having proved him higher
   Than those he lived with, proved his competence   940
In helping them to wonder and aspire.

My words are guiltless of the bigot's sense.
My soul has fire to mingle with the fire
   Of all these souls, within or out of doors

Of Rome's church or another. I believe
　　In one Priest, and one temple, with its floors
Of shining jasper gloom'd at morn and eve
　　By countless knees of earnest auditors,
And crystal walls, too lucid to perceive,
　　That none may take the measure of the place   950
And say, 'So far the porphyry, then, the flint –
　　To this mark, mercy goes, and there, ends grace,'
Though still the permeable crystals hint
　　At some white starry distance, bathed in space.
I feel how nature's ice-crusts keep the dint
　　Of undersprings of silent Deity.
I hold the articulated gospels, which
　　Show Christ among us, crucified on tree.
I love all who love truth, if poor or rich
　　In what they have won of truth possessively.   960
No altars and no hands defiled with pitch
　　Shall scare me off, but I will pray and eat
With all these – taking leave to choose my ewers
　　And say at last, 'Your visible churches cheat
Their inward types, – and, if a church assures
　　Of standing without failure and defeat,
The same both fails and lies.'

　　　　　　　　　　　　　　To leave which lures
　　Of wider subject through past years, – behold,
We come back from the popedom to the pope,
　　To ponder what he *must* be, ere we are bold   970
For what he *may* be, with our heavy hope
　　To trust upon his soul. So, fold by fold,
Explore this mummy in the priestly cope,
　　Transmitted through the darks of time, to catch
The man within the wrappage, and discern
　　How he, an honest man, upon the watch
Full fifty years, for what a man may learn,
　　Contrived to get just there; with what a snatch
Of old-world oboli he had to earn
　　The passage through; with what a drowsy sop,   980
To drench the busy barkings of his brain;
　　What ghosts of pale tradition, wreathed with hop
'Gainst wakeful thought, he had to entertain

For heavenly visions; and consent to stop
The clock at noon, and let the hour remain
    (Without vain windings up) inviolate,
Against all chimings from the belfry. Lo,
    From every given pope you must abate,
Albeit you love him, some things – good, you know –
    Which every given heretic you hate,   990
Assumes for his, as being plainly so.
    A pope must hold by popes a little, – yes,
By councils, – from Nicæa up to Trent, –
    By hierocratic empire, more or less
Irresponsible to men, – he must resent
    Each man's particular conscience, and repress
Inquiry, meditation, argument,
    As tyrants faction. Also, he must not
Love truth too dangerously, but prefer
    'The interests of the Church,' (because a blot   1000
Is better than a rent, in miniver)
    Submit to see the people swallow hot
Husk-porridge, which his chartered churchmen stir
    Quoting the only true God's epigraph,
'Feed my lambs, Peter!' – must consent to sit
    Attesting with his pastoral ring and staff,
To such a picture of our Lady, hit
    Off well by artist angels, (though not half
As fair as Giotto would have painted it) –
    To such a vial, where a dead man's blood   1010
Runs yearly warm beneath a churchman's finger;
    To such a holy house of stone and wood,
Whereof a cloud of angels was the bringer
    From Bethlehem to Loreto. – Were it good
For any pope on earth to be a flinger
    Of stones against these high-niched counterfeits?
Apostates only are iconoclasts.
    He dares not say, while this false thing abets
That true thing, 'this is false.' He keeps his fasts
    And prayers, as prayer and fast were silver frets   1020
To change a note upon a string that lasts,
    And make a lie a virtue. Now, if he
Did more than this, higher hoped, and braver dared,
    I think he were a pope in jeopardy,

Or no pope rather, for his truth had barred
    The vaulting of his life, – and certainly,
If he do only this, mankind's regard
    Moves on from him at once, to seek some new
Teacher and leader. He is good and great
    According to the deeds a pope can do;   1030
Most liberal, save those bonds; affectionate,
    As princes may be, and, as priests are, true;
But only the ninth Pius after eight,
    When all's praised most. At best and hopefullest,
He's pope – we want a man! his heart beats warm,
    But, like the prince enchanted to the waist,
He sits in stone, and hardens by a charm
    Into the marble of his throne high-placed.
Mild benediction, waves his saintly arm –
    So, good! but what we want's a perfect man,   1040
Complete and all alive: half travertine
    Half suits our need, and ill subserves our plan.
Feet, knees, nerves, sinews, energies divine
    Were never yet too much for men who ran
In such hard ways as must be this of thine,
    Deliverer whom we seek, whoe'er thou art,
Pope, prince, or peasant! If, indeed, the first,
    The noblest, therefore! since the heroic heart
Within thee must be great enough to burst
    Those trammels buckling to the baser part   1050
Thy saintly peers in Rome, who crossed and cursed
    With the same finger.

                                    Come, appear, be found,
If pope or peasant, come! we hear the cock,
    The courtier of the mountains when first crowned
With golden dawn; and orient glories flock
    To meet the sun upon the highest ground.
Take voice and work! we wait to hear thee knock
    At some one of our Florentine nine gates,
On each of which was imaged a sublime
    Face of a Tuscan genius, which, for hate's   1060
And love's sake, both, our Florence in her prime
    Turned boldly on all comers to her states,
As heroes turned their shields in antique time,

Emblazoned with honourable acts. And though
The gates are blank now of such images,
  And Petrarch looks no more from Nicolo
Toward dear Arezzo, 'twixt the acacia trees,
  Nor Dante, from gate Gallo – still we know,
Despite the razing of the blazonries,
  Remains the consecration of the shield!   1070
The dead heroic faces will start out
  On all these gates, if foes should take the field,
And blend sublimely, at the earliest shout,
  With living heroes who will scorn to yield
A hair's-breadth even, when gazing round about,
  They find in what a glorious company
They fight the foes of Florence. Who will grudge
  His one poor life, when that great man we see
Has given five hundred years, the world being judge,
  To help the glory of his Italy?   1080
Who, born the fair side of the Alps, will budge,
  When Dante stays, when Ariosto stays,
When Petrarch stays for ever? Ye bring swords,
  My Tuscans? Ay, if wanted in this haze,
Bring swords. But first bring souls! – bring thoughts and
    words,
  Unrusted by a tear of yesterday's,
Yet awful by its wrong, – and cut these cords,
  And mow this green lush falseness to the roots,
And shut the mouth of hell below the swathe!
  And, if ye can bring songs too, let the lute's   1090
Recoverable music softly bathe
  Some poet's hand, that, through all bursts and bruits
Of popular passion, all unripe and rathe
  Convictions of the popular intellect,
Ye may not lack a finger up the air,
  Annunciative, reproving, pure, erect,
To show which way your first Ideal bare
  The whiteness of its wings, when (sorely pecked
By falcons on your wrists) it unaware
  Arose up overhead, and out of sight.   1100

Meanwhile, let all the far ends of the world
  Breathe back the deep breath of their old delight,

To swell the Italian banner just unfurled.
  Help, lands of Europe! for, if Austria fight,
The drums will bar your slumber. Had ye curled
  The laurel for your thousand artists' brows,
If these Italian hands had planted none?
  Can any sit down idle in the house,
Nor hear appeals from Buonarroti's stone
  And Raffael's canvas, rousing and to rouse?   1110
Where's Poussin's master? Gallic Avignon
  Bred Laura, and Vaucluse's fount has stirred
The heart of France too strongly, as it lets
  Its little stream out, (like a wizard's bird
Which bounds upon its emerald wing and wets
  The rocks on each side) that she should not gird
Her loins with Charlemagne's sword when foes beset
  The country of her Petrarch. Spain may well
Be minded how from Italy she caught,
  To mingle with her tinkling Moorish bell,   1120
A fuller cadence and a subtler thought.
  And even the New World, the receptacle
Of freemen, may send glad men, as it ought,
  To greet Vespucci Amerigo's door.
While England claims, by trump of poetry,
  Verona, Venice, the Ravenna-shore,
And dearer holds John Milton's Fiesole
  Than Langlande's Malvern with the stars in flower.

And Vallombrosa, we two went to see
  Last June, beloved companion, – where sublime   1130
The mountains live in holy families,
  And the slow pinewoods ever climb and climb
Half up their breasts, just stagger as they seize
  Some grey crag, drop back with it many a time,
And straggle blindly down the precipice!
  The Vallombrosan brooks were strewn as thick
That June-day, knee-deep, with dead beechen leaves,
  As Milton saw them, ere his heart grew sick
And his eyes blind. I think the monks and beeves
  Are all the same too. Scarce they have changed the wick 1140
On good St Gualbert's altar, which receives
  The convent's pilgrims, – and the pool in front

(Wherein the hill-stream trout are cast, to wait
 The beatific vision and the grunt
Used at refectory) keeps its weedy state,
 To baffle saintly abbots who would count
The fish across their breviary nor 'bate
 The measure of their steps. O waterfalls
And forests! sound and silence! mountains bare,
 That leap up peak by peak, and catch the palls 1150
Of purple and silver mist to rend and share
 With one another, at electric calls
Of life in the sunbeams, – till we cannot dare
 Fix your shapes, count your number! we must think
Your beauty and your glory helped to fill
 The cup of Milton's soul so to the brink,
He never more was thirsty, when God's will
 Had shattered to his sense the last chain-link
By which he had drawn from Nature's visible
 The fresh well-water. Satisfied by this, 1160
He sang of Adam's paradise and smiled,
 Remembering Vallombrosa. Therefore is
The place divine to English man and child,
 And pilgrims leave their souls here in a kiss.

For Italy's the whole earth's treasury, piled
 With reveries of gentle ladies, flung
Aside, like ravelled silk, from life's worn stuff;
 With coins of scholars' fancy, which, being rung
On work-day counter, still sound silver-proof;
 In short, with all the dreams of dreamers young, 1170
Before their heads have time for slipping off
 Hope's pillow to the ground. How oft, indeed,
We've sent our souls out from the rigid north,
 On bare white feet which would not print nor bleed,
To climb the Alpine passes and look forth,
 Where booming low the Lombard rivers lead
To gardens, vineyards, all a dream is worth, –
 Sights, thou and I, Love, have seen afterward
From Tuscan Bellosguardo, wide awake,
 When, standing on the actual blessed sward 1180
Where Galileo stood at nights to take
 The vision of the stars, we have found it hard,

Gazing upon the earth and heaven, to make
  A choice of beauty.

               Therefore let us all
Refreshed in England or in other land,
  By visions, with their fountain-rise and fall,
Of this earth's darling, – we, who understand
  A little how the Tuscan musical
Vowels do round themselves as if they planned
  Eternities of separate sweetness, – we,   1190
Who loved Sorrento vines in picture-book,
  Or ere in wine-cup we pledged faith or glee, –
Who loved Rome's wolf, with demi-gods at suck,
  Or ere we loved truth's own divinity, –
Who loved, in brief, the classic hill and brook,
  And Ovid's dreaming tales, and Petrarch's song,
Or ere we loved Love's self even! – let us give
  The blessing of our souls, (and wish them strong
To bear it to the height where prayers arrive,
  When faithful spirits pray against a wrong,)   1200
To this great cause of southern men, who strive
  In God's name for man's rights, and shall not fail!

Behold, they shall not fail. The shouts ascend
  Above the shrieks, in Naples, and prevail.
Rows of shot corpses, waiting for the end
  Of burial, seem to smile up straight and pale
Into the azure air and apprehend
  That final gun-flash from Palermo's coast
Which lightens their apocalypse of death.
  So let them die! The world shows nothing lost;   1210
Therefore, not blood. Above or underneath,
  What matter, brothers, if ye keep your post
On duty's side? As sword returns to sheath,
  So dust to grave, but souls find place in Heaven.
Heroic daring is the true success,
  The eucharistic bread requires no leaven;
And though your ends were hopeless, we should bless
  Your cause as holy. Strive – and, having striven,
Take, for God's recompense, that righteousness!

From

AURORA LEIGH
(1856)

FROM AURORA LEIGH

Aurora Leigh is the daughter of an English father and an Italian mother. Her mother having died when Aurora was four years old, Aurora is brought up by her father in Italy. Her father dies when she is thirteen and Aurora moves to England. Her father's sister becomes her guardian, and tries to educate Aurora in the manner of the English gentry. Aurora is both self-conscious about and resistant to the forms of education favoured by her aunt and uses her father's library secretly to give herself an alternative education.

At the age of twenty her cousin, Romney Leigh, proposes to her, asking her to abandon her poetic and intellectual enterprises and to aid him in his quest for social and political reforms. Aurora refuses Romney's proposal to the anger of her aunt. When her aunt dies Aurora is left with only £300 – marriage to Romney would have guaranteed her financial security.

Aurora moves to London and attempts to make a living as a writer. Romney, meanwhile, continues his philanthropic adventures, during which he rescues and gets employment for Marian Erle, a working-class girl who has run away from violent parents. Having been refused by Aurora, Romney decides to marry for principles rather than love and proposes to Marian. Aurora is informed of the proposed marriage by Lady Waldemar, who is also in love with Romney and who believes that Aurora will be able to stop the marriage. Aurora, however, does not attempt to prevent Romney marrying, though on the wedding day Romney is left standing at the altar, receiving a letter from Marian explaining that she could not marry someone who did not love her.

Aurora, on a trip to the continent, sees Marian, who now has a son. Marian reveals that Lady Waldemar persuaded her not to marry Romney and that after arriving in France (with the 'help' of Lady Waldemar) she was deserted and later raped. Aurora and Marian go to Florence together to bring up Marian's child, Aurora believing that Romney has married Lady Waldemar. Aurora hears from England that Romney has been ill, and when he arrives in Florence, it transpires that he has not married after all, and that he is still willing to marry Marian (though she will now not marry him). Romney has been blinded during a riot at Leigh Hall and has decided to turn away from his philanthropy. His blindness leads him to review Aurora's profession as a poet, and they confess their love for each other.

Of writing many books there is no end;
And I who have written much in prose and verse
For others' uses, will write now for mine, –
Will write my story for my better self,
As when you paint your portrait for a friend,
Who keeps it in a drawer and looks at it
Long after he has ceased to love you, just
To hold together what he was and is.
I, writing thus, am still what men call young;
I have not so far left the coasts of life   10
To travel inland, that I cannot hear
That murmur of the outer Infinite
Which unweaned babies smile at in their sleep
When wondered at for smiling; not so far,
But still I catch my mother at her post
Beside the nursery door, with finger up,
'Hush, hush – here's too much noise!' while her sweet eyes
Leap forward, taking part against her word
In the child's riot. Still I sit and feel
My father's slow hand, when she had left us both,   20
Stroke out my childish curls across his knee,
And hear Assunta's daily jest (she knew
He liked it better than a better jest)
Inquire how many golden scudi went
To make such ringlets. O my father's hand,
Stroke heavily, heavily the poor hair down,
Draw, press the child's head closer to thy knee!
I'm still too young, too young, to sit alone.
I write. My mother was a Florentine,
Whose rare blue eyes were shut from seeing me   30
When scarcely I was four years old, my life
A poor spark snatched up from a failing lamp
Which went out therefore. She was weak and frail;
She could not bear the joy of giving life,
The mother's rapture slew her. If her kiss
Had left a longer weight upon my lips
It might have steadied the uneasy breath,
And reconciled and fraternised my soul
With the new order. As it was, indeed,

I felt a mother-want about the world,   40
And still went seeking, like a bleating lamb
Left out at night in shutting up the fold, –
As restless as a nest-deserted bird
Grown chill through something being away, though what
It knows not. I, Aurora Leigh, was born
To make my father sadder, and myself
Not overjoyous, truly. Women know
The way to rear up children (to be just),
They know a simple, merry, tender knack
Of tying sashes, fitting baby-shoes,   50
And stringing pretty words that make no sense,
And kissing full sense into empty words,
Which things are corals to cut life upon,
Although such trifles: children learn by such,
Love's holy earnest in a pretty play
And get not over-early solemnised,
But seeing, as in a rose-bush, Love's Divine
Which burns and hurts not, – not a single bloom, –
Become aware and unafraid of Love.
Such good do mothers. Fathers love as well   60
– Mine did, I know, – but still with heavier brains,
And wills more consciously responsible,
And not as wisely, since less foolishly;
So mothers have God's license to be missed.

[FIRST BOOK, ll. 135–215]

I, a little child, would crouch
For hours upon the floor with knees drawn up,
And gaze across them, half in terror, half
In adoration, at the picture there, –
That swan-like supernatural white life
Just sailing upward from the red stiff silk   70
Which seemed to have no part in it nor power
To keep it from quite breaking out of bounds.
For hours I sat and stared. Assunta's awe
And my poor father's melancholy eyes
Still pointed that way. That way went my thoughts
When wandering beyond sight. And as I grew
In years, I mixed, confused, unconsciously,

Whatever I last read or heard or dreamed,
Abhorrent, admirable, beautiful,
Pathetical, or ghastly, or grotesque,   80
With still that face . . . which did not therefore change,
But kept the mystic level of all forms,
Hates, fears, and admirations, was by turns
Ghost, fiend, and angel, fairy, witch, and sprite,
A dauntless Muse who eyes a dreadful Fate,
A loving Psyche who loses sight of Love,
A still Medusa with mild milky brows
All curdled and all clothed upon with snakes
Whose slime falls fast as sweat will; or anon
Our Lady of the Passion, stabbed with swords   90
Where the Babe sucked; or Lamia in her first
Moonlighted pallor, ere she shrunk and blinked
And shuddering wriggled down to the unclean;
Or my own mother, leaving her last smile
In her last kiss upon the baby-mouth
My father pushed down on the bed for that, –
Or my dead mother, without smile or kiss,
Buried at Florence. All which images,
Concentred on the picture, glassed themselves
Before my meditative childhood, as   100
The incoherencies of change and death
Are represented fully, mixed and merged,
In the smooth fair mystery of perpetual Life.
And while I stared away my childish wits
Upon my mother's picture (ah, poor child!),
My father, who through love had suddenly
Thrown off the old conventions, broken loose
From chin-bands of the soul, like Lazarus,
Yet had no time to learn to talk and walk
Or grow anew familiar with the sun, –   110
Who had reached to freedom, not to action, lived,
But lived as one entranced, with thoughts, not aims, –
Whom love had unmade from a common man
But not completed to an uncommon man, –
My father taught me what he had learnt the best
Before he died and left me, – grief and love.
And, seeing we had books among the hills,
Strong words of counselling souls confederate

With vocal pines and waters, – out of books
He taught me all the ignorance of men,   120
And how God laughs in heaven when any man
Says 'Here I'm learned; this, I understand;
In that, I am never caught at fault or doubt.'
He sent the schools to school, demonstrating
A fool will pass for such through one mistake,
While a philosopher will pass for such,
Through said mistakes being ventured in the gross
And heaped up to a system.
                                        I am like,
They tell me, my dear father. Broader brows
Howbeit, upon a slenderer undergrowth   130
Of delicate features, – paler, near as grave;
But then my mother's smile breaks up the whole,
And makes it better sometimes than itself.
So, nine full years, our days were hid with God
Among his mountains: I was just thirteen,
Still growing like the plants from unseen roots
In tongue-tied Springs, – and suddenly awoke
To full life and life's needs and agonies
With an intense, strong, struggling heart beside
A stone-dead father. Life, struck sharp on death,   140
Makes awful lightning. His last word was 'Love – '
'Love, my child, love, love!' – (then he had done with grief)
'Love, my child.' Ere I answered he was gone,
And none was left to love in all the world.

There, ended childhood.

[FIRST BOOK, ll. 385–465]

                              So it was.
I broke the copious curls upon my head
In braids, because she liked smooth-ordered hair.
I left off saying my sweet Tuscan words
Which still at any stirring of the heart   150
Came up to float across the English phrase
As lilies (*Bene* or *Che che*), because
She liked my father's child to speak his tongue.
I learnt the collects and the catechism,

The creeds, from Athanasius back to Nice,
The Articles, the Tracts *against* the times
(By no means Buonaventure's 'Prick of Love'),
And various popular synopses of
Inhuman doctrines never taught by John,
Because she liked instructed piety.   160
I learnt my complement of classic French
(Kept pure of Balzac and neologism)
And German also, since she liked a range
Of liberal education, – tongues, not books.
I learnt a little algebra, a little
Of the mathematics, – brushed with extreme flounce
The circle of the sciences, because
She misliked women who are frivolous.
I learnt the royal genealogies
Of Oviedo, the internal laws   170
Of the Burmese empire, – by how many feet
Mount Chimborazo outsoars Teneriffe,
What navigable river joins itself
To Lara, and what census of the year five
Was taken at Klagenfurt, – because she liked
A general insight into useful facts.
I learnt much music, – such as would have been
As quite impossible in Johnson's day
As still it might be wished – fine sleights of hand
And unimagined fingering, shuffling off   180
The hearer's soul through hurricanes of notes
To a noisy Tophet; and I drew . . . costumes
From French engravings, nereids neatly draped
(With smirks of simmering godship): I washed in
Landscapes from nature (rather say, washed out).
I danced the polka and Cellarius,
Spun glass, stuffed birds, and modelled flowers in wax,
Because she liked accomplishments in girls.
I read a score of books on womanhood
To prove, if women do not think at all,   190
They may teach thinking (to a maiden aunt
Or else the author), – books that boldly assert
Their right of comprehending husband's talk
When not too deep, and even of answering
With pretty 'may it please you,' or 'so it is,' –

Their rapid insight and fine aptitude,
Particular worth and general missionariness,
As long as they keep quiet by the fire
And never say 'no' when the world says 'ay,'
For that is fatal, – their angelic reach   200
Of virtue, chiefly used to sit and darn,
And fatten household sinners, – their, in brief,
Potential faculty in everything
Of abdicating power in it: she owned
She liked a woman to be womanly,
And English women, she thanked God and sighed
(Some people always sigh in thanking God),
Were models to the universe. And last
I learnt cross-stitch, because she did not like
To see me wear the night with empty hands   210
A-doing nothing. So, my shepherdess
Was something after all (the pastoral saints
Be praised for't), leaning lovelorn with pink eyes
To match her shoes, when I mistook the silks;
Her head uncrushed by that round weight of hat
So strangely similar to the tortoise-shell
Which slew the tragic poet.
                                        By the way,
The works of women are symbolical.
We sew, sew, prick our fingers, dull our sight,
Producing what? A pair of slippers, sir,   220
To put on when you're weary – or a stool
To stumble over and vex you . . . 'curse that stool!'
Or else at best, a cushion, where you lean
And sleep, and dream of something we are not
But would be for your sake. Alas, alas!
This hurts most, this – that, after all, we are paid
The worth of our work, perhaps.

[FIRST BOOK, ll. 832–95]

                    Books, books, books!
I had found the secret of a garret-room
Piled high with cases in my father's name,
Piled high, packed large, – where, creeping in and out   230
Among the giant fossils of my past,

Like some small nimble mouse between the ribs
Of a mastodon, I nibbled here and there
At this or that box, pulling through the gap,
In heats of terror, haste, victorious joy,
The first book first. And how I felt it beat
Under my pillow, in the morning's dark,
An hour before the sun would let me read!
My books! At last because the time was ripe,   240
I chanced upon the poets.

                              As the earth
Plunges in fury, when the internal fires
Have reached and pricked her heart, and, throwing flat
The marts and temples, the triumphal gates
And towers of observation, clears herself
To elemental freedom – thus, my soul,
At poetry's divine first finger-touch,
Let go conventions and sprang up surprised,
Convicted of the great eternities
Before two worlds.

                              What's this, Aurora Leigh,   250
You write so of the poets, and not laugh?
Those virtuous liars, dreamers after dark,
Exaggerators of the sun and moon,
And soothsayers in a tea-cup?

                              I write so
Of the only truth-tellers now left to God,
The only speakers of essential truth,
Opposed to relative, comparative,
And temporal truths; the only holders by
His sun-skirts, through conventional gray glooms;
The only teachers who instruct mankind   260
From just a shadow on a charnel-wall
To find man's veritable stature out
Erect, sublime, – the measure of a man,
And that's the measure of an angel, says
The apostle. Ay, and while your common men
Lay telegraphs, gauge railroads, reign, reap, dine,
And dust the flaunty carpets of the world
For kings to walk on, or our president,
The poet suddenly will catch them up
With his voice like a thunder, – 'This is soul,   270

This is life, this word is being said in heaven,
Here's God down on us! what are you about?'
How all those workers start amid their work,
Look round, look up, and feel, a moment's space,
That carpet-dusting, though a pretty trade,
Is not the imperative labour after all.

My own best poets, am I one with you,
That thus I love you, – or but one through love?
Does all this smell of thyme about my feet
Conclude my visit to your holy hill   280
In personal presence, or but testify
The rustling of your vesture through my dreams
With influent odours? When my joy and pain,
My thought and aspiration, like the stops
Of pipe or flute, are absolutely dumb
Unless melodious, do you play on me
My pipers, – and if, sooth, you did not blow,
Would no sound come? or is the music mine,
As a man's voice or breath is called his own,
Inbreathed by the Life-breather? There's a doubt   290
For cloudy seasons!

[SECOND BOOK, ll. 323–67]

                        Then I spoke.
'I have not stood long on the strand of life,
And these salt waters have had scarcely time
To creep so high up as to wet my feet:
I cannot judge these tides – I shall, perhaps.
A woman's always younger than a man
At equal years, because she is disallowed
Maturing by the outdoor sun and air,
And kept in long-clothes past the age to walk.   300
Ah well, I know you men judge otherwise!
You think a woman ripens, as a peach,
In the cheeks chiefly. Pass it to me now;
I'm young in age, and younger still, I think,
As a woman. But a child may say amen
To a bishop's prayer and feel the way it goes,
And I, incapable to loose the knot

Of social questions, can approve, applaud
August compassion, Christian thoughts that shoot
Beyond the vulgar white of personal aims.   310
Accept my reverence.'

                There he glowed on me
With all his face and eyes. 'No other help?'
Said he – 'no more than so?'

                      'What help?' I asked.
'You'd scorn my help, – as Nature's self, you say,
Has scorned to put her music in my mouth
Because a woman's. Do you now turn round
And ask for what a woman cannot give?'

'For what she only can, I turn and ask,'
He answered, catching up my hands in his,
And dropping on me from his high-eaved brow   320
The full weight of his soul, – 'I ask for love,
And that, she can; for life in fellowship
Through bitter duties – that, I know she can;
For wifehood – will she?'

                 'Now,' I said, 'may God
Be witness 'twixt us two!' and with the word,
Meseemed I floated into a sudden light
Above his stature, – 'am I proved too weak
To stand alone, yet strong enough to bear
Such leaners on my shoulder? poor to think,
Yet rich enough to sympathise with thought?   330
Incompetent to sing, as blackbirds can,
Yet competent to love, like HIM?'

                    I paused;
Perhaps I darkened, as the lighthouse will
That turns upon the sea. 'It's always so.
Anything does for a wife.'

[THIRD BOOK, ll. 758–826]

            Two hours afterward,
Within Saint Margaret's Court I stood alone,
Close-veiled. A sick child, from an ague-fit,
Whose wasted right hand gambled 'gainst his left
With an old brass button in a blot of sun,   340

Jeered weakly at me as I passed across
The uneven pavement; while a woman, rouged
Upon the angular cheek-bones, kerchief torn,
Thin dangling locks, and flat lascivious mouth,
Cursed at a window both ways, in and out,
By turns some bed-rid creature and myself, –
'Lie still there, mother! liker the dead dog
You'll be to-morrow. What, we pick our way,
Fine madam, with those damnable small feet!
We cover up our face from doing good,   350
As if it were our purse! What brings you here,
My lady? Is't to find my gentleman
Who visits his tame pigeon in the eaves?
Our cholera catch you with its cramps and spasms,
And tumble up your good clothes, veil and all,
And turn your whiteness dead-blue.' I looked up;
I think I could have walked through hell that day,
And never flinched. 'The dear Christ comfort you,'
I said, 'you must have been most miserable
To be so cruel,' – and I emptied out   360
My purse upon the stones: when, as I had cast
The last charm in the cauldron, the whole court
Went boiling, bubbling up, from all its doors
And windows, with a hideous wail of laughs
And roar of oaths, and blows perhaps . . . I passed
Too quickly for distinguishing . . . and pushed
A little side-door hanging on a hinge,
And plunged into the dark, and groped and climbed
The long, steep, narrow stair 'twixt broken rail
And mildewed wall that let the plaster drop   370
To startle me in the blackness. Still, up, up!
So high lived Romney's bride. I paused at last
Before a low door in the roof, and knocked.
There came an answer like a hurried dove –
'So soon?' can that be Mister Leigh? so soon?'
And, as I entered, an ineffable face
Met mine upon the threshold. 'Oh, not you,
Not you!' – the dropping of the voice implied;   380
'Then, if not you, for me not any one.'
I looked her in the eyes, and held her hands,
And said 'I am his cousin, – Romney Leigh's;

And here I come to see my cousin too.'
She touched me with her face and with her voice,
This daughter of the people. Such soft flowers
From such rough roots? The people, under there,
Can sin so, curse so, look so, smell so . . . faugh!
Yet have such daughters?
               Nowise beautiful
Was Marian Erle. She was not white nor brown,
But could look either, like a mist that changed
According to being shone on more or less: 390
The hair, too, ran its opulence of curls
In doubt 'twixt dark and bright, nor left you clear
To name the colour. Too much hair perhaps
(I'll name a fault here) for so small a head,
Which seemed to droop in that side and on this,
As a full-blown rose uneasy with its weight
Though not a wind should trouble it. Again,
The dimple in the cheek had better gone
With redder, fuller rounds; and somewhat large
The mouth was, though the milky little teeth   400
Dissolved it to so infantine a smile.
For soon it smiled at me; the eyes smiled too,
But 'twas as if remembering they had wept,
And knowing they should, some day, weep again.

[FIFTH BOOK, ll. 1–73]

Aurora Leigh, be humble. Shall I hope
To speak my poems in mysterious tune
With man and nature? – with the lava-lymph
That trickles from successive galaxies
Still drop by drop adown the finger of God
In still new worlds? – with summer-days in this   410
That scarce dare breathe they are so beautiful?
With spring's delicious trouble in the ground,
Tormented by the quickened blood of roots,
And softly pricked by golden crocus-sheaves
In token of the harvest-time of flowers?
With winters and with autumns, – and beyond
With the human heart's large seasons, when it hopes
And fears, joys, grieves, and loves? – with all that strain

Of sexual passion, which devours the flesh
In a sacrament of souls? with mother's breasts   420
Which, round the new-made creatures hanging there,
Throb luminous and harmonious like pure spheres? –
With multitudinous life, and finally
With the great escapings of ecstatic souls,
Who, in a rush of too long prisoned flame,
Their radiant faces upward, burn away
This dark of the body, issuing on a world
Beyond our mortal? – can I speak my verse
So plainly in tune to these things and the rest
That men shall feel it catch them on the quick   430
As having the same warrant over them
To hold and move them if they will or no,
Alike imperious as the primal rhythm
Of that theurgic nature? – I must fail,
Who fail at the beginning to hold and move
One man, – and he my cousin, and he my friend,
And he born tender, made intelligent,
Inclined to ponder the precipitous sides
Of difficult questions; yet, obtuse to *me*,
Of *me*, incurious! likes me very well,   440
And wishes me a paradise of good,
Good looks, good means, and good digestion, – ay,
But otherwise evades me, puts me off
With kindness, with a tolerant gentleness, –
Too light a book for a grave man's reading! Go,
Aurora Leigh: be humble.
                              There it is,
We women are too apt to look to one,
Which proves a certain impotence in art.
We strain our natures at doing something great,
Far less because it's something great to do,   450
Than haply that we, so, commend ourselves
As being not small, and more appreciable
To some one friend. We must have mediators
Betwixt our highest conscience and the judge;
Some sweet saint's blood must quicken in our palms,
Or all the life in heaven seems slow and cold:
Good only being perceived as the end of good,
And God alone pleased, – that's too poor, we think,

And not enough for us by any means.
Ay – Romney, I remember, told me once   460
We miss the abstract when we comprehend.
We miss it most when we aspire, – and fail.

Yet, so, I will not. – This vile woman's way
Of trailing garments shall not trip me up:
I'll have no traffic with the personal thought
In Art's pure temple. Must I work in vain,
Without the approbation of a man?
It cannot be; it shall not. Fame itself,
That approbation of the general race,
Presents a poor end (though the arrow speed   470
Shot straight with vigorous finger to the white),
And the highest fame was never reached except
By what was aimed above it. Art for art,
And good for God Himself, the essential Good!
We'll keep our aims sublime, our eyes erect,
Although our woman-hands should shake and fail;
And if we fail . . . But must we? –
                              Shall I fail?

[FIFTH BOOK, ll. 139–229]

The critics say that epics have died out
With Agamemnon and the goat-nursed gods;
I'll not believe it. I could never deem,   480
As Payne Knight did (the mythic mountaineer
Who travelled higher than he was born to live,
And showed sometimes the goitre in his throat
Discoursing of an image seen through fog),
That Homer's heroes measured twelve feet high.
They were but men: – his Helen's hair turned grey
Like any plain Miss Smith's who wears a front;
And Hector's infant whimpered at a plume
As yours last Friday at a turkey-cock.
All actual heroes are essential men,   490
And all men possible heroes: every age,
Heroic in proportions, double-faced,
Looks backward and before, expects a morn
And claims an epos.

               Ay, but every age
Appears to souls who live in't (ask Carlyle)
Most unheroic. Ours, for instance, ours:
The thinkers scout it, and the poets abound
Who scorn to touch it with a finger-tip:
A pewter age, – mixed metal, silver-washed;
An age of scum, spooned off the richer past,   500
An age of patches for old gaberdines,
An age of mere transition, meaning nought
Except that what succeeds must shame it quite
If God please. That's wrong thinking, to my mind,
And wrong thoughts make poor poems.
                          Every age,
Through being beheld too close, is ill-discerned
By those who have not lived past it. We'll suppose
Mount Athos carved, as Alexander schemed,
To some colossal statue of a man.
The peasants, gathering brushwood in his ear   510
Had guessed as little as the browsing goats
Of form or feature of humanity
Up there, – in fact, had travelled five miles off
Or ere the giant image broke on them,
Full human profile, nose and chin distinct,
Mouth, muttering rhythms of silence up the sky
And fed at evening with the blood of suns;
Grand torso, – hand, that flung perpetually
The largesse of a silver river down
To all the country pastures. 'Tis even thus   520
With times we live in, – evermore too great
To be apprehended near.
                      But poets should
Exert a double vision; should have eyes
To see near things as comprehensively
As if afar they took their point of sight,
And distant things as intimately deep
As if they touched them. Let us strive for this.
I do distrust the poet who discerns
No character or glory in his times,
And trundles back his soul five hundred years,   530
Past moat and drawbridge, into a castle-court,
To sing – oh, not of lizard or of toad

Alive i' the ditch there, – 'twere excusable,
But of some black chief, half knight, half sheep-lifter,
Some beauteous dame, half chattel and half queen,
As dead as must be, for the greater part,
The poems made on their chivalric bones;
And that's no wonder: death inherits death.

Nay, if there's room for poets in this world
A little overgrown (I think there is),   540
Their sole work is to represent the age,
Their age, not Charlemagne's, – this live, throbbing age,
That brawls, cheats, maddens, calculates, aspires,
And spends more passion, more heroic heat,
Betwixt the mirrors of its drawing-rooms,
Than Roland with his knights at Roncesvalles.
To flinch from modern varnish, coat or flounce,
Cry out for togas and the picturesque,
Is fatal, – foolish too. King Arthur's self
Was commonplace to Lady Guenever;   550
And Camelot to minstrels seemed as flat
As Fleet Street to our poets.
                              Never flinch,
But still, unscrupulously epic, catch
Upon the burning lava of a song
The full-veined, heaving, double-breasted Age:
That, when the next shall come, the men of that
May touch the impress with reverent hand, and say
'Behold, – behold the paps we all have sucked!
This bosom seems to beat still, or at least
It sets ours beating: this is living art,   560
Which thus presents and thus records true life.'

What form is best for poems? Let me think
Of forms less, and the external. Trust the spirit,
As sovran nature does, to make the form;
For otherwise we only imprison spirit
And not embody. Inward evermore
To outward, – so in life, and so in art
Which still is life.

[SIXTH BOOK, ll. 736-93]

                'Kill! O Christ,' she said,
And turned her wild sad face from side to side   570
With most despairing wonder in it, 'What,
What have you in your souls against me then,
All of you? am I wicked, do you think?
God knows me, trusts me with the child; but you,
You think me really wicked?'
                    'Complaisant,'
I answered softly, 'to a wrong you've done,
Because of certain profits, – which is wrong
Beyond the first wrong, Marian. When you left
The pure place and the noble heart, to take
The hand of a seducer' . . .   580
               'Whom? whose hand?
I took the hand of' . . .
                Springing up erect,
And lifting up the child at full arm's length,
As if to bear him like an oriflamme
Unconquerable to armies of reproach, –
'By *him*,' she said, 'my child's head and its curls,
By these blue eyes no woman born could dare
A perjury on, I make my mother's oath,
That if I left that Heart, to lighten it,
The blood of mine was still, except for grief!
No cleaner maid than I was took a step   590
To a sadder end, – no matron-mother now
Looks backward to her early maidenhood
Through chaster pulses. I speak steadily;
And if I lie so, . . . if, being fouled in will
And paltered with in soul by devil's lust,
I dared to bid this angel take my part, . . .
Would God sit quiet, let us think, in heaven,
Nor strike me dumb with thunder? Yet I speak:
He clears me therefore. What, "seduced"'s your word!
Do wolves seduce a wandering fawn in France?   600
Do eagles, who have pinched a lamb with claws,
Seduce it into carrion? So with me.
I was not ever, as you say, seduced,
But simply, murdered.'

There she paused, and sighed
With such a sigh as drops from agony
To exhaustion, – sighing while she let the babe
Slide down upon her bosom from her arms,
And all her face's light fell after him
Like a torch quenched in falling. Down she sank,   610
And sat upon the bedside with the child.

But I, convicted, broken utterly,
With woman's passion clung about her waist
And kissed her hair and eyes, – 'I have been wrong,
Sweet Marian' . . . (weeping in a tender rage) . . .
'Sweet holy Marian! And now, Marian, now,
I'll use your oath although my lips are hard,
And by the child, my Marian, by the child,
I swear his mother shall be innocent
Before my conscience, as in the open Book   620
Of Him who reads for judgment. Innocent,
My sister! let the night be ne'er so dark
The moon is surely somewhere in the sky;
So surely is your whiteness to be found
Through all dark facts. But pardon, pardon me,
And smile a little, Marian, – for the child,
If not for me, my sister.'

[SEVENTH BOOK, ll. 174–227]

It is strange,
To-day while Marian told her story like
To absorb most listeners, how I listened chief   630
To a voice not hers, nor yet that enemy's,
Nor God's in wrath, . . . but one that mixed with mine
Long years ago among the garden-trees,
And said to *me*, to *me* too, 'Be my wife,
Aurora.' It is strange with what a swell
Of yearning passion, as a snow of ghosts
Might beat against the impervious door of heaven,
I thought, 'Now, if I had been a woman, such
As God made women, to save men by love, –
By just my love I might have saved this man,   640
And made a nobler poem for the world

Than all I have failed in.' But I failed besides
In this; and now he's lost! through me alone!
And, by my only fault, his empty house
Sucks in, at this same hour, a wind from hell
To keep his hearth cold, make his casements creak
For ever to the tune of plague and sin –
O Romney, O my Romney, O my friend,
My cousin and friend! my helper, when I would,
My love, that might be! mine!
                         Why, how one weeps   650
When one's too weary! Were a witness by,
He'd say some folly . . . that I loved the man,
Who knows? . . . and make me laugh again for scorn.
At strongest, women are as weak in flesh,
As men, at weakest, vilest, are in soul:
So, hard for women to keep pace with men!
As well give up at once, sit down at once,
And weep as I do. Tears, tears! why
'Tis worth inquiry? – that we've shamed a life,
Or lost a love, or missed a world, perhaps?   660
By no means. Simply that we've walked too far,
Or talked too much, or felt the wind;' the east, –
And so we weep, as if both body and soul
Broke up in water – this way.
                         Poor mixed rags
Forsooth we're made of, like those other dolls
That lean with pretty faces into fairs.
It seems as if I had a man in me,
Despising such a woman.
                        Yet indeed,
To see a wrong or suffering moves us all
To undo it though we should undo ourselves,   670
Ay, all the more, that we undo ourselves;
That's womanly, past doubt, and not ill-moved.
A natural movement therefore, on my part,
To fill the chair up of my cousin's wife,
And save him from a devil's company!
We're all so, – made so – 'tis our woman's trade
To suffer torment for another's ease.
The world's male chivalry has perished out,
But women are knights-errant to the last;

And if Cervantes had been Shakespeare too,   680
He had made his Don a Donna.

[SEVENTH BOOK, ll. 749–94]

            I have written truth,
And I a woman, – feebly, partially,
Inaptly in presentation, Romney'll add,
Because a woman. For the truth itself,
That's neither man's nor woman's, but just God's,
None else has reason to be proud of truth:
Himself will see it sifted, disenthralled,
And kept upon the height and in the light,
As far as and no farther than 'tis truth;   690
For, now He has left off calling firmaments
And strata, flowers and creatures, very good,
He says it still of truth, which is His own.
Truth, so far, in my book; the truth which draws
Through all things upwards – that a twofold world
Must go to a perfect cosmos. Natural things
And spiritual, – who separates those two
In art, in morals, or the social drift,
Tears up the bond of nature and brings death,
Paints futile pictures, writes unreal verse,   700
Leads vulgar days, deals ignorantly with men,
Is wrong, in short, at all points. We divide
This apple of life, and cut it through the pips:
The perfect round which fitted Venus' hand
Has perished as utterly as if we ate
Both halves. Without the spiritual, observe,
The natural's impossible – no form,
No motion: without sensuous, spiritual
Is inappreciable, – no beauty or power:
And in this twofold sphere the twofold man   710
(For still the artist is intensely a man)
Holds firmly by the natural, to reach
The spiritual beyond it, – fixes still
The type with mortal vision, to pierce through,
With eyes immortal, to the antitype
Some call the ideal, – better called the real,
And certain to be called so presently

When things shall have their names. Look long enough
On any peasant's face here, coarse and lined,
You'll catch Antinous somewhere in that clay,   720
As perfect featured as he yearns at Rome
From marble pale with beauty; then persist,
And, if your apprehension's competent,
You'll find some fairer angel at his back,
As much exceeding him as he the boor,
And pushing him with empyreal disdain
For ever out of sight.

[EIGHT BOOK, ll. 261–352]

               'I have read your book,
Aurora.'
           'You have read it,' I replied,
'And I have writ it, – we have done with it.   730
And now the rest?'
                 'The rest is like the first,'
He answered, – 'for the book is in my heart,
Lives in me, wakes in me, and dreams in me:
My daily bread tastes of it, – and my wine
Which has no smack of it, I pour it out,
It seems unnatural drinking.'
                   Bitterly
I took the word up; 'Never waste your wine.
The book lived in me ere it lived in you;
I know it closer than another does,
And how it's foolish, feeble, and afraid,   740
And all unworthy so much compliment.
Beseech you, keep your wine, – and, when you drink,
Still wish some happier fortune to a friend,
Than even to have written a far better book.'

He answered gently, 'That is consequent:
The poet looks beyond the book he has made,
Or else he had not made it. If a man
Could make a man, he'd henceforth be a god
In feeling what a little thing is man:
It is not my case. And this special book,   750
I did not make it, to make light of it:

It stands above my knowledge, draws me up;
'Tis high to me. It may be that the book
Is not so high, but I so low, instead;
Still high to me. I mean no compliment:
I will not say there are not, young or old,
Male writers, ay, or female, let it pass,
Who'll write us richer and completer books.
A man may love a woman perfectly,
And yet by no means ignorantly maintain   760
A thousand women have not larger eyes:
Enough that she alone has looked at him
With eyes that, large or small, have won his soul.
And so, this book, Aurora, – so, your book.'

'Alas,' I answered, 'is it so, indeed?'
And then was silent.
                          'Is it so, indeed,'
He echoed, 'that *alas* is all your word?'
I said, 'I'm thinking of a far-off June,
When you and I, upon my birthday once,
Discoursed of life and art, with both untried.   770
I'm thinking, Romney, how 'twas morning then,
And now 'tis night.'
                          'And now,' he said, 'tis night.'

'I'm thinking,' I resumed, ''tis somewhat sad,
That if I had known, that morning in the dew,
My cousin Romney would have said such words
On such a night at close of many years,
In speaking of a future book of mine,
It would have pleased me better as a hope,
Than as an actual grace it can at all:
That's sad, I'm thinking.'
                          'Ay,' he said, ''tis night.'   780

'And there,' I added lightly, 'are the stars!
And here, we'll talk of stars and not of books.'

'You have the stars,' he murmured, – 'it is well:
Be like them! shine, Aurora, on my dark,
Though high and cold and only like a star,

And for this short night only, – you, who keep
The same Aurora of the bright June-day
That withered up the flowers before my face,
And turned me from the garden evermore
Because I was not worthy. Oh, deserved,   790
Deserved! that I, who verily had not learnt
God's lesson half, attaining as a dunce
To obliterate good words with fractious thumbs
And cheat myself of the context, – I
Aside, with male ferocious impudence,
The world's Aurora who had conned her part
On the other side the leaf! ignore her so,
Because she was a woman and a queen,
And had no beard to bristle through her song,
My teacher, who has taught me with a book,   800
My Miriam, whose sweet mouth, when nearly drowned
I still heard singing on the shore! Deserved,
That here I should look up unto the stars
And miss the glory' . . .

                        'Can I understand?'
I broke in. 'You speak wildly, Romney Leigh,
Or I hear wildly. In that morning-time
We recollect, the roses were too red,
The trees too green, reproach too natural
If one should see not what the other saw:
And now, it's night, remember; we have shades   810
In place of colours; we are now grown cold,
And old, my cousin Romney. Pardon me, –
I'm very happy that you like my book,
And very sorry that I quoted back
A ten years' birthday. 'Twas so mad a thing
In any woman, I scarce marvel much
You took it for a venturous piece of spite,
Provoking such excuses as indeed
I cannot call you slack in.'

[NINTH BOOK, ll. 321–452]

'. . . The truth is, I am grown so proud with grief,   820
And He has said so often through His nights
And through His mornings, "Weep a little still,

Thou foolish Marian, because women must,
But do not blush at all except for sin" –
That I, who felt myself unworthy once
Of virtuous Romney and his high-born race,
Have come to learn, – a woman, poor or rich,
Despised or honoured, is a human soul,
And what her soul is, that she is herself,
Although she should be spit upon of men,   830
As is the pavement of the churches here,
Still good enough to pray in. And being chaste
And honest, and inclined to do the right,
And love the truth, and live my life out green
And smooth beneath his steps, I should not fear
To make him thus a less uneasy time
Than many a happier woman. Very proud
You see me. Pardon, that I set a trap
To hear a confirmation in your voice,
Both yours and yours. It is so good to know   840
'Twas really God who said the same before;
And thus it is in heaven, that first God speaks,
And then His angels. Oh, it does me good,
It wipes me clean and sweet from devil's dirt,
That Romney Leigh should think me worthy still
Of being his true and honourable wife!
Henceforth I need not say, on leaving earth,
I had no glory in it. For the rest,
The reason's ready (master, angel, friend,
Be patient with me) wherefore you and I   850
Can never, never, never join hands so.
I know you'll not be angry like a man
(For *you* are none) when I shall tell the truth,
Which is, I do not love you, Romney Leigh,
I do not love you. Ah well! catch my hands,
Miss Leigh, and burn into my eyes with yours –
I swear I do not love him. Did I once?
'Tis said that women have been bruised to death
And yet, if once they loved, that love of theirs
Could never be drained out with all their blood: 860
I've heard such things and pondered. Did I indeed
Love once; or did I only worship? Yes,
Perhaps, O friend, I set you up so high

Above all actual good or hope of good
Or fear of evil, all that could be mine,
I haply set you above love itself,
And set out reach of these poor woman's arms,
Angelic Romney. What was in my thought?
To be your slave, your help, your toy, your tool.
To be your love . . . I never thought of that: 870
To give you love . . . still less. I gave you love?
I think I did not give you anything;
I was but only yours – upon my knees,
All yours, in soul and body, in head and heart,
A creature you had taken from the ground
Still crumbling through your fingers to your feet
To join the dust she came from. Did I love,
Or did I worship? judge, Aurora Leigh!
But, if indeed I loved, 'twas long ago –
So long! before the sun and moon were made,   880
Before the hells were open, – ah, before
I heard my child cry in the desert night,
And knew he had no father. It may be
I'm not as strong as other women are,
Who, torn and crushed, are not undone from love:
It may be I am colder than the dead,
Who, being dead, love always. But for me,
Once killed, this ghost of Marian loves no more,
No more . . . except the child! . . . no more at all.
I told your cousin, sir, that I was dead;   890
And now, she thinks I'll get up from my grave,
And wear my chin-cloth for a wedding-veil,
And glide along the churchyard like a bride
While all the dead keep whispering through the withes,
"You would be better in your place with us,
You pitiful corruption!" At the thought,
The damps break out on me like leprosy
Although I'm clean. Ay, clean as Marian Erle!
As Marian Leigh, I know, I were not clean:
Nor have I so much life that I should love,   900
Except the child. Ah God! I could not bear
To see my darling on a good man's knees,
And know, by such a look, or such a sigh,
Or such a silence, that he thought sometimes,

"This child was fathered by some cursèd wretch" . . .
For, Romney, angels are less tender-wise
Than God and mothers: even *you* would think
What *we* think never. He is ours, the child;
And we would sooner vex a soul in heaven   910
By coupling with it the dead body's thought,
It left behind it in a last month's grave,
Than, in my child, see other than . . . my child.
We only never call him fatherless
Who has God and his mother. O my babe,
My pretty, pretty blossom, an ill wind
Once blew upon my breast! can any think
I'd have another – one called happier,
A fathered child, with father's love and race
That's worn as bold and open as a smile,
To vex my darling when he's asked his name   920
And has no answer? What! a happier child
Than mine, my best – who laughed so loud to-night
He could not sleep for pastime? Nay, I swear,
By life and love, that, if I lived like some,
And loved like . . . *some*, ay, loved you, Romney Leigh,
As some love (eyes that have wept so much, see clear),
I've room for no more children in my arms,
My kisses are all melted on one mouth,
I would not push my darling to a stool
To dandle babies. Here's a hand shall keep   930
For ever clean without a marriage-ring,
To tend my boy until he cease to need
One steadying finger of it, and desert
(Not miss) his mother's lap, to sit with men.
And when I miss him (not he me), I'll come
And say "Now give me some of Romney's work,
To help your outcast orphans of the world
And comfort grief with grief." For you, meantime,
Most noble Romney, wed a noble wife,
And open on each other your great souls –   940
I need not farther bless you. If I dared
But strain and touch her in her upper sphere,
And say "Come down to Romney – pay my debt!"
I should be joyful with the stream of joy
Sent through me. But the moon is in my face . . .

I dare not – though I guess the name he loves;
I'm learned with my studies of old days,
Remembering how he crushed his under-lip
When some one came and spoke, or did not come.
Aurora, I could touch her with my hand,   950
And fly because I dare not.'

[NINTH BOOK, ll. 624–760]

'. . . No matter: let the truth
Stand high; Aurora must be humble: no,
My love's not pity merely. Obviously
I'm not a generous woman, never was,
Or else, of old, I had not looked so near
To weights and measures, grudging you the power
To give, as first I scorned your power to judge
For me, Aurora. I would have no gifts,
Forsooth, but God's, – and I would use *them* too   960
According to my pleasure and my choice,
As He and I were equals, you below,
Excluded from that level of interchange
Admitting benefaction. You were wrong
In much? you said so. I was wrong in most.
Oh, most! You only thought to rescue men
By half-means, half-way, seeing half their wants,
While thinking nothing of your personal gain.
But I, who saw the human nature broad
At both sides, comprehending too the soul's,   970
And all the high necessities of Art,
Betrayed the thing I saw, and wronged my own life
For which I pleaded. Passioned to exalt
The artist's instinct in me at the cost
Of putting down the woman's, I forgot
No perfect artist is developed here
From any imperfect woman. Flower from root,
And spiritual from natural, grade by grade
In all our life. A handful of the earth
To make God's image! the despised poor earth,   980
The healthy, odorous earth. – I missed with it
The divine Breath that blows the nostrils out
To ineffable inflatus, – ay, the breath

Which love is. Art is much, but Love is more.
O Art, my Art, thou'rt much, but Love is more!
Art symbolises heaven, but Love is God
And makes heaven. I, Aurora, fell from mine.
I would not be a woman like the rest,
A simple woman who believes in love
And owns the right of love because she loves,   990
And, hearing she's beloved, is satisfied
With what contents God: I must analyse,
Confront, and question; just as if a fly
Refused to warm itself in any sun
Till such was *in Leone*: I must fret,
Forsooth, because the month was only May,
Be faithless of the kind of proffered love,
And captious, lest it miss my dignity,
And scornful, that my lover sought a wife
To use . . . to use! O Romney, O my love,   1000
I am changed since then, changed wholly, – for indeed
If now you'd stoop so low to take my love
And use it roughly, without stint or spare,
As men use common things with more behind
(And, in this, ever would be more behind)
To any mean and ordinary end, –
The joy would set me like a star, in heaven,
So high up, I should shine because of height
And not of virtue. Yet in one respect,
Just one, beloved, I am in nowise changed: 1010
I love you, loved you . . . loved you first and last,
And love you on for ever. Now I know
I loved you always, Romney. She who died
Knew that, and said so; Lady Waldemar
Knows that; . . . and Marian. I had known the same,
Except that I was prouder than I knew,
And not so honest. Ay, and, as I live,
I should have died so, crushing in my hand
This rose of love, the wasp inside and all,
Ignoring ever to my soul and you   1020
Both rose and pain – except for this great loss,
This great despair – to stand before your face
And know you do not see me where I stand.
You think, perhaps, I am not changed from pride

And that I chiefly bear to say such words,
Because you cannot shame me with your eyes?
O calm, grand eyes, extinguished in a storm,
Blown out like lights o'er melancholy seas,
Though shrieked for by the shipwrecked, – O my Dark,
My Cloud, – to go before me every day   1030
While I go ever toward the wilderness, –
I would that you could see me bare to the soul!
If this be pity, 'tis so for myself,
And not for Romney! *he* can stand alone;
A man like *him* is never overcome:
No woman like me counts him pitiable
While saints applaud him. He mistook the world;
But I mistook my own heart, and that slip
Was fatal. Romney, – will you leave me here?
So wrong, so proud, so weak, so unconsoled,   1040
So mere a woman! – and I love you so,
I love you, Romney – '
                Could I see his face,
I wept so? Did I drop against his breast,
Or did his arms constrain me? were my cheeks
Hot, overflooded, with my tears – or his?
And which of our two large explosive hearts
So shook me? That, I know not. There were words
That broke in utterance . . . melted, in the fire, –
Embrace, that was convulsion, . . . then a kiss
As long and silent as the ecstatic night,   1050
And deep, deep, shuddering breaths, which meant beyond
Whatever could be told by word or kiss.
But what he said . . . I have written day by day,
With somewhat even writing. Did I think
That such a passionate rain would intercept
And dash this last page? what he said, indeed,
I fain would write it down here like the rest,
To keep it in my eyes, as in my ears,
The heart's sweet scripture it be read at night
When weary, or at morning when afraid,   1060
And lean my heaviest oath on when I swear
That, when all's done, all tried, all counted here,
All great arts, and all good philosophies,
This love just puts its hand out in a dream

And straight outstretches all things.
                         What he said,
I fain would write. But if an angel spoke
In thunder, should we haply know much more
Than that it thundered? If a cloud came down
And wrapped us wholly, could we draw its shape,
As if on the outside and not overcome?   1070
And so he spake. His breath against my face
Confused his words, yet made them more intense
(As when the sudden finger of the wind
Will wipe a row of single city-lamps
To a pure white line of flame, more luminous
Because of obliteration), more intense,
The intimate presence carrying in itself
Complete communication, as with souls
Who, having put the body off, perceive
Through simply being. Thus, 'twas granted me   1080
To know he loved me to the depth and height
Of such large natures, ever competent,
With grand horizons by the sea or land,
To love's grand sunrise. Small spheres hold small fires,
But he loved largely, as a man can love
Who, baffled in his love, dares live his life,
Accepts the ends which God loves, for his own,
And lift a constant aspect.

[NINTH BOOK, ll. 900–64]

           '. . . O poet, O my love,
Since *I* was too ambitious in my deed,   1090
And thought to distance all men in success
(Till God came on me, marked the place, and said
"Ill-doer, henceforth keep within this line,
Attempting less than others," – and I stand
And work among Christ's little ones, content),
Come thou, my compensation, my dear sight,
My morning-star, my morning, – rise and shine,
And touch my hills with radiance not their own.
Shine out for two, Aurora, and fulfil
My falling-short that must be! work for two,   1100
As I, though thus restrained, for two, shall love!

Gaze on, with inscient vision toward the sun,
And, from his visceral heat, pluck out the roots
Of light beyond him. Art's a service, – mark:
A silver key is given to thy clasp,
And thou shalt stand unwearied, night and day,
And fix it in the hard, slow-turning wards,
To open, so, that intermediate door
Betwixt the different planes of sensuous form
And form insensuous, that inferior men   1110
May learn to feel on still through these to those,
And bless thy ministration. The world waits
For help. Beloved, let us love so well,
Our work shall still be better for our love,
And still our love be sweeter for our work,
And both commended, for the sake of each,
By all true workers and true lovers born.
Now press the clarion on thy woman's lip
(Love's holy kiss shall still keep consecrate)
And breathe thy fine keen breath along the brass,   1120
And blow all class-walls level as Jericho's
Past Jordan, – crying from the top of souls,
To souls, that, here assembled on earth's flats,
They get them to some purer eminence
Than any hitherto beheld for clouds!
What height we know not, – but the way we know,
And how by mounting ever we attain,
And so climb on. It is the hour for souls,
That bodies, leavened by the will and love,
Be lightened to redemption. The world's old,   1130
But the old world waits the time to be renewed,
Toward which, new hearts in individual growth
Must quicken, and increase to multitude
In new dynasties of the race of men;
Developed whence, shall grow spontaneously
New churches, new œconomies, new laws
Admitting freedom, new societies
Excluding falsehood: HE shall make all new.'

My Romney! – Lifting up my hand in his,
As wheeled by Seeing spirits toward the east,   1140
He turned instinctively, where, faint and far,

Along the tingling desert of the sky,
Beyond the circle of the conscious hills,
Were laid in jasper-stone as clear as glass
The first foundations of that new, near Day
Which should be builded out of heaven to God.

He stood a moment with erected brows,
In silence, as a creature might who gazed, –
Stood calm, and fed his blind, majestic eyes
Upon the thought of perfect noon: and when   1150
I saw his soul saw, – 'Jasper first,' I said;
'And second, sapphire; third, chalcedony;
The rest in order: – last, an amethyst.'

From

POEMS BEFORE CONGRESS
(1860)

A CURSE FOR A NATION

PROLOGUE

I heard an angel speak last night,
    And he said 'Write!
Write a Nation's curse for me,
And send it over the Western Sea.'

I faltered, taking up the word:
    'Not so, my lord!
If curses must be, choose another
To send thy curse against my brother.

'For I am bound by gratitude,
    By love and blood,   10
To brothers of mine across the sea,
Who stretch out kindly hands to me.'

'Therefore,' the voice said, 'shalt thou write
    My curse to-night.
From the summits of love a curse is driven,
As lightning is from the tops of heaven.'

'Not so,' I answered. 'Evermore
    My heart is sore
For my own land's sins: for little feet
Of children bleeding along the street: 20

'For parked-up honours that gainsay
    The right of way:
For almsgiving through a door that is
Not open enough for two friends to kiss:

'For love of freedom which abates
    Beyond the Straits:
For patriot virtue starved to vice on
Self-praise, self-interest, and suspicion:

'For an oligarchic parliament,
        And bribes well-meant.
What curse to another land assign,
When heavy-souled for the sins of mine?'

'Therefore,' the voice said, 'shalt thou write
        My curse to-night.
Because thou hast strength to see and hate
A foul thing done *within* thy gate.'

'Not so,' I answered once again.
        'To curse, choose men.
For I, a woman, have only known
How the heart melts and the tears run down.'

'Therefore,' the voice said, 'shalt thou write
        My curse to-night.
Some women weep and curse, I say
(And no one marvels), night and day.

'And thou shalt take their part to-night,
        Weep and write.
A curse from the depths of womanhood
Is very salt, and bitter, and good.'

So thus I wrote, and mourned indeed,
        What all may read.
And thus, as was enjoined on me,
I send it over the Western Sea.

THE CURSE

I

Because ye have broken your own chain
        With the strain
Of brave men climbing a Nation's height,
Yet thence bear down with brand and thong
On souls of others, – for this wrong
        This is the curse. Write.

Because yourselves are standing straight
    In the state   60
Of Freedom's foremost acolyte,
Yet keep calm footing all the time
On writhing bond-slaves, – for this crime
    This is the curse. Write.

Because ye prosper in God's name,
    With a claim
To honour in the old world's sight,
Yet do the fiend's work perfectly
In strangling martyrs, – for this lie
    This is the curse. Write.   70

II

Ye shall watch while kings conspire
Round the people's smouldering fire,
    And, warm for your part,
Shall never dare – O shame!
To utter the thought into flame
    Which burns at your heart.
    This is the curse. Write.

Ye shall watch while nations strive
With the bloodhounds, die or survive,
    Drop faint from their jaws,   80
Or throttle them backward to death,
And only under your breath
    Shall favour the cause.
    This is the curse. Write.

Ye shall watch while strong men draw
The nets of feudal law
    To strangle the weak,
And, counting the sin for a sin,
Your soul shall be sadder within
    Than the word ye shall speak.   90
    This is the curse. Write.

When good men are praying erect
That Christ may avenge His elect
   And deliver the earth,
The prayer in your ears, said low,
Shall sound like the tramp of a foe
   That's driving you forth.
      This is the curse. Write.

When wise men give you their praise,
They shall pause in the heat of the phrase,   100
   As if carried too far.
When ye boast your own charters kept true,
Ye shall blush; – for the thing which ye do
   Derives what ye are.
      This is the curse. Write.

When fools cast taunts at your gate,
Your scorn ye shall somewhat abate
   As ye look o'er the wall,
For your conscience, tradition, and name
Explode with a deadlier blame   110
   Than the worst of them all.
      This is the curse. Write.

Go, wherever ill deeds shall be done,
Go, plant your flag in the sun
   Beside the ill-doers!
And recoil from clenching the curse
Of God's witnessing Universe
   With a curse of yours.
      THIS is the curse. Write.

A COURT LADY

I

Her hair was tawny with gold, her
    eyes with purple were dark,
Her cheeks' pale opal burnt with a red
    and restless spark.

II

Never was lady of Milan nobler in name
    and in race;
Never was lady of Italy fairer to see in
    the face.

III

Never was lady on earth more true as
    woman and wife,
Larger in judgement and instinct, prouder
    in manners and life.

10

IV

She stood in the early morning, and
    said to her maidens, 'Bring
That silken robe made ready to wear at
    the court of the king.

V

'Bring me the clasps of diamond, lucid,
    clear of the mote,
Clasp me the large at the waist, and
    clasp me the small at the throat.

20

VI

'Diamonds to fasten the hair, and
    diamonds to fasten the sleeves,
Laces to drop from their rays, like
    a powder of snow from the eaves.'

VII

Gorgeous she entered the sunlight
    which gathered her up in a flame,
While, straight in her open carriage,
    she to the hospital came.

VIII

In she went at the door, and gazing
    from end to end,
'Many and low are the pallets, but   30
    each is the place of a friend.'

IX

Up she passed through the wards, and
    stood at a young man's bed:
Bloody the band on his brow, and livid
    the droop of his head.

X

'Art thou a Lombard, my brother?
    Happy art thou,' she cried,
And smiled like Italy on him: he
    dreamed in her face and died.   40

XI

Pale with his passing soul, she went on
    still to a second:
He was a grave hard man, whose years
    by dungeons were reckoned.

XII

Wounds in his body were sore, wounds
  in his life were sorer.
'Art thou a Romagnole?' Her eyes
  drove lightnings before her.

XIII

'Austrian and priest had joined to double
  and tighten the cord
Able to bind thee, O strong one, – free
  by the stroke of a sword.

XIV

'Now be grave for the rest of us, using
  the life overcast
To ripen our wine of the present, (too
  new) in glooms of the past.'

XV

Down she stepped to a pallet where lay
  a face like a girl's,
Young, and pathetic with dying, – a deep
  black hole in the curls.

XVI

'Art thou from Tuscany, brother? and
  seest thou, dreaming in pain,
Thy mother stand in the piazza, search-
  ing the List of the slain?'

XVII

Kind as a mother herself, she touched
  his cheeks with her hands:
'Blessed is she who has borne thee,
  although she should weep as she stands.'

50

60

XVIII

On she passed to a Frenchman, his arm
    carried off by a ball: 70
Kneeling, . . . 'O more than my brother!
    how shall I thank thee for all?

XIX

'Each of the heroes around us has fought
    for his land and line,
But *thou* hast fought for a stranger, in
    hate of a wrong not thine.

XX

'Happy are all free peoples, too strong
    to be dispossessed.
But blessed are those among nations, who
    dare to be strong for the rest!'   80

XXI

Ever she passed on her way, and came
    to a couch where pined
One with a face from Venetia, white with
    a hope out of mind.

XXII

Long she stood and gazed, and twice she
    tried at the name,
But two great crystal tears were all that
    faltered and came.

XXIII

Only a tear for Venice? – she turned as
    in passion and loss,   90
And stooped to his forehead and kissed
    it, as if she were kissing the cross.

XXIV

Faint with that strain of heart she moved
    on then to another,
Stern and strong in his death. 'And
    dost thou suffer, my brother?'

XXV

Holding his hands in hers: – 'Out of the
    Piedmont lion
Cometh the sweetness of freedom!
    sweetest to live or to die on.'

      100

XXVI

Holding his cold rough hands, – 'Well,
    oh, well have ye done
In noble, noble Piedmont, who would
    not be noble alone.'

XXVII

Back he fell while she spoke. She rose
    to her feet with a spring, –
'That was a Piedmontese! and this is
    the Court of the King.'

A TALE OF VILLAFRANCA

I

My little son, my Florentine,
   Sit down beside my knee,
And I will tell you why the sign
   Of joy which flushed our Italy,
Has faded since but yesternight;
And why your Florence of delight
   Is mourning as you see.

II

A great man (who was crowned one day)
   Imagined a great Deed:
He shaped it out of cloud and clay,   10
   He touched it finely till the seed
Possessed the flower: from heart and brain
He fed it with large thoughts humane,
   To help a people's need.

III

He brought it out into the sun –
   They blessed it to his face:
'O great pure Deed, that hast undone
   So many bad and base!
O generous Deed, heroic Deed,
Come forth, be perfected, succeed,   20
   Deliver by God's grace.'

IV

Then sovereigns, statesmen, north and south,
  Rose up in wrath and fear,
And cried, protesting by one mouth,
  'What monster have we here?
A great Deed at this hour of day?
A great just Deed – and not for pay?
  Absurd, – or insincere.

V

'And if sincere, the heavier blow
  In that case we shall bear,
For where's our blessed "status quo,"   30
  Our holy treaties, where, –
Our rights to sell a race, or buy,
Protect and pillage, occupy,
  And civilize despair?'

VI

Some muttered that the great Deed meant
  A great pretext to sin;
And others, the pretext, so lent,
  Was heinous (to begin).
Volcanic terms of 'great' and 'just'?   40
Admit such tongues of flame, the crust
  Of time and law falls in.

VII

A great Deed in this world of ours?
  Unheard of the pretence is:
It threatens plainly the great Powers;
  Is fatal in all senses.
A just Deed in the world? – call out
The rifles! be not slack about
  The national defences.

VIII

And many murmured, 'From this source   50
   What red blood must be poured!'
And some rejoined, ''Tis even worse;
   What red tape is ignored!'
All cursed the Doer for an evil
Called here, enlarging on the Devil, –
   There, monkeying the Lord!

IX

Some said, it could not be explained,
   Some, could not be excused;
And others, 'Leave it unrestrained,
   Gehenna's self is loosed.'   60
And all cried, 'Crush it, maim it, gag it!
Set dog-toothed lies to tear it ragged,
   Truncated and traduced!'

X

But HE stood sad before the sun
   (The peoples felt their fate).
'The world is many, – I am one;
   My great Deed was too great.
God's fruit of justice ripens slow:
Men's souls are narrow; let them grow.
   My brothers, we must wait.'   70

XI

The tale is ended, child of mine,
   Turned graver at my knee.
They say your eyes, my Florentine,
   Are English: it may be:
And yet I've marked as blue a pair
Following the doves across the square
   At Venice by the sea.

XII

Ah, child! ah, child! I cannot say
    A word more. You conceive
The reason now, why just to-day   80
    We see our Florence grieve.
Ah, child, look up into the sky!
In this low world, where great Deeds die,
    What matter if we live?

THE DANCE

I

You remember down at Florence our Cascine,
    Where the people on the feast-days walk and drive,
And, through the trees, long-drawn in many a green way,
    O'er-roofing hum and murmur like a hive,
    The river and the mountains look alive?

II

You remember the piazzone there, the stand-place
    Of carriages a-brim with Florence Beauties,
Who lean and melt to music as the band plays,
    Or smile and chat with some one who afoot is,
    Or on horseback, in observance of male duties?   10

III

'Tis so pretty, in the afternoons of summer,
    So many gracious faces brought together!
Call it rout, or call it concert, they have come here,
    In the floating of the fan and of the feather,
    To reciprocate with beauty the fine weather.

IV

While the flower-girls offer nosegays (because *they* too
   Go with other sweets) at every carriage-door;
Here, by shake of a white finger, signed away to
   Some next buyer, who sits buying score on score,
   Piling roses upon roses evermore.   20

V

And last season, when the French camp had its station
   In the meadow-ground, things quickened and grew gayer
Through the mingling of the liberating nation
   With this people; groups of Frenchmen everywhere,
   Strolling, gazing, judging lightly . . . 'who was fair.'

VI

Then the noblest lady present took upon her
   To speak nobly from her carriage for the rest;
'Pray these officers from France to do us honour
   By dancing with us straightway.' – The request
   Was gravely apprehended as addressed.   30

VII

And the men of France bareheaded, bowing lowly,
   Led out each a proud signora to the space
Which the startled crowd had rounded for them – slowly,
   Just a touch of still emotion in his face,
   Not presuming, through the symbol, on the grace.

VIII

There was silence in the people: some lips trembled,
   But none jested. Broke the music, at a glance:
And the daughters of our princes, thus assembled,
   Stepped the measure with the gallant sons of France.
   Hush! it might have been a Mass, and not a dance.   40

IX

And they danced there till the blue that overskied us
   Swooned with passion, though the footing seemed sedate;
And the mountains, heaving mighty hearts beside us,
   Sighed a rapture in a shadow, to dilate,
    And touch the holy stone where Dante sate.

X

Then the sons of France bareheaded, lowly bowing,
   Led the ladies back where kinsmen of the south
Stood, received them; – till, with burst of overflowing
   Feeling . . . husbands, brothers, Florence's male youth,
    Turned, and kissed the martial strangers mouth to mouth. 50

XI

And a cry went up, a cry from all that people!
   – You have heard a people cheering, you suppose,
For the Member, Mayor . . with chorus from the steeple?
   This was different: scarce as loud perhaps (who knows?),
    For we saw wet eyes around us ere the close.

XII

And we felt as if a nation, too long borne in
   By hard wrongers, comprehending in such attitude
That God had spoken somewhere since the morning,
   That men were somehow brothers, by no platitude,
    Cried exultant in great wonder and free gratitude. 60

From

LAST POEMS
(1862)

LORD WALTER'S WIFE

I

'But why do you go,' said the lady, while both sat under the
  yew,
And her eyes were alive in their depth, as the kraken beneath
  the sea-blue.

II

'Because I fear you,' he answered; – 'because you are far too
  fair,
And able to strangle my soul in a mesh of your gold-coloured
  hair.'

III

'Oh, that,' she said, 'is no reason! Such knots are quickly
  undone,
And too much beauty, I reckon, is nothing but too much sun.'

IV

'Yet farewell so,' he answered; – 'the sun-stroke's fatal at
  times.
I value your husband, Lord Walter, whose gallop rings still
  from the limes.'

V

'Oh, that,' she said, 'is no reason. You smell a rose through a
  fence:
If two should smell it, what matters? who grumbles, and
  where's the pretence?'   10

VI

'But I,' he replied, 'have promised another, when love was free,
To love her alone, alone, who alone and afar loves me.'

VII

'Why, that,' she said, 'is no reason. Love's always free, I am
    told.
Will you vow to be safe from the headache on Tuesday, and
    think it will hold?'

VIII

'But you,' he replied, 'have a daughter, a young little child,
    who was laid
In your lap to be pure; so, I leave you: the angels would make
    me afraid.'

IX

'Oh, that,' she said, 'is no reason. The angels keep out of the
    way;
And Dora, the child, observes nothing, although you should
    please me and stay.'

X

At which he rose up in his anger, – 'Why, now, you no longer
    are fair!
Why, now, you no longer are fatal, but ugly and hateful, I
    swear.'   20

XI

At which she laughed out in her scorn. – 'These men! Oh,
    these men overnice,
Who are shocked if a colour, not virtuous, is frankly put on
    by a vice.'

XII

Her eyes blazed upon him – 'And *you!* You bring us your
    vices so near
That we smell them! You think in our presence a thought
    'twould defame us to hear!

XIII

'What reason had you, and what right, – I appeal to your soul
  from my life, –
To find me too fair as a woman? Why, sir, I am pure, and a
  wife.

XIV

'Is the day-star too fair up above you? It burns you not. Dare
  you imply
I brushed you more close than the star does, when Walter had
  set me as high?

XV

'If a man finds a woman too fair, he means simply adapted
  too much
To uses unlawful and fatal. The praise! – shall I thank you
  for such?   30

XVI

'Too fair? – not unless you misuse us! and surely if, once in a
  while,
You attain to it, straightway you call us no longer too fair,
  but too vile.

XVII

'A moment? I pray your attention! – I have a poor word in
  my head
I must utter, though womanly custom would set it down
  better unsaid.

XVIII

'You grew, sir, pale to impertinence, once when I showed
  you a ring.
You kissed my fan when I dropped it. No matter! – I've
  broken the thing.

XIX

'You did me the honour, perhaps, to be moved at my side
   now and then
In the senses – a vice, I have heard, which is common to
   beasts and some men.

XX

'Love's a virtue for heroes! – as white as the snow on high hills,
And immortal as every great soul is that struggles, endures,
   and fulfils.   40

XXI

'I love my Walter profoundly, – you, Maude, though you
   faltered a week,
For the sake of . . . what was it? an eyebrow? or, less still, a
   mole on a cheek?

XXII

'And since, when all's said, you're too noble to stoop to the
   frivolous cant
About crimes irresistible, virtues that swindle, betray and
   supplant,

XXIII

'I determined to prove to yourself that, whate'er you might
   dream or avow
By illusion, you wanted precisely no more of me than you
   have now.

XXIV

'There! look me full in the face! – in the face. Understand, if
   you can,
That the eyes of such women as I am, are clean as the palm
   of a man.

XXV

'Drop his hand, you insult him. Avoid us for fear we should
    cost you a scar –
You take us for harlots, I tell you, and not for the women we
    are.   50

XXVI

'You wronged me: but then I considered . . . there's Walter!
    And so at the end,
I vowed that he should not be mulcted, by me, in the hand
    of a friend.

XXVII

'Have I hurt you indeed? We are quits then. Nay, friend of
    my Walter, be mine!
Come Dora, my darling, my angel, and help me to ask him to
    dine.'

AMY'S CRUELTY

I

Fair Amy of the terraced house,
    Assist me to discover
Why you who would not hurt a mouse
    Can torture so your lover.

II

You give your coffee to the cat,
    You stroke the dog for coming,
And all your face grows kinder at
    The little brown bee's humming.

III

But when *he* haunts your door . . . the town
    Marks coming and marks going . . .   10
You seem to have stitched your eyelids down
    To that long piece of sewing!

IV

You never give a look, not you,
    Nor drop him a 'Good-morning,'
To keep his long day warm and blue,
    So fretted by your scorning.

V

She shook her head – 'The mouse and bee
    For crumb or flower will linger:
The dog is happy at my knee,
    The cat purrs at my finger.   20

VI

But *he* . . . to *him*, the least thing given
    Means great things at a distance;
He wants my world, my sun, my heaven,
    Soul, body, whole existence.

VII

'They say love gives as well as takes;
    But I'm a simple maiden, –
My mother's first smile when she wakes
    I still have smiled and prayed in.

VIII

'I only know my mother's love
    Which gives all and asks nothing;   30
And this new loving sets the groove
    Too much the way of loathing.

IX

'Unless he gives me all in change,
  I forfeit all things by him:
The risk is terrible and strange –
  I tremble, doubt, . . . deny him.

X

'He's sweetest friend, or hardest foe,
  Best angel, or worst devil;
I either hate or . . . love him so,
  I can't be merely civil!   40

XI

'You trust a woman who puts forth,
  Her blossoms thick as summer's?
You think she dreams what love is worth,
  Who casts it to new-comers?

XII

'Such love's a cowslip-ball to fling,
  A moment's pretty pastime;
I give . . . all me, if anything,
  The first time and the last time.

XIII

'Dear neighbour of the trellised house,
  A man should murmur never,   50
Though treated worse than dog and mouse,
  Till doted on for ever!'

A FALSE STEP

I

Sweet, thou hast trod on a heart.
  Pass! there's a world full of men,
And women as fair as thou art
  Must do such things now and then.

II

Thou only hast stepped unaware, –
  Malice, not one can impute;
And why should a heart have been there
  In the way of a fair woman's foot?

III

It was not a stone that could trip,
  Nor was it a thorn that could rend:
Put up thy proud underlip!
  'Twas merely the heart of a friend.

IV

And yet peradventure one day
  Thou, sitting alone at the glass,
Remarking the bloom gone away,
  Where the smile in its dimplement was,

V

And seeking around thee in vain
  From hundreds who flattered before,
Such a word as, 'Oh, not in the main
  Do I hold thee less precious, but more!' . . .

VI

Thou'lt sigh, very like, on thy part,
   'Of all I have known or can know,
I wish I had only that Heart
   I trod upon ages ago!'

MY HEART AND I

I

Enough! we're tired, my heart and I.
   We sit beside the headstone thus,
   And wish that name were carved for us.
The moss reprints more tenderly
   The hard types of the mason's knife,
   As Heaven's sweet life renews earth's life
With which we're tired, my heart and I.

II

You see we're tired, my heart and I.
   We dealt with books, we trusted men,
   And in our own blood drenched the pen,   10
As if such colours could not fly.
   We walked too straight for fortune's end,
   We loved too true to keep a friend;
At last we're tired, my heart and I.

III

How tired we feel, my heart and I!
   We seem of no use in the world;
   Our fancies hang grey and uncurled
About men's eyes indifferently;
   Our voice which thrilled you so, will let
   You sleep; our tears are only wet: 20
What do we here, my heart and I?

IV

So tired, so tired, my heart and I!
　　It was not thus in that old time
　　When Ralph sat with me 'neath the lime
To watch the sunset from the sky.
　　'Dear love, you're looking tired,' he said;
　　I, smiling at him, shook my head:
'Tis now we're tired, my heart and I.

V

So tired, so tired, my heart and I!
　　Though now none takes me on his arm   30
　　To fold me close and kiss me warm
Till each quick breath end in a sigh
　　Of happy languor. Now, alone,
　　We lean upon this graveyard stone,
Uncheered, unkissed, my heart and I.

VI

Tired out we are, my heart and I.
　　Suppose the world brought diadems
　　To tempt us, crusted with loose gems
Of powers and pleasures? Let it try.
　　We scarcely care to look at even   40
　　A pretty child, or God's blue heaven,
We feel so tired, my heart and I.

VII

Yet who complains? My heart and I?
　　In this abundant earth no doubt
　　Is little room for things worn out:
Disdain them, break them, throw them by!
　　And if before the days grew rough
　　We *once* were loved, used, – well enough,
I think, we've fared, my heart and I.

BIANCA AMONG THE NIGHTINGALES

I

The cypress stood up like a church
   That night we felt our love would hold,
And saintly moonlight seemed to search
   And wash the whole world clean as gold;
The olives crystallized the vales'
   Broad slopes until the hills grew strong:
The fireflies and the nightingales
   Throbbed each to either, flame and song.
The nightingales, the nightingales.

II

Upon the angle of its shade
   The cypress stood, self-balanced high;
Half up, half down, as double made,
   Along the ground, against the sky.
And *we* too! from such soul-height went
   Such leaps of blood, so blindly driven,
We scarce knew if our nature meant
   Most passionate earth or intense heaven.
The nightingales, the nightingales.

III

We paled with love, we shook with love,
   We kissed so close we could not vow;
Till Giulio whispered, 'Sweet, above
   God's Ever guarantees this Now.'
And through his words the nightingales
   Drove straight and full their long clear call,
Like arrows through heroic mails,
   And love was awful in it all.
The nightingales, the nightingales.

IV

O cold white moonlight of the north,
   Refresh these pulses, quench this hell!
O coverture of death drawn forth   30
   Across this garden-chamber . . . well!
But what have nightingales to do
   In gloomy England, called the free . . .
(Yes, free to die in! . . .) when we two
   Are sundered, singing still to me?
And still they sing, the nightingales.

V

I think I hear him, how he cried
   'My own soul's life' between their notes.
Each man has but one soul supplied,
   And that's immortal. Though his throat's   40
On fire with passion now, to *her*
   He can't say what to me he said!
And yet he moves her, they aver.
   The nightingales sing through my head,
The nightingales, the nightingales.

VI

He says to *her* what moves her most.
   He would not name his soul within
Her hearing, – rather pays her cost
   With praises to her lips and chin.
Man has but one soul, 'tis ordained,   50
   And each soul but one love, I add;
Yet souls are damned and love's profaned.
   These nightingales will sing me mad!
The nightingales, the nightingales.

VII

I marvel how the birds can sing.
  There's little difference, in their view,
Betwixt our Tuscan trees that spring
  As vital flames into the blue,
And dull round blots of foliage meant
  Like saturated sponges here   60
To suck the fogs up. As content
  Is *he* too in this land, 'tis clear.
And still they sing, the nightingales.

VIII

My native Florence! dear, foregone!
  I see across the Alpine ridge
How the last feast-day of St John
  Shot rockets from Carraia bridge.
The luminous city, tall with fire,
  Trod deep down in that river of ours,
While many a boat with lamp and choir   70
  Skimmed birdlike over glittering towers.
I will not hear these nightingales.

IX

I seem to float, *we* seem to float
  Down Arno's stream in festive guise;
A boat strikes flame into our boat
  And up that lady seems to rise
As then she rose. The shock had flashed
  A vision on us! What a head,
What leaping eyeballs! – beauty dashed
  To splendour by a sudden dread.   80
And still they sing, the nightingales.

X

Too bold to sin, too weak to die;
    Such women are so. As for me,
I would we had drowned there, he and I,
    That moment, loving perfectly.
He had not caught her with her loosed
    Gold ringlets . . . rarer in the south . . .
Nor heard the 'Grazie tanto' bruised
    To sweetness by her English mouth.
And still they sing, the nightingales.   90

XI

She had not reached him at my heart
    With her fine tongue, as snakes indeed
Kill flies; nor had I, for my part,
    Yearned after, in my desperate need,
And followed him as he did her
    To coasts left bitter by the tide,
Whose very nightingales, elsewhere
    Delighting, torture and deride!
For still they sing, the nightingales.

XII

A worthless woman! mere cold clay   100
    As all false things are! but so fair,
She takes the breath of men away
    Who gaze upon her unaware.
I would not play her larcenous tricks
    To have her looks! She lied and stole,
And spat into my lover's pure pyx
    The rank saliva of her soul.
And still they sing, the nightingales.

XIII

I would not for her white and pink,
   Though such he likes – her grace of limb,   110
Though such he has praised – nor yet, I think,
   For life itself, though spent with him,
Commit such sacrilege, affront
   God's nature which is love, intrude
'Twixt two affianced souls, and hunt
   Like spiders, in the altar's wood.
I cannot bear these nightingales.

XIV

If she chose sin, some gentler guise
   She might have sinned in, so it seems:
She might have pricked out both my eyes,   120
   And I still seen him in my dreams!
– Or drugged me in my soup or wine,
   Nor left me angry afterward:
To die here with his hand in mine
   His breath upon me, were not hard.
(Our Lady hush these nightingales!)

XV

But set a springe for *him*, 'mio ben,'
   My only good, my first last love! –
Though Christ knows well what sin is, when
   He sees some things done they must move   130
Himself to wonder. Let her pass.
   I think of her by night and day.
Must *I* too join her . . . out, alas! . . .
   With Giulio, in each word I say?
And evermore the nightingales!

XVI

Giulio, my Giulio! – sing they so,
  And you be silent? Do I speak,
And you not hear? An arm you throw
  Round some one, and I feel so weak?
– Oh, owl-like birds! They sing for spite,   140
  They sing for hate, they sing for doom!
They'll sing through death who sing through night,
  They'll sing and stun me in the tomb –
The nightingales, the nightingales!

VOID IN LAW

I

Sleep, little babe, on my knee,
  Sleep, for the midnight is chill,
And the moon has died out in the tree,
  And the great human world goeth ill.
Sleep, for the wicked agree:
  Sleep, let them do as they will.
Sleep.

II

Sleep, thou hast drawn from my breast
  The last drop of milk that was good;
And now, in a dream, suck the rest,   10
  Lest the real should trouble thy blood.
Suck, little lips dispossessed,
  As we kiss in the air whom we would.
Sleep.

III

O lips of thy father! the same,
 So like! Very deeply they swore
When he gave me his ring and his name,
 To take back, I imagined, no more!
And now is all changed like a game,
 Though the old cards are used as of yore?   20
Sleep.

IV

'Void in law,' said the courts. Something wrong
 In the forms? Yet, 'Till death part us two,
I, James, take thee, Jessie,' was strong,
 And ONE witness competent. True
Such a marriage was worth an old song,
 Heard in Heaven, though, as plain as the New.
Sleep.

V

Sleep, little child, his and mine!
 Her throat has the antelope curve,   30
And her cheek just the colour and line
 Which fade not before him nor swerve:
Yet *she* has no child! – the divine
 Seal of right upon loves that deserve.
Sleep.

VI

My child! though the world take her part,
 Saying, 'She was the woman to choose,
He had eyes, was a man in his heart,' –
 We twain the decision refuse:
We . . . weak as I am, as thou art, . . .   40
 Cling on to him, never to loose.
Sleep.

VII

He thinks that, when done with this place,
    All's ended? he'll new-stamp the ore?
Yes, Cæsar's – but not in our case.
    Let him learn we are waiting before
The grave's mouth, the Heaven's gate, God's face,
    With implacable love evermore.
Sleep.

VIII

He's ours, though he kissed her but now;   50
    He's ours, though she kissed in reply;
He's ours, though himself disavow,
    And God's universe favour the lie;
Ours to claim, ours to clasp, ours below,
    Ours above, . . . if we live, if we die.
Sleep.

IX

Ah baby, my baby, too rough
    Is my lullaby? What have I said?
Sleep? When I've wept long enough
    I shall learn to weep softly instead,   60
And piece with some alien stuff
    My heart to lie smooth for thy head.
Sleep.

X

Two souls met upon thee, my sweet;
    Two loves led thee out to the sun:
Alas, pretty hands, pretty feet,
    If the one who remains (only one)
Set her grief at thee, turned in a heat
    To thine enemy, – were it well done?
Sleep.   70

XI

May He of the manger stand near
   And love thee! An infant He came
To His own who rejected Him here,
   But the Magi brought gifts all the same.
I hurry the cross on my Dear!
   My gifts are the griefs I declaim!
Sleep.

FIRST NEWS FROM VILLAFRANCA

I

Peace, peace, peace, do you say?
   What! – with the enemy's guns in our ears?
   With the country's wrong not rendered back?
What! – while Austria stands at bay
   In Mantua, and our Venice bears
   The cursed flag of the yellow and black?

II

Peace, peace, peace, do you say?
   And this the Mincio? Where's the fleet,
   And where's the sea? Are we all blind
Or mad with the blood shed yesterday,
   Ignoring Italy under our feet,
   And seeing things before, behind?

10

III

Peace, peace, peace, do you say?
   What! – uncontested, undenied?
   Because we triumph, we succumb?
A pair of Emperors stand in the way,
   (One of whom is a man, beside)
To sign and seal our cannons dumb?

IV

No, not Napoleon! – he who mused
  At Paris, and at Milan spake,   20
  And at Solferino led the fight:
Not he we trusted, honoured, used
  Our hope and hearts for . . . till they break –
  Even so, you tell us . . . in his sight.

V

Peace, peace, is still your word?
  We say you lie then! – that is plain.
  There *is* no peace, and shall be none.
Our very dead would cry 'Absurd!'
  And clamour that they died in vain,
  And whine to come back to the sun.   30

VI

Hush! more reverence for the dead!
  They've done the most for Italy
  Evermore since the earth was fair.
Now would that *we* had died instead,
  Still dreaming peace meant liberty,
  And did not, could not mean despair.

VII

Peace, you say? – yes, peace, in truth!
  But such a peace as the ear can achieve
  'Twixt the rifle's click and the rush of the ball,
'Twixt the tiger's spring and the crunch of the tooth,   40
  'Twixt the dying atheist's negative
  And God's face – waiting, after all!

THE FORCED RECRUIT

SOLFERINO 1859

I

In the ranks of the Austrian you found him,
   He died with his face to you all;
Yet bury him here where around him
   You honour your bravest that fall.

II

Venetian, fair-featured and slender,
   He lies shot to death in his youth,
With a smile on his lips over-tender
   For any mere soldier's dead mouth.

III

No stranger, and yet not a traitor,
   Though alien the cloth on his breast,
Underneath it how seldom a greater
   Young heart, has a shot sent to rest!

10

IV

By your enemy tortured and goaded
   To march with them, stand in their file,
His musket (see) never was loaded,
   He facing your guns with that smile!

V

As orphans yearn on to their mothers,
   He yearned to your patriot bands; –
'Let me die for our Italy, brothers,
   If not in your ranks, by your hands!

20

VI

'Aim straightly, fire steadily! spare me
  A ball in the body which may
Deliver my heart here, and tear me
  This badge of the Austrian away!'

VII

So thought he, so died he this morning.
  What then? many others have died.
Aye, but easy for men to die scorning
  The death-stroke, who fought side by side –

VIII

One tricolor floating above them;
  Struck down 'mid triumphant acclaims   30
Of an Italy rescued to love them
  And blazon the brass with their names.

IX

But he, – without witness or honour,
  Mixed, shamed in his country's regard,
With the tyrants who march in upon her,
  Died faithful and passive: 'twas hard.

X

'Twas sublime. In a cruel restriction
  Cut off from the guerdon of sons,
With most filial obedience, conviction,
  His soul kissed the lips of her guns.   40

XI

That moves you? Nay, grudge not to show it,
  While digging a grave for him here:
The others who died, says your poet,
  Have glory, – let *him* have a tear.

MOTHER AND POET

(TURIN, AFTER NEWS FROM GAETA, 1861)

I

Dead! One of them shot by the sea in the east,
    And one of them shot in the west by the sea.
Dead! both my boys! When you sit at the feast
    And are wanting a great song for Italy free,
        Let none look at *me*!

II

Yet I was a poetess only last year,
    And good at my art, for a woman, men said;
But *this* woman, *this*, who is agonised here,
    – The east sea and west sea rhyme on in her head
        For ever instead.   10

III

What art can a woman be good at? Oh, vain!
    What art *is* she good at, but hurting her breast
With the milk-teeth of babes, and a smile at the pain?
    Ah boys, how you hurt! you were strong as you pressed,
        And I proud, by that test.

IV

What art's for a woman? To hold on her knees
    Both darlings! to feel all their arms round her throat,
Cling, strangle a little! to sew by degrees
    And 'broider the long-clothes and neat little coat;
        To dream and to doat.   20

V

To teach them . . . It stings there! *I* made them indeed
    Speak plain the word *country*. *I* taught them, no doubt,
That a country's a thing men should die for at need.
    I prated of liberty, rights, and about
        The tyrant cast out.

VI

And when their eyes flashed . . . O my beautiful eyes! . . .
    I exulted; nay, let them go forth at the wheels
Of the guns, and denied not. But then the surprise
    When one sits quite alone! Then one weeps, then one kneels!
        God, how the house feels!   30

VII

At first, happy news came, in gay letters moiled
    With my kisses, – of camp-life and glory, and how
They both loved me; and, soon coming home to be spoiled
    In return would fan off every fly from my brow
        With their green laurel-bough.

VIII

Then was triumph at Turin: 'Ancona was free!'
    And some one came out of the cheers in the street,
With a face pale as stone, to say something to me.
    My Guido was dead! I fell down at his feet,
        While they cheered in the street.   40

IX

I bore it; friends soothed me; my grief looked sublime
    As the ransom of Italy. One boy remained
To be leant on and walked with, recalling the time
    When the first grew immortal, while both of us strained
        To the height he had gained.

X

And letters still came, shorter, sadder, more strong,
　　Writ now but in one hand, 'I was not to faint, –
One loved me for two – would be with me ere long:
　　And *Viva l'Italia!* – *he* died for, our saint,
　　　　Who forbids our complaint.'　　　　　　　　50

XI

My Nanni would add, 'he was safe, and aware
　　Of a presence that turned off the balls, – was imprest
It was Guido himself, who knew what I could bear,
　　And how 'twas impossible, quite dispossessed
　　　　To live on for the rest.'

XII

On which, without pause, up the telegraph line
　　Swept smoothly the next news from Gaeta: – *Shot*.
Tell his mother. Ah, ah, 'his,' 'their' mother, – not 'mine,'
　　No voice says '*My* mother' again to me. What!
　　　　You think Guido forgot?　　　　　　　　60

XIII

Are souls straight so happy that, dizzy with Heaven,
　　They drop earth's affections, conceive not of woe?
I think not. Themselves were too lately forgiven
　　Through THAT Love and Sorrow which reconciled so
　　　　The Above and Below.

XIV

O Christ of the five wounds, who look'dst through the dark
　　To the face of Thy mother! consider, I pray,
How we common mothers stand desolate, mark,
　　Whose sons, not being Christs, die with eyes turned away,
　　　　And no last word to say!　　　　　　　　70

XV

Both boys dead? but that's out of nature. We all
   Have been patriots, yet each house must always keep one.
'Twere imbecile, hewing out roads to a wall;
   And, when Italy's made, for what end is it done
      If we have not a son?

XVI

Ah, ah, ah! when Gaeta's taken, what then?
   When the fair wicked queen sits no more at her sport
Of the fire-balls of death crashing souls out of men?
   When the guns of Cavalli with final retort
      Have cut the game short?   80

XVII

When Venice and Rome keep their new jubilee,
   When your flag takes all heaven for its white, green, and red,
When *you* have your country from mountain to sea,
   When King Victor has Italy's crown on his head,
      (And *I* have my Dead) –

XVIII

What then? Do not mock me. Ah, ring your bells low,
   And burn your lights faintly! *My* country is *there*,
Above the star pricked by the last peak of snow:
   My Italy's THERE, with my brave civic Pair,
      To disfranchise despair!   90

XIX

Forgive me. Some women bear children in strength,
   And bite back the cry of their pain in self-scorn;
But the birth-pangs of nations will wring us at length
   Into wail such as this – and we sit on forlorn
      When the man-child is born.

XX

Dead! One of them shot by the sea in the east,
  And one of them shot in the west by the sea.
Both! both my boys! If in keeping the feast
  You want a great song for your Italy free,
    Let none look at *me*!   100

A MUSICAL INSTRUMENT

I

What was he doing, the great god Pan,
  Down in the reeds by the river?
Spreading ruin and scattering ban,
Splashing and paddling with hoofs of a goat,
And breaking the golden lilies afloat
  With the dragon-fly on the river.

II

He tore out a reed, the great god Pan,
  From the deep cool bed of the river:
The limpid water turbidly ran,
And the broken lilies a-dying lay,   10
And the dragon-fly had fled away,
  Ere he brought it out of the river.

III

High on the shore sate the great god Pan,
  While turbidly flowed the river;
And hacked and hewed as a great god can,
With his hard bleak steel at the patient reed,
Till there was not a sign of a leaf indeed
  To prove it fresh from the river.

IV

He cut it short, did the great god Pan,
   (How tall it stood in the river!)   20
Then drew the pith, like the heart of a man,
Steadily from the outside ring,
And notched the poor dry empty thing
   In holes, as he sate by the river.

V

'This is the way,' laughed the great god Pan,
   (Laughed while he sate by the river,)
'The only way, since gods began
To make sweet music, they could succeed.'
Then, dropping his mouth to a hole in the reed,
   He blew in power by the river.   30

VI

Sweet, sweet, sweet, O Pan!
   Piercing sweet by the river!
Blinding sweet, O great god Pan!
The sun on the hill forgot to die,
And the lilies revived, and the dragon-fly
   Came back to dream on the river.

VII

Yet half a beast is the great god Pan,
   To laugh as he sits by the river,
Making a poet out of a man:
The true gods sigh for the cost and pain, –   40
For the reed which grows nevermore again
   As a reed with the reeds in the river.

THE NORTH AND THE SOUTH

ROME, MAY 1861

I

'Now give us lands where the olives grow,'
    Cried the North to the South,
'Where the sun with a golden mouth can blow
Blue bubbles of grapes down a vineyard-row!'
    Cried the North to the South.

II

'Now give us men from the sunless plain,'
    Cried the South to the North,
'By need of work in the snow and the rain,
Made strong, and brave by familiar pain!'
    Cried the South to the North.   10

III

'Give lucider hills and intenser seas,'
    Said the North to the South,
'Since ever by symbols and bright degrees
Art, childlike, climbs to the dear Lord's knees,'
    Said the North to the South.

IV

'Give strenuous souls for belief and prayer,'
    Said the South to the North,
'That stand in the dark on the lowest stair,
While affirming of God, "He is certainly there,"'
    Said the South to the North.   20

V

'Yet oh, for the skies that are softer and higher!'
        Sighed the North to the South;
'For the flowers that blaze, and the trees that aspire,
And the insects made of a song or a fire!'
        Sighed the North to the South.

VI

'And oh, for a seer to discern the same!'
        Sighed the South to the North!
'For a poet's tongue of baptismal flame,
To call the tree or the flower by its name!'
        Sighed the South to the North.   30

VII

The North sent therefore a man of men,
        As a grace to the South;
And thus to Rome came Andersen.
– '*Alas, but must you take him again?*'
        Said the South to the North.

NOTES

'To My Father on His Birthday' (p. 5)

Causa fuit Pater his: 'My father was the reason for these things' (Horace, *Satires*, I.6.71).

l. 19 sylphic: a sylph is a mythical creature supposedly inhabiting the air.

l. 23 Echo: (in Greek myth) a nymph loved by Pan. She was torn apart by shepherds; fragments of her are hidden in the earth.

l. 27 Aonian: Aonia was a district of ancient Boeotia, containing Mount Helicon, sacred to the Muses.

l. 44 Maecenas: Gaius Maecenas, a Roman statesman, patron of the poets Virgil, Horace and Propertius.

'The Dream' (p. 7)

l. 12 Hespery: (in Greek myth) the garden of the Hesperides, beyond the Atlas mountains in which there was a tree bearing golden apples guarded by the Hesperides, daughters of Night and Erebus, or, in some versions, Hesperis and Atlas.

l. 13 Aegyptus: Egypt.

l. 53 'Pan *was not*': Pan (Greek god of Arcadia) was associated both with fertility and an ability to induce panic in humans – both may be possible explanations for his repression at this point in the poem.

'Epitaph (p. 11)

l. 7 Hyblan: Hybla was the ancient name of several sites in Sicily.

'A Sea-side Meditation' (p. 12)

Ut per aquas quae nunc rerum simulacra videmus: 'like the images which we now see reflected by water' (Lucretius, *De Rerum Natura*, I. 1060).

l. 7   **thymele:** the altar of Dionysus in the centre of the orchestra in an ancient Greek theatre (*OED*).

l. 46   **pandemonic:** a rare usage referring primarily to Milton's Pandemonium (in Hell), *Paradise Lost* l. 756.

l. 60   **God's creation, man's intelligence:** again, and as with l. 62, evocative of themes and language in Milton's *Paradise Lost*.

l. 62   **like the serpent, once erect as they:** Miltonic.

l. 64   **Phylacteries:** probably used here in its meaning as a preservative against disease; though there may be a play on its connotations of religious observance.

l. 74   **Cyrene's fount:** Cyrene was a Greek colony founded *c.* 630 BC.

ll. 108–9   **as martyrs lie/Wheel-bound:** the origin of the wheel as a punishment lies in the story of Ixion who offended Zeus and was fixed to a burning wheel that rotated continually.

l. 133   **eterne volution:** never-ending revolution, turning. 'Eterne' is an archaic form of eternal.

l. 137   **Babel:** see Genesis 11.

l. 142   **Hell's angel:** the angel referred to is probably Uriel.

'The Tempest' (p. 16)

Based on an actual storm which EBB experienced in 1826.

Mors erat ante oculos: 'death was before our eyes' (Lucan, *De Bello Civile*, IX.763).

l. 8   **Titans:** (in Greek myth) some of the oldest of the gods, who preceded the Olympians.

l. 9   **Aethiopian queen:** Aethiopian because black; a common metaphor, though slightly archaic by the time EBB uses it.

l. 12   **sulph'rous:** yellow

l. 67   **Nathless:** nevertheless (archaic).

l. 107   **scathèd:** harmed or harmful.

l. 109   **Eleusis:** a town in Attica where the Eleusinian Mysteries, in honour of Demeter and Persephone, were celebrated.

l. 119   **Janus:** as a god, Janus is double-faced, looking both ways simultaneously. But the origins of the word suggest a gate or barbican, which is the primary meaning here.

l. 129   **sans:** without.

l. 142 **tusky:** a rare usage of this adjective.

l. 153 **corse:** corpse (archaic).

l. 158 **pale-steedèd Death:** see Revelation 6:8.

l. 161 **charnel-houses:** burial-places, cemeteries.

l. 162 **scath:** injury, hurt, damage.

l. 176 **Laocoon:** a legendary Trojan prince who protested against bringing the Wooden Horse inside Troy's walls. As a result of his protests, two serpents came from Tenedos and killed him and his two sons.

l. 182 **sophists:** a school of Greek philosophy known for encouraging an attitude of scepticism (sometimes cynicism). While the word in English has taken on pejorative meanings, EBB is probably using it in a more straightforward 'classical' sense.

l. 186 **wassail:** either a salutation which is drunk, or a revelry. The latter seems more likely here.

l. 190 **Stoic:** the Stoics were a group of Greek (and later) philosophers who emphasised wisdom, harmony and virtue in their teachings. They were criticised both for their belief that knowledge was absolutely reliable as a path to virtue and for their tendency to encourage acceptance as an attitude to life.

'A True Dream' (p. 25)

'Dreamed at Sidmouth, 1833': EBB and her family lived at Sidmouth from 1832–5.

l. 5 **vial:** a small vessel for holding liquid.

l. 8 **unshuddering:** this word is not specifically cited in the *OED*.

l. 26 **swart:** dark or black (archaic).

l. 39 **eyne:** an obscure and poetic plural of eye.

l. 51 **Besprent:** sprinkled.

l. 63 **vitriol:** literally a medicinal chemical, the word has come to have connotations of acrimony.

'Man and Nature' (p. 29)

l. 6 **bosky:** bushy.

l. 26 **horrent:** bristling; can also mean shuddering.

'The Deserted Garden' (p. 30)

l. 53   ken: a word used in different ways by EBB, here perhaps in its archaic sense of 'birth'.

l. 54   sward: grassy turf (the earth in general here).

'The Sea-Mew': p. 33

The 'sea-mew' is a seagull.

ll. 31–2   The green trees ... shade: alluding to Andrew Marvell's poem 'The Garden'.

'A Sea-side Walk' (p. 35)

ll. 3–7   like the princess ... So runs the Arab tale: in *The Arabian Nights*.

l. 26   supernal: heavenly; from on high.

'My Doves' (p. 37)

O Weisheit! Du red'st wie eine Taube!: 'O Wisdom! You speak like a dove!'

l. 38   mart: market.

'Night and the Merry Man' (p. 39)

l. 37   trysted: made an appointment or agreement with.

l. 104   sealeth up the darksome pit: a possible allusion to Psalm 140:10 and/or to Milton's *Paradise Lost*.

l. 107   Queen Titania: (usually) queen of the fairies.

l. 109   αι αι: an expression of astonishment.

l. 103   shoon: a plural of shoe.

'The Romaunt of Margret' (p. 43)

The story appears to be of EBB's own devising. The quotation is from Francis Quarles (1594–1644), English poet.

l. 26   ween: believe.

l. 34   certes: certainly, for certain (archaic).

l. 57   swound: swoon, fainting fit (an unusual usage).

l. 63   **pall:** rich cloth.

l. 110   **goss-hawk:** bird of prey, sometimes used in falconry.

l. 166   **tourney show:** joust.

l. 169   **tryst:** appointment.

l. 225   **corse:** corpse.

'A Romance of the Ganges' (p. 52)

Written for Mary Russell Mitford's *Finden's Tableaux* (1838).

l. 28   **coco:** coconut.

l. 106   **three broad worlds:** it is not clear where EBB finds this apparent Hindu world-view.

l. 111   **peepul:** Indian species of fig-tree, often thought sacred and often mentioned in Western writings on India.

'De Profundis' (p. 63)

This poem explores the grief which EBB felt at the death of her brother Edward Moulton-Barrett ('Bro') in 1840.

l. 83   **seraphs:** heavenly entities.

l. 85   **Ancient of Days:** biblical name for God. See Daniel 7:9 and 22; also William Blake's painting of the same name.

l. 88   **sovran:** sovereign.

'Tears' (p. 69)

l. 4   **Adam forfeited the primal lot:** through original sin.

'Substitution' (p. 69)

l. 8   **Faunus:** a god often identified with Pan (cf. 'The Dream', l. 53, above).

'Lady Geraldine's Courtship' (p. 70)

l. 41   **vassals:** servants or subordinates.

l. 49   **the Commons:** the exact meaning of this reference could vary depending on the time at which the poem is intended to be set; in general it is to the main, elected chamber of the British Parliament.

l. 63   **nympholeptic:** describing the love of a mortal for a nymph. See Robert Browning's poem 'Numpholeptos' (1876).

l. 98   **regnant:** regal, dominating.

l. 184   **abeles:** white poplar trees.

l. 215   **lindens:** lime trees.

l. 230   **Lough the sculptor:** John Graham Lough (1798–1876), sculptor whose work often caused controversy.

l. 252   **ken:** knowledge, knowing, believing.

l. 306   **gowans:** daisies, or daisy-like wild flowers.

l. 317   **the pastoral parts of Spenser:** Edmund Spenser (c. 1552–97), poet. EBB is primarily thinking of his poem *The Shepheardes Calender* (1579).

l. 319   **Petrarch's sonnets:** Francesco Petrarch (1304–74), Italian poet.

ll. 321–2   **Wordsworth's/solemn-thoughted idyl:** William Wordsworth (1770–1850), leading Romantic poet and Poet Laureate.

l. 323   **Howitt's ballad verse:** William Howitt (1792–1879), poet. Like EBB, he was interested in spiritualism.

l. 323   **Tennyson's:** Alfred, Lord Tennyson (1809–92), Poet Laureate after Wordsworth.

l. 325   **from Browning some 'Pomegranate':** referring to Robert Browning's series of books *Bells and Pomegranates* (1841–6). This praise of Browning led him to write his first letter to EBB.

l. 343   **naiad:** a water nymph.

l. 367   **birchen-wood:** birch wood (archaic formulation).

l. 400   **cars:** chariots, carriages.

l. 453   **Camoëns:** Luis de Camões (1542–80), Portuguese poet, author of *The Lusiads*. See EBB's poem 'Catarina to Camoëns', below.

l. 461   **osier:** a species of willow.

l. 535   **Pythian height:** probably a reference to the Pythian games (in Ancient Greece second only to the Olympian).

l. 582   **infidels:** unbelievers.

l. 621   **Parias:** probably meaning social outcasts (but see note to l. 756).

l. 635   **tost:** tossed.

l. 705   **lacqueys:** servants.

l. 721   oriel: a large window forming a balcony.

l. 734   **Phemius:** shortened version of Polyphemus, the Cyclops in the *Odyssey*.

l. 756   **Parian statue-stone:** from the island of Paros, known for its white marble often used in sculpture.

'The Lost Bower' (p. 96)

ll. 43-5   **Malvern Hills ... Piers Plowman's visions:** William Langland (*c.* 1330-87), poet, author of *The Vision of Piers Plowman*, which is set in the Malvern Hills. EBB described the poem as 'the earliest classic ground of English poetry'.

l. 68   **Rinaldo's lovely lady:** refers either to Rinaldo in Torquato Tasso's (1544-95) poems *Gerusalemme Liberata* (1580-81) or *Rinaldo* (1562), in which case the 'lady' is Armida, or to Ariosto's *Orlando Furioso* (1532), in which Rinaldo is the suitor of Angelica.

l. 70   **Rosalinda:** either Shakespeare's heroine in *As You Like It* or a character in Spenser's *Shepheardes Calender*.

l. 71   **Chaucer:** Geoffrey Chaucer (*c.* 1340-1400), poet. These lines seem to refer to the poem 'The Assembly of Ladies' which, up to and including Thomas Tyrwhitt's 1778 Glossary to his edition of Chaucer's works, was thought to have been written by Chaucer. EBB had evidently not registered the poem's disappearance from the Chaucer canon in the nineteenth century. She might have been interested to read Skeat referring to the 'authoress' of the poem in 1900.

l. 79   **gyve and thong:** a gyve is a shackle; a thong is a long piece of leather used either on a whip or as a method of binding.

l. 85   **astonied:** astonished, stupefied.

l. 117   **eglantine:** a type of briar.

l. 118   **wild hop:** a climbing plant.

l. 119   **columbine:** a flowering plant.

l. 120   **mullion:** a vertical bar dividing the lights in a window, especially used in Gothic architecture.

l. 162   **Dryad:** a wood nymph.

l. 168   **Unassoiled:** not absolved from sin.

l. 170   **St Catherine's:** the sound of bells from a church of this name (EBB does not seem to have a specific setting in mind for this poem).

l. 180   **Naiad:** a river nymph.

l. 183   **Pan or Faunus:** cf. note to 'The Dream', p. 7, l. 53, above.

ll. 201–2   **a bird, it seemëd/Most like Chaucer's:** unclear. The lady with the 'silent mouth' suggests Philomela and thus 'The Legend of Philomela' in Chaucer's *The Legend of Good Women*. But the imagery used by EBB appears to allude more closely to lines from 'The Seinte's Legend of Cupide' in the same work (in which the bird is a lark).

l. 208   **nympholeptic:** see note to 'Lady Geraldine's Courtship', p. 70, l. 63.

l. 209   **virëlay:** a short lyric, originating in fourteenth-century France.

l. 213   **geste:** gesture, movement, action.

l. 238   **lusus:** a *lusus naturae* (a play or sport of nature) was a notion used to explain deviations from the perceived norm in the natural world (thus 'freak of nature').

l. 244   **benison:** blessing.

l. 280   **Œdipus's grave-place 'mid Colone's olives swart:** Oedipus, King of Thebes, unwittingly slept with/married his mother. EBB is perhaps making an ironic reference to the disappearance of Oedipus at the end of Sophocles' *Oedipus at Colonus*.

ll. 281–4: **As Aladdin ... to the sun:** presumably from *The Arabian Nights*.

'Rime of the Duchess May' (p. 113)

l. 6   **rebecks:** a rebeck is a medieval form of fiddle with three strings and played with a bow.

l. 7   **abeles:** white poplar trees.

l. 38   **Linteged:** this appears to be EBB's coinage of a fictive place.

l. 84   **churl:** of low rank and/or rude, uncouth.

l. 89   **sovranly:** regally.

l. 122   **sward:** grass, earth.

l. 134   **amain:** quickly, forcefully.

l. 146   **red-roan:** a horse which has a red-grey colouring.

l. 158   **fetlocks:** joint in a horse's leg above the pastern.

l. 188   **blee:** colour.

l. 208   **faulchion:** usually falchion, a sword.

l. 251   **gauds:** decorations.

l. 397   **bower chambère:** bedroom.

l. 494   **pardiè**: a form of oath; here meaning assuredly, certainly.

l. 505   **selle**: cell, room (obscure usage).

l. 560   **coping-stone**: the uppermost part of a wall.

l. 581   **chapelle**: chapel.

'Bertha in the Lane' (p. 141)

l. 37   **jasper**: a green precious stone.

l. 59   **fever-bale**: torment from sickness.

l. 200   **rosemary**: a flower often associated with death and funerals.

l. 229   **Mystic Dove**: the dove is biblically associated with purity and innocence. See Matthew 3:16 where Jesus sees the Spirit of God ascend into heaven in the shape of a dove.

'Catarina to Camoëns' (p. 150)

Written in 1831 and later revised. EBB read Camoëns in a translation by Lord Strangford, who portrays Camoëns as the Byronic lover of Catarina, a lady of the Portuguese court.

l. 45   **unweeting**: unwitting, unknowingly.

l. 81   **angelus**: the angelus bell, which is rung at morning, noon and sunset as a call to devotional prayers in Roman Catholicism.

l. 98   **gittern**: an old guitar-like instrument.

l. 117   *Miserere*: a prayer derived from the fifty-first Psalm.

l. 151   **terrene**: earthly, material.

'The Romance of the Swan's Nest' (p. 156)

l. 68   **guerdon**: reward.

'The Cry of the Human' (p. 160)

l. 21   **wains**: large vehicles for carrying heavy loads, usually agricultural.

l. 39   **chimar**: probably referring to a loose robe (often worn by bishops).

l. 40   **centaur**: a mythological creature with the upper body of a man and the lower body of a horse; often thought savage.

l. 43   **'Change**: exchange, barter.

l. 70 'Till death us part!' said as part of the marriage ceremony.

l. 109 wist: knew, often implying a nostalgic yearning.

'The Cry of the Children' (p. 165)

Written after reading a report by R. H. Horne on the conditions and employment of children in mines and factories.

l. 40 rime: frozen mist.

l. 50 kirk-chime: church bell.

l. 56 cerement: a shroud.

'A Sabbath Morning at Sea' (p. 175)

Probably written at Sidmouth.

l. 33 inurning: entombing.

l. 45 dedicature: act of dedication (the OED credits EBB with first usage here).

'Human Life's Mystery' (p. 178)

l. 1 glebe: earth, land.

l. 27 diapason: loud resonance.

l. 28 pinions: part (sometimes whole) of a bird's wing.

l. 55 swound: (presumably) swoon.

'A Denial' (p. 187)

l. 3 forecome: arrive before (expected) time.

'Hector in the Garden' (p. 190)

Hector, who may be an invention of Homer's, was a champion of the Trojans. In the *Iliad* his body is ransomed and the poem ends with his burial.

l. 6 Ilium: Ilium was established in the seventh century BC on the site of Troy.

l. 19 Canidian: Canidia was a sorceress.

l. 23 Lydian: one of the Greek scales in music.

l. 49   **gentianellas:** a plant with blue flowers.

l. 82   ὀτοτοτοτοῖ: a grief stricken exclamation (Greek).

'Flush or Faunus' (p. 195)

Flush was EBB's spaniel. See Virginia Woolf's *Flush* (1933).

l. 9   **Arcadian:** Arcadia was the region where Pan (the 'goatly god') supposedly lived.

'Hiram Powers' Greek Slave' (p. 195)

Hiram Powers was an American sculptor. 'The Greek Slave' was shown at the Great Exhibition in 1851. It is a nude female figure representing a Greek Christian being sold in a Turkish slave market.

'The Runaway Slave at Pilgrim's Point* (p. 196)

See the Introduction for a discussion of this poem. The poem was written in response to a request by the Anti-Slavery Bazaar in Boston in 1845, and was sent in February 1847. The poem was first published in *The Liberty Bell* (1848).

l. 2   **the first white pilgrim:** where the Pilgrim Fathers landed in North America.

l. 55   **the whip-poor-will or the cat of the glen:** both presumably instruments of corporal punishement.

l. 221   **the Washington-race:** white Americans. It is worth noting additionally that one of EEB's father's illegitimate half-brothers bore the name Charles Washington. If, as Julia Markus suggests, EBB believed herself to have 'mixed blood' then the allusion to this branch of the family further strengthens the case for this poem being an uncovering of that belief.

'Confessions' (p. 205)

See RB's poem of the same name in *Dramatis Personae* (1864).

l. 11   **lees:** dregs.

ll. 110–11   **unguent of love ... Saviour's feet:** alluding to John 12:3 where Mary Magdalene anoints Jesus' feet.

Sonnets from the Portuguese (p. 210)

These are original poems rather than translations. The Brownings agreed that the title would obscure their autobiographical nature. The title supposedly originates in the fact that RB liked EBB's poem 'Catarina to Camoëns'.

I
l. 1   **Theocritus:** (*c.* 308–*c.* 240 BC), Greek poet.

II
l. 5   **amerce:** to punish or put a penalty upon.

III
l. 7   **gages:** pledges.

l. 13   **chrism:** a sacramental sign of anointment.

V
l. 2   **Electra:** the daughter of Agamemnon and Clytemnestra. At her father's tomb she recognised her brother and they subsequently plotted to kill her adulterous mother.

VIII
l. 6   **largesse:** liberality, generosity.

IX
l. 12   **Venice-glass:** properly a particularly delicate type of glass made in Venice. The term is also at times used to refer to a form of glazing known as Venice turpentine. Here the most likely meaning is a Venetian mirror.

XI
l. 6   **Aornus:** probably the mountain Aornus, near the Indus, captured by Alexander in 327–6 BC.

XV
l. 6   **a bee shut in a crystalline:** i.e. fossilised.

XIX
l. 1   **Rialto:** a bridge in Venice, giving its name to the mercantile quarter of the city.

l. 4   **argosies:** large and heavily laden merchant ships.

l. 5   **Pindar:** (*c.* 522–443 BC), Greek poet.

l. 6   **purpureal:** of purple colour.

l. 7   **nine white Muse-brows:** in classical mythology there are nine muses, goddesses of literature and the arts.

l. 8   **bay-crown:** crown of bay leaves awarded to poets.

XXI
l. 13   **iterance:** repetition.

XXIV
l. 1   **clasping knife:** the blade of which folds into its handle.

XXVII
l. 10   **dewless asphodel:** a flowering plant; in classical poetry often said to cover the meadows of Elysium.

XXX
l. 4   **acolyte:** an attendant upon a priest; more generally, a novice or junior assistant.

XXXIII
l. 10   **exanimate:** lifeless.

XL
l. 5   **Mussulmans:** Muslims (see Byron's poem 'The Gaiour').

l. 7   **Polypheme's:** the Cyclops in the *Odyssey*.

XLII
l. 1   *'My future will not copy fair my past'*: EBB quotes from her own poem 'Past and Future', which had been published in *Poems* (1844) [cf. p. 68].

'Casa Guidi Windows': Part One (p. 235)

l. 3   *O bella libertà, O bella*: 'O beautiful freedom, O beautiful' (Italian).

l. 20   **Filicaja:** Vincenzo da Filicaia (1642–1707), Florentine poet. His texts were read as predictions of Italian unity.

l. 32   **Cybele:** originally a mother-goddess of Anatolia, Cybele's cult was widespread in Greece and Rome. She is often associated with her young lover, Attis, and with wild nature. EBB's reference appears to be to the images of Cybele (often with attendant lion) used by her worshippers.

l. 32   **Niobe:** in mythology, daughter of Tantalus and wife of Amphion. When her children were killed by Apollo and Artemis she turned into stone on Mount Sipylon.

l. 36   **Juliet:** EBB regarded Cybele, Niobe and Shakespeare's Juliet as symptomatic of the fated feminine roles in which Italy was personified.

l. 53   **Arno:** the river on which Florence stands.

l. 54   **her bridges four:** the bridges across the Arno in Florence.

l. 68   Giotto: Giotto di Bondone (1267–1337), Florentine artist. His campanile of the Duomo remained unfinished at his death.

ll. 73–4   Michel's Night and Day/And Dawn and Twilight: statues by Michelangelo in the Sagrestia Nuova.

l. 76   Medicean: of the Medici's, the once-powerful family in Florence.

l. 81   St Lawrence: the church of San Lorenzo in Florence.

l. 93   Urbino: Michelangelo's servant. Vasari relates Michelangelo's distress at Urbino's death.

l. 98   Angelo: Michelangelo (1475–1564), painter and sculptor.

ll. 99–100   Via Larga . . . build a statue up in snow: untraced.

l. 168   Se tu men bella fossi, Italia: 'If only you were less beautiful, O Italy' (Italian).

l. 176   Virgil: Publius Vergilius Maro (70–19 BC), Roman poet, author of *Aeneid*, *Eclogues*, *Georgics*.

l. 176   Cicero: Marcus Tullius Cicero (106–43 BC), Roman orator and writer.

l. 177   Catullus: Gaius Valerius Catullus (c. 84–c. 54 BC), Roman poet.

l. 177   Caesar: Gaius Julius Caesar (102/100–44 BC), Roman politician, general and statesman, approvingly discussed by Cicero.

l. 178   Boccaccio: Giovanni Boccaccio (1313–75), Italian writer, author of *Decameron*.

l. 179   Dante: Dante Alighieri (1265–1321), Florentine poet, author of *Divina Commedia*.

l. 179   Petrarca: see note to 'Lady Geraldine's Courtship', p. 358, l. 319.

l. 181   Angelo: Michelangelo.

l. 181   Raffael: Raphael Sanzio (1483–1520), Italian painter.

l. 181   Pergolese: Giovanni Battista Pergolesi (1710–36), Italian composer.

l. 185   chaplets: a string of beads.

l. 186   ken: knowledge (here, perhaps memory).

l. 195   phylacteries: amulets worn against disease (also has a more specific meaning of religious texts or observances, which seems less appropriate here).

l. 256 **Savonarola:** Italian monk and patriot, burned for protesting against Papal corruption in 1498.

l. 270 **Luther:** Martin Luther (1483–1546), German leader of the Reformation.

l. 274 **cowl:** an outer robe with a hood worn by monks (sometimes refers to the hood alone).

l. 307 **Jubal:** referred to in Genesis 4:20 as the inventor of musical instruments.

l. 309 **Asaph:** chief musician at David's festival sacrifice (see I Chronicles 15 and 16).

l. 314 **Miriam clashed her cymbals:** see Exodus 15:20: 'Miriam . . . took a timbrel in her hand'.

l. 316 **David's strings:** King David, the psalmist.

l. 321 **St Maria Novella:** church in Florence (see notes for ll. 332 and 338, below).

ll. 322–3 **Macchiavel . . . One:** Niccolo Machiavelli (1469–1527), Florentine political theorist. Machiavelli records this incident in his account of the plague in Florence.

ll. 328–9 **Orgagnas save/Of Dante's daemons:** may refer to an altarpiece by Orcagna in St Maria Novella.

l. 332 **Cimabue's Virgin:** Giovanni Cimabue (1240–1302), artist. See Giorgio Vasari's account of his life in *Lives of the Artists*.

l. 338 **Glad Borgo:** Vasari says that while Cimabue was painting his Virgin in St Maria Novella, King Charles of Anjou came to see him. Because of the rejoicing accompanying this visit, the neighbourhood has since been known as Borgo Allegri (Joyful Quarter).

l. 346 **The Lady:** presumably Cimabue's Virgin.

l. 346 **empyreal:** heavenly, celestial.

l. 353 **Raffaelhood:** the 'realm' of Raphael.

ll. 358–63: EBB cites this incident to illustrate how close the Italian people were to what she perceives as their culture at this time.

ll. 362–3: **Giotto . . . Cimabue found among the sheep:** Cimabue was said to be Giotto's teacher.

l. 379 **Margheritone:** a painter supposedly jealous of Cimabue.

l. 390 **Angelico:** Fra Angelico (1387–1455), painter. EBB associates him with Raphael.

l. 424 **Troy:** site of the siege in the *Iliad*.

l. 425   **Marathon:** a plain near Athens where the Greeks won a famous victory over the invading Persians (cf. EBB's *Battle of Marathon*).

l. 427   **benison:** blessing.

l. 442   **lachrymals:** tears.

l. 457   **palace-Pitti:** the palace of Grand Duke Leopold II in Florence.

ll. 458–61: see note l. 476.

l. 476   **Magistracy, with insignia:** referring to the significant step taken by the Grand Duke in granting a Tuscan guard. The insignia of the officials thence takes on a symbolism of greater power.

l. 490   **'vivas':** literally, hurrahs. Shortened version of 'viva Italia' ('long live Italy').

l. 493   **new Pope:** Pius IX.

l. 499   **'Il popolo':** 'the people'.

ll. 505–9   **Siena's she-wolf ... Arezzo's steed:** the insignia of the various Tuscan states carried in the procession which the Brownings observed from Casa Guidi, 12 September 1847.

l. 513   **Greeks, English, French:** supporters from these nations marched in the same procession mentioned above.

l. 532   **'tired:** attired, dressed.

l. 543   **charta:** charter, granting permission to form a guard.

l. 543   **liberal Duke's excess:** i.e. Duke Leopold.

l. 544   **Guelf's or Ghibelline's:** ancient rival factions in Italy.

l. 580   **tryst:** pact, agreement.

l. 581   **Loggia:** the Loggia dei Lanzi.

l. 582   **Cellini's godlike Perseus:** statue by Benvenuto Cellini (1500–71), in the Loggia. See Cellini's lively account of its commission and execution in his *Autobiography*.

l. 586   **Gorgon:** a mythical figure whose face turned people into stone (from the Perseus myth).

l. 590   **Brutus:** Marcus Iunius Brutus, conspirator against Julius Caesar.

l. 591   **Buonarroti:** Michelangelo.

l. 593   **Rome's sublimest homicide:** the murder of Julius Caesar.

ll. 601–2   **stone/Called Dante's:** a stone which EBB assumes was a favourite resting place of Dante (it is cited also in RB's poem 'Old Pictures in Florence').

l. 605 **Brunelleschi's church:** Filipo Brunelleschi (1373–1446), builder of the church of San Lorenzo.

l. 608 **a banished Florentine:** while Dante was on a mission to Rome in October 1306 the Black Guelfs took power in Florence. Dante, sympathetic to the White Guelfs, never returned.

l. 616 **Ravenna's bones:** Ravenna is a town on the north-east coast of Italy. The Ravennans refused to hand Dante's body over to the Florentines.

l. 623 **Santa Croce church:** in Florence.

l. 631 **ordures:** dirt, excrement.

l. 633 **Bargello chamber:** alludes to a fresco-painting by Giotto uncovered in the nineteenth century.

l. 634 **Beatrix:** the object of Dante's love poetry, especially in the *Vita Nuova*.

l. 653 **the Pitti:** a royal palace in Florence.

l. 659 **puissant:** possessed of power.

l. 662 **Austrian Metternich:** Clement Van Metternich-Winneburg (1773–1859), Austrian chancellor.

l. 670 **dew-laps:** the folds of loose skin under the throat of a cow (or other animal).

l. 694 **knightly Roland on the coward's flinch:** see RB's poem 'Childe Roland to the Dark Tower Came' in *Men and Women* (1855). RB took his title from Shakespeare's *King Lear* III.4.139.

l. 695 **chloroform and ether-gas:** both anaesthetics.

l. 707 **my England:** EBB chastising Britain's foreign policy.

ll. 733–4 **'that Achillean wrath ... heroes':** see the opening of Homer's *Iliad*.

l. 738 **Ledas:** Leda was the daughter of Thestius and mother of Helen. Zeus, assuming the shape of a swan, raped her.

l. 747 **lappets:** ornamental, overlapping pieces of cloth.

l. 750 **festa-days:** feast-days, holidays.

l. 754 **sallow kine:** brownish yellow cattle.

l. 789 **'Væ! meâ culpâ':** 'Vae!' is an exclamation of pain or dread. 'Mea culpa!': 'It is my fault' (Latin).

l. 792 **suo jure:** 'under his/her/one's own jurisdiction' (Latin).

l. 804 **donna:** woman.

l. 821 **Tell:** the legend of William Tell is appropriate here because of its anti-Austrian themes.

l. 822 **Masaniello:** Tommaso Aniello (1622–47), Italian fisherman who became the leader of a revolt against Spanish rule in Naples in 1647.

l. 834 **oriflamme:** originally the sacred banner of St Denis which the King of France received before setting out for war.

l. 846 **Rienzi:** Nicolas di Rienzi (1313–54), Roman patriot and politician.

l. 846 **fasces:** in Rome these were a bundle of rods carried before magistrates as a symbol of their power.

l. 847 **fife:** a small, shrill (often military) flute.

l. 848 **Pallas:** stock epithet of the goddess Athena.

l. 868 **Pio nono:** Pope Pius IX.

ll. 872–3 **Pellico's/Venetian dungeon:** Silvio Pellico (1788–1854), Italian dramatist and activist against Austrian rule. He was arrested in October 1820 and imprisoned in Santa Margharita.

l. 873 **Spielberg's gate:** Pellico's death sentence was commuted to fifteen years' imprisonment and he was moved to prison in Spielberg, Brünn.

ll. 874–82: see note on 'Mother and Poet' (p. 376) for a possible explanation of these lines.

l. 896 **Ninth Pius in Seventh Gregory's chair:** Gregory VII (formerly Hildebrand) became Pope in 1073. He made great claims for the worldly power of the church.

l. 897 **Andrea Doria:** Genoese admiral (1466–1560). Often regarded as treacherous because of his ability to switch allegiances quickly.

l. 906 **oubliettes:** secret dungeons.

l. 906 **plash:** the sound of water being struck (usually with a hoof or foot).

l. 910 **apophthegms:** pithy maxims.

l. 913 **Calvin:** (1509–64), French theologian and reformer.

l. 914 **Servetus:** Miguel Serveto (1511–53), Spanish physician and theologian. He was burnt on Calvin's orders.

l. 919 **pourpoint:** a quilted doublet worn in the fourteenth and fifteen centuries as armour.

l. 919 **'quotha' . . . 'I ween':** archaic phrases.

l. 945ff.   I believe . . . : echoing the Credo.

l. 979   oboli: ancient Greek coins.

l. 980   sop: an appeasement, bribe or pacification.

l. 993   Nicæa up to Trent: the Council of Nicaea (AD 325) and the Council of Trent (1545–63). EBB encapsulates the history of the pre-Reformation church constitution.

l. 994   hierocratic empire: a hierocracy is under the rule of priests.

l. 1001   miniver: fur trimming in a ceremonial robe.

l. 1005   'Feed my lambs, Peter': see John 21:15.

l. 1041   travertine: limestone; its porous nature is alluded to here.

l. 1082   Ariosto: Ludovico Ariosto (1474–1533), Italian writer, author of Orlando Furioso.

l. 1083   Petrarch: see note to 'Lady Geraldine's Courtship', p. 358, l. 319.

l. 1092   bruits: loud, public noises.

l. 1109   Buonarroti's stone: Michelangelo's sculptures.

l. 1110   Raffael's canvas: i.e. a painting by Raphael.

l. 1111   Poussin's master: presumably meaning Raphael whose style greatly influenced Nicolas Poussin (1593/4–1665), French painter active in Rome.

l. 1112   Laura: the addressee of many of Petrarch's love poems.

l. 1112   Vaucluse's fount: Petrarch lived for a time at Vaucluse in south-eastern France.

l. 1117   Charlemagne's sword: Charlemagne was king of the Franks. He and his Paladins figure in the Chanson de Roland.

l. 1124   Vespucci Amerigo: Amerigo Vespucci (1451–1512), merchant and adventurer, from whose name 'America' is derived. He was a friend of Savonarola (see note to l. 256, above).

l. 1127   John Milton's Fiesole: John Milton (1608–74), poet, author of Paradise Lost. He visited the European continent 1637–9.

l. 1128   Langlande's Malvern: see note to 'The Lost Bower', pp. 358–9, ll. 43–5.

l. 1129   Vallombrosa: province, and town, of Tuscany, east of Florence; site of a Benedictine abbey set amidst the wooded slopes of the Appenines. The beauty of its valley inspired some famous lines by Milton.

ll. 1138–9: Milton's eyesight worsened in the 1640s. By 1651 he was completely blind.

l. 1139   **beeves:** oxen, cattle (poetic usage).

l. 1141   **St Gualbert's:** Giovanni Gualbert was founder of the Vallombrosan order.

l. 1161   **sang of Adam's paradise:** in Milton's *Paradise Lost*.

l. 1176   **Lombard:** the region of northern Italy around Milan.

l. 1181   **Galileo:** (1564–1641), astronomer and scientist.

l. 1191   **Sorrento:** on the west coast of Italy, south of Naples.

l. 1193   **Rome's wolf:** Romulus and Remus, the brothers who founded Rome, were nursed by a she-wolf.

l. 1196   **Ovid's dreaming tales:** Ovid's *Metamorphoses* consisting of linked tales describing various shape-changes.

l. 1208   **Palermo's coast:** Palermo is the chief town of Sicily.

from Aurora Leigh (p. 269)

l. 4   **my better self:** usually at the beginning of an 'epic' poem (which *Aurora Leigh* in some ways purports to be) there is an invocation to the muse. Joyce Zonana (1996, p. 56) points out that Aurora's invocation of herself as the muse can be read in terms of a quest for a feminist poetic.

l. 12   **outer Infinite:** i.e. eternity.

l. 22   **Assunta's:** the Leigh's servant.

l. 24   **scudi:** Italian coins.

l. 53   **corals to cut life upon:** teething rings made from coral.

l. 57   **rose-bush:** see the image of the burning bush in Exodus 3:2.

FIRST BOOK, ll. 135–215: here Aurora gazes at a portrait of her dead mother.

l. 86   **Psyche:** Psyche, who was in love with Cupid, had been told by Cupid not to look at him – when she did he disappeared.

l. 87   **Medusa:** one of the Gorgons, a mythical female with snakes in her hair and whose look could turn people to stone.

l. 90   **Lady of the Passion, stabbed with swords:** McSweeney notes that in Italy the Virgin is sometimes depicted in this way, the swords representing her sufferings at Christ's crucifixion.

l. 108   **chin-bands:** devices for keeping closed the mouths of the dead.

l. 108   **Lazarus:** biblical character who rose from the dead.

FIRST BOOK, ll. 385–465: Aurora describes her educational experiences with her aunt in England.

l. 152   *Bene* or Che che: exclamations (Italian).

ll. 154–5   the collects ... creeds: all shortened versions of Christian teaching; what is noticeable here is that Aurora is given digests of the Bible rather than the text itself.

l. 156   articles: the thirty-nine articles of the Church of England.

l. 156   Tracts *against* the times: *Tracts for the Time* (1833–) were the main writings of the Oxford Movement.

l. 157   Buonaventure's 'Prick of Love': St Bonaventure, thirteenth-century theologian.

l. 162   Balzac: Honoré de Balzac (1799–1850), French novelist. His novels were often thought of as corrupting.

l. 162   neologism: new words or ideas.

l. 170   Oviedo: Spanish historian.

l. 172   Chimborazo: highest peak in the Andes.

l. 174   Lara: Spanish town.

l. 175   Klagenfurt: Austrian city.

l. 178   Johnson: Samuel Johnson (1709–84), English writer.

l. 182   Tophet: hell.

l. 183   nereids: sea-nymphs.

l. 183   Cellarius: French waltz.

FIRST BOOK, ll. 832–95: Aurora develops alternative ideas to those of her aunt by secretly reading her father's library.

SECOND BOOK, ll. 323–77: an early conversation between Aurora and Romney on marriage and the status of the female intellect.

l. 310   white: McSweeney quotes Reynolds (from the *Variorum* edition) who notes that the centre of the target in archery is white.

THIRD BOOK, ll. 758–826: Aurora visits Marian Erle.

FIFTH BOOK, ll. 1–73: Aurora contemplates the nature of women's poetry and how it is and will be considered by men.

l. 407   -lymph: stream.

l. 434   theurgic: relating to the action of the divine among humans.

FIFTH BOOK, ll. 139–229 Aurora on the need for a contemporary epic.

l. 479 **Agamemnon**: in Homer's *Iliad*.

l. 481 **Payne Knight**: Richard Payne Knight (1750–1824), classicist. Best known for proclaiming the Elgin Marbles to be imitations.

ll. 486–8 **Helen . . . Hector**: referring to Helen of Troy and the Trojan hero Hector, both in the *Iliad*.

l. 494 **epos**: an epic poem.

l. 495 **Carlyle**: Thomas Carlyle (1795–1881), Victorian writer; the reference is specifically to his *On Heroes, Hero-Worship and the Heroic in History* (1841).

l. 497 **scout**: reject or scorn.

l. 501 **gaberdines**: usually smocks or topcoats.

ll. 508–9: from a suggestion in Plutarch's life of Alexander.

l. 546 **Roland with his knights at Roncesvalles**: alluding to *The Song of Roland* in which Roland dies at the battle of Roncesvalles.

ll. 549–51: Arthurian legend in general is alluded to here, though a more particular reference is undoubtedly to Tennyson's 'The Epic'/ 'Morte d'Arthur' and his *Idylls of the King*, publication of which was ongoing at the time EBB was writing. 'The Epic' contains a contemplation of the status of the epic genre in Victorian literature which parallels EBB's.

SIXTH BOOK, ll. 737–93: Aurora and Marian discuss her status as the mother of an illegitimate child. Aurora, initially condemnatory, comes to a realisation of Marian's 'innocence'.

l. 583 **oriflamme**: sacred banner.

SEVENTH BOOK, ll. 174–229: Aurora on Marian and the position of women.

ll. 680–81 **Cervantes**: Spanish author; wrote *Don Quixote* (which mocks the heroic literature discussed in FIFTH BOOK).

SEVENTH BOOK, ll.749–94: Aurora on the nature of women's creativity.

l. 704 **the perfect round**: referring to the apple Venus won from Paris.

l. 720 **Antinous**: a beautiful Roman youth; more specifically a statue of Antinous in Rome.

EIGHTH BOOK, ll.261–352: (in Italy) Romney tells Aurora that he has read her work and they begin to retrace old arguments.

l. 801   Miriam: see Exodus 2.

NINTH BOOK, ll. 321–452: Marian speaking to Aurora and Romney.

l. 892   chin-cloth: see note for l. 108, p. 372.

NINTH BOOK, ll. 624–760: Aurora speaking to Romney.

l. 983   inflatus: breathing into, inspiration.

l. 995   in Leone: i.e. in Leo, the zodiacal sign.

NINTH BOOK, ll. 900–64: begins with Romney speaking. Line 964 ends the poem.

l. 1102   inscient: having inward knowledge, insight.

l. 1103   visceral: inward, deepest.

ll. 1121–22: see Joshua 6.

l. 1138: see Revelation 21:5.

l. 1146: see Revelation 21:19 and following.

'A Curse for a Nation' (p. 305)

At the time this poem was interpreted as an attack on Britain because of its attitude to Napoleon III and Italian nationalism. However, the poem was written, like 'A Runaway Slave at Pilgrim's Point' (see above, p. 363), at the request of the Anti-Slavery Bazaar in Boston, and American slave laws are thus its primary theme.

ll. 93–4   Christ may avenge . . . the earth: see Luke 18:7.

'A Court Lady' (p. 309)

l. 47   Romagnole: from Romagnano in Piedmont.

l. 98   Piedmont: region of northern Italy around Turin.

'A Tale of Villafranca' (p. 314)

A defence of Napoleon III.

l. 60   Gehenna's self: place of torment, hell.

'The Dance' (p. 317)

Written about Florentine women who danced with French soldiers in order to show their patriotic gratitude.

l. 6   **piazzone:** piazza, square.

'Lord Walter's Wife' (p. 323)

l. 2   **kraken:** a sea monster. Cf. Tennyson's poem 'The Kraken'.

l. 18   **Dora:** possibly derived from, or alluding to, Tennyson's poem 'Dora'.

l. 52   **mulcted:** penalized.

'Bianca Among the Nightingales' (p. 333)

l. 67   **Carraia bridge:** one of the four bridges across the River Arno in Florence.

l. 88   **'Grazie tanto':** 'many thanks' (Italian).

l. 106   **pyx:** generally a box or coffer, but religiously the box in which the sacrament is kept.

l. 127   **springe:** a snare, trap.

l. 127   **'mio ben':** my sweetheart (Italian).

'First News from Villafranca' (p. 341)

The armistice of Villafranca (6 July 1859) followed the battle of Solferino (see 'The Forced Recruit', below) and was signed by Napoleon III and Francis Joseph.

l. 5   **Mantua:** under the armistice agreement the Austrians retained the fortress at Mantua.

l. 5   **Venice:** Venice also remained temporarily under Austrian control.

l. 8   **Mincio:** River in northern Italy, which flows into the Po near Mantua, site of the battle of Solferino, 1859.

ll. 19–21:   'he' being Napoleon III (1808–73), French emperor. The reference to Paris alludes to his support for Italy at the Congress of Paris (1856).

'The Forced Recruit' (p. 343)

The battle at Solferino in 1859 was decisive in securing Italian victory in the Second War of Independence.

l. 38   **guerdon:** reward, recompense.

'Mother and Poet' (p. 345)

The speaker is the female poet of the Risorgimento, Laura Savio, whose son died fighting for Italian unity. Gaeta was the last stronghold of the King of Naples, Francis II.

l. 7 **good at my art, for a woman, men said:** see 'Elizabeth Barrett Browning and Her Critics', below, for an explanation of this statement.

l. 36 **'Ancona was free!':** as part of the continuing gains of the Italian forces. Ancona was besieged in 1859.

l. 79 **Cavalli:** Giovanni Cavalli (1801–79), Italian general.

l. 84 **King Victor:** Victor Emmanuel II was proclaimed King of Italy in March 1861.

'The North and the South' (p. 351)

l. 33 **Andersen:** probably Hans Christian Andersen (1805–75), Danish writer, who visited Rome in October 1834.

ELIZABETH BARRETT BROWNING
AND HER CRITICS

———

In their seminal work on gender and writing in the nineteenth century, Sandra M. Gilbert and Susan Gubar describe how the woman writer:

> must come to terms with the images on the surface of the glass, with, that is, those mythic masks male artists have fastened over her human face both to lessen their dread of her 'inconstancy' and – by identifying her with the 'eternal types' they themselves have invented – to possess her more thoroughly.

The Madwoman In the Attic: The Woman Writer and the Nineteenth-Century Literary Imagination (London: Yale University Press, 1979), pp. 16–17.

Criticism of Elizabeth Barrett Browning has tended to exist within these interlocking critical discourses, and under the cover of such 'mythic masks'. A 'purely' aesthetic critique of her work (in which it is often devalued) acts as a cover for a gendered critique: Elizabeth Barrett Browning thus becomes, at best, a good *woman* writer, where the gender implies a lessened aesthetic capability.

This critical process can be seen at work in the reviews which her early work received in *The Athenaeum*. Her anonymity as author may have saved her from a more severe review of her translation of Aeschylus (*Prometheus Bound* [1833]). The short notice said:

> ... we advise those who adventure in the hazardous lists of poetic translation, to touch anyone rather than Aeschylus; and they may take warning by the author before us.

The Athenaeum, 8 June 1833, p. 362.

When her volume *The Seraphim, and Other Poems* [1838] was published, the gender of the 'authoress' of *Prometheus Bound* was clear and the response to her poetry became embedded in the 'mythic masks' which Gilbert and Gubar suggest are placed upon the female writer. The review begins:

> This is an extraordinary volume – especially welcome as evidence of female genius and accomplishment – but it is hardly less disappointing than extraordinary. Miss Barrett's genius is of a higher order; active, vigorous, and versatile, but unaccompanied by discriminating taste. A thousand strange and beautiful visions flit across her mind, but she cannot look on them with steady gaze; – her descriptions, therefore, are often shadowy and indistinct, and her language wanting in the simplicity of unaffected earnestness.

The Athenaeum, 7 July 1838, p. 466.

Elizabeth Barrett thus becomes 'the best a woman could be' – accomplished 'as evidence of female genius' but retaining those 'feminine' characteristics of flightiness and unsteadiness. The call for 'simplicity' in her work is echoed at the end of the review, where the critic suggests that her poetics should have 'a simpler and less mannered clothing than ... at present'. The notion of simplicity, desired here as a corrective to mannerism, later becomes an accusation levelled at Elizabeth Barrett – it serves the function of being an expected (and therefore potentially devaluing) trope in women's poetry. It is at once the way women should write and the reason that their writing is always only 'women's writing'.

In 1840 *The Quarterly Review* vol. 65, p. 132, assessed a range of 'Modern English Poetesses', describing Elizabeth Barrett as a poet who 'may justly claim to stand alone anywhere else, as well for her extraordinary acquaintance with classic literature, as for the boldness of her poetic attempts' (pp. 382–3). The article went on to discuss her version of *Prometheus Bound*:

> Miss Barrett's version of the 'Prometheus' is a remarkable performance for a young lady; but it is not a good translation in and by itself. It is too frequently uncouth, without being faithful, and, under a pile of sounding words, lets the fire go out (p. 386).

Again the value of Elizabeth Barrett's work is seen as laudable only as a woman's attempt at translation, but by a universal (male) standard is seen to fall short. The notion of her writing as 'uncouth', straying beyond the often undisclosed boundaries of poetic discourse set for the woman poet, was to surface again later.

With the publication of *Poems* in 1844, Elizabeth Barrett was able to consolidate her reputation, and *The Athenaeum* had reified its response to her work into an instinctive, qualified and gendered praise:

> Whatever be the place which will be finally adjudged to Miss Barrett among the poetesses of England, there can be no question as to the earnest inspiration she brings to the completion of her verse, or the holy aims to which it is devoted. Between her poems and the slighter lyrics of her sisterhood, there is all the difference which exists between the putting on of 'singing-robes' for the altar-service, and the taking up [of] lute or harp to enchant an indulgent circle of friends and kindred (p. 763).

The review ends:

> We have been so often indebted to Miss Barrett's kindness, that it behoved us to prove the high opinion expressed in the outset of this article by letting her volumes speak for themselves. Though they have done this eloquently, musically, and loftily, they contain still many other voices (to speak figuratively) to which we can give no utterance. Assuredly they ought to be sought for – respectfully by men, affectionately by women; as remarkable manifestations of female power (p. 764).

While Elizabeth Barrett's poetry could be acknowledged as excelling within its prescribed critical parameters – as good women's writing – there was little disruption of this paradigmatic response: *The Athenaeum*, for example, reviewed *Casa Guidi Windows* (1848) relatively positively despite its political content. (In fact the review concurs with Elizabeth Barrett Browning's [as she had become] own political stance.)

With the publication of *Aurora Leigh* (1856) the circle of the encapsulating value-gender-criticism was overtly alluded to and potentially broken. Reaction to the volume thus became more heated than previous criticism (and bound to the scandal of her elopement with and marriage to Robert Browning). The reviewer in *Blackwood's Edinburgh Magazine* (vol. 81, p. 395 January 1857) felt drawn into a complete reassessment of the relationship of critic to text before he (presumably) could begin to discuss the poem. Having (with pointed incredulity) described the narrative of *Aurora Leigh*, he says:

> Such is the story, which no admirer of Mrs Browning's high genius ought in prudence to defend. In our opinion it is fantastic, unnatural, exaggerated; and all the worse, because it professes to be a tale of our own times (p. 32).

The nature of the poem's narrative (the biography and development of the woman poet) tends to make analysis of Aurora's character slide easily into criticism of Elizabeth Barrett Browning herself. The *Blackwood's* reviewer goes on:

> Aurora Leigh is not an attractive character. After making the most liberal allowance for pride, and fanaticism for art, and inflexible independence, she is incongruous and contradictory both in her sentiments and in her actions. She is not a genuine woman; one half of her heart seems bounding with the beat of humanity, while the other half is ossified. . . . with all deference to Mrs Browning, and with ideas of our own perhaps more chivalric than are commonly promulgated, we must maintain that woman was created to be dependent on the man, and not in the primary sense his lady and his mistress. The extreme independence of Aurora detracts from the feminine charm, and mars the interest which we might otherwise have felt in so intellectual a heroine (pp. 32–3).

The success of *Aurora Leigh* is surely its ability to expose such flanks in the masculinised discourse of literature and criticism, forcing utterance of the delineative boundaries of what woman as writer could or should do.

Having narrated her position as woman poet in the public realm, Barrett Browning then went on to her most publicly political (and final) volume *Poems Before Congress* (1860). Her 'safe' status as feminine 'poetess' now challenged, the political ambition of the volume came in for close scrutiny and criticism by reviewers – her interest in politics was seen to confirm the 'unwomanly' turn her verse had taken. *Blackwood's* entitled its review of *Poems Before Congress* 'Poetic Aberrations' (vol. 87, April 1860). The review began:

> We are strongly of the opinion that, for the peace and welfare of society, it is a good and wholesome rule that women should not interfere with politics. We love the fairer sex too well, to desire that they should be withdrawn from their own sphere, which is that of adorning the domestic circle, and tempering by their

gentleness the asperities of our ruder nature, to figure in the public arena, or involve themselves in party contests (p. 490).

The 'appropriate' provenance of women's writing is then sardonically described:

> We have a tender side for ladies who delight in enveloping their pretty ancles [sic] in azure. Whether, inspired by verse, they warble like larks in the firmament, or dole like doves in a coppice, or coo like pigeons in spring – whether, in less ambitious prose, they conduct hero and heroine through a love story, 'passing sweet and amorous withal', through three octavo volumes, to the inevitable hymeneal altar – or whether they apply themselves to the exposition of the finer arts, or the collection of culinary maxims – we listen, read, comment, perpend, and approve without the slightest feeling that they have in any degree over-stepped the pale of propriety.... But very different is the case when women addict themselves to politics. Then they resemble, to our shuddering fancy, in spite of all their charms, not angels, but so many *tricoteuses* in the gallery of the National Convention. Of all imaginable inflictions and torments, defend us from a female partisan! (p. 490)

This is, of course, a prologue to a criticism of Elizabeth Barrett Browning for her engagement with Italian politics in *Poems Before Congress*. As an extension of *Aurora Leigh*, this volume steps outside the 'sphere' this critic describes for her (a notably more constricted female sphere than was allowed before *Aurora Leigh*), and into a public and contentious realm. By this time, in contrast to *Casa Guidi Windows*, the political situation has also changed, and woven into the review's dislike for the very fact of her political poetry is a distaste for her siding with Italian nationalism (she becomes traitorous in gender and national terms):

> ... very sincerely do we regret, for her sake, that [Elizabeth Barrett Browning] has fallen into the error of publishing anything so ineffably bad, if we regard it as poetical composition – so strangely blind, if we look upon it as political confession of faith – or so utterly unfair to England and English feeling, as has been penned by one of England's most gifted daughters (p. 491).

The course of critical understanding of Barrett Browning during her lifetime was thus set in terms of gender and writerly authority; her challenge to this constriction in *Aurora Leigh* marked the beginning of a marginalisation of her work – as it became more complex, it was aesthetically derided for what were often (in the broadest sense) political reasons. This decline from potential Laureate-status to 'minor' poet was aided by the fame Robert Browning achieved, and the ambivalence with which the Pre-Raphaelites viewed her work. Writing about Christina Rossetti in 1882, to whom Elizabeth Barrett Browning was to be increasingly and unfavourably compared, Edmund Gosse repeats various tropes concerning the quality of women's writing:

> Woman, for some reason which seems to have escaped the philosopher, has never taken a very prominent position in the history of poetry. . . . Men like Dryden and Victor Hugo can strike every chord of the lyre, every mode and species of the art, and impress us by their bulk and volume. One very gifted and ambitious Englishwoman essayed to do the same. But her success, it must be admitted, grows every day more dubious. Where she strove to be passionate she was often hysterical; a sort of scream spoils the effect of her full tirades. She remains readable mainly where she is exquisite, and one small volume would suffice to contain her probable bequest to posterity.

'Christina Rossetti' in *The Victorian Poet: Poetics and Persona*, edited by Joseph Bristow (London: Croom Helm, 1987), p. 138.

As the century moved towards its end and assessment of the Victorian age began, the decline in Elizabeth Barrett Browning's poetic fortunes continued – increasingly she was remembered as the wife of Robert Browning (whose work managed to retain a status because of its complexity and resistance to easy categorisation) or as a poet (quaintly) liked by the Victorians. Typical of this placing of Barrett Browning in a structured pantheon of the era is George Saintsbury, writing in his major critical survey *A History of Nineteenth-Century Literature, 1780–1900* (London: Macmillan [1896], 1901):

> [Elizabeth Barrett Browning's] popularity, we have said, long anticipated her husband's; indeed, years after her death, it was possible, and not uncommon, to meet persons, not uncultivated, who were fairly well acquainted with her verse and entirely ignorant of his. The case has since altered; but it is believed that Mrs Browning still retains, and it is probable that she will always retain, no small measure of general favour. It has been usual to

speak of her as the chief English poetess, which she certainly is if bulk and character of work as distinguished from perfection of workmanship are considered. Otherwise, she must certainly give place to Miss Christina Rossetti. But Mrs Browning no doubt combined, in very unusual and interesting manner, the qualities which appeal to what may be called, with no disdainful intention, the crowd of readers of poetry, and those which appeal to the elect (p. 277).

Hugh Walker, in his *The Age of Tennyson* (London: George Bell, 1897), makes what was to become an increasingly common inversion of the status of Robert Browning and Elizabeth Barrett Browning – while Saintsbury can note and contextualise the shift in opinion from Elizabeth to Robert, Walker's analysis of Elizabeth Barrett Browning's importance is seen entirely through her relationship with her husband and concomitantly her gender:

> Mrs Browning's influence upon her husband was remarkably slight; his influence upon her was of mixed effect, but good predominated. . . . Mrs Browning was not really a thinker; woman-like, she felt first, and the attempt to translate her feeling into thought was an error. . . . Minor influences of Robert Browning may be traced in his wife's rhymes and rhythms; but while his effects, though often grotesque and uncouth, are striking and memorable, hers are feeble and commonplace. . . . Beyond question, the *Sonnets from the Portuguese* (1850) are Mrs Browning's most valuable contribution to literature. They are valuable even beyond their intrinsic merits. Good as they are, these sonnets have neither massiveness and subtlety of thought on the one hand, nor melody and charm on the other, sufficient to secure a place beside the greatest poetry. But they are the genuine utterance of a woman's heart, at once humbled and exalted by love; and in this respect they are unique (pp. 234–5).

Walker's notion of the 'lacks' and deficiencies in Browning's verse is echoed by Clement Shorter in his *Victorian Literature: Sixty Years of Books and Bookmen* (London: James Bowden, 1900, p. 14); Shorter notes the comparative lack of obscurity in Elizabeth Barrett Browning's verse (he has just discussed Robert Browning), and described *Aurora Leigh* as having a 'note of extreme simplicity' and being 'a very readable romance', thus denying any of the questioning of sanctified issues of gender and writing which the text embodied.

The status being accorded at the end of the century to Elizabeth Barrett Browning in terms of surveys of the literature of the Victorian era continued throughout the twentieth century. Oliver Elton, for example, writing in his *Survey of English Literature, 1830–1880* (London: Edward Arnold, 1920), encapsulates Elizabeth Barrett Browning in a chapter on 'The Brownings' which has thirteen sections on Robert and three on Elizabeth Barrett. Elton reverts to the gendered critical discourse of the nineteenth century in order to 'place' Elizabeth Barrett Browning:

> There have been few good poetesses at any time or in any country. Amongst those who have written in English, it is equally certain that Mrs Browning is the surest artist and that she 'has the largest and most comprehensive soul'. . . . As to her performance, it is well to approach it with some critical precautions. It would be a mistake, within a week of doing so, to read either Robert Browning or Christina Rossetti, and it is best, perhaps, to begin with a prejudice of the right kind, in order to find how often it is disarmed. Prepare from the first to come, almost anywhere, on a sudden lapse of language into almost every fault except vulgarity, or on a vicious rhyme or a defect of rhythm, or on queer vague matter, diffuse and high-flown, or on hectic writing. Expect all this, – and again and again you will not find it; but instead will come on passages of melody unbroken and imagery unimpaired; on gorgeous things, and also on simple things, which are successful, and which leave you free to admire the generous poetic vision which inspires them (p. 399).

Contemporary histories of Victorian literature are apt to continue this denial of status to Elizabeth Barrett Browning. Paul Turner includes her in his *English Literature, 1832–1890, Excluding the Novel* (Oxford: Clarendon, 1988) in a chapter entitled 'Four Lesser Poets'. Of *Aurora Leigh* he says:

> Today it seems . . . open to criticism for its implausible plot, its over-emotional tone, and its prolixity. But this last was caused by the very richness of the poet's imagination. The style seems like a spontaneous chain-reaction of vivid and ingenuous images, which carry the thought along by a series of intellectual explosions. Certainly one often wishes that the process could be halted; but the pyrotechnics are always worth watching. In retrospect the poem's faults are glaring: at the time of reading it one is more conscious of its immense vitality (p. 101).

The changes in the status and function of women's writing in the twentieth century should have seen a reassessment of Elizabeth Barrett Browning as a precursor of feminist discourses in literature. But by 1923, in Marjory A. Bald's *Women-Writers of the Nineteenth Century* (Cambridge: Cambridge University Press), the well-worn critical tropes of the nineteenth century were resurfacing:

> Christina Rossetti was never garrulous like Mrs Browning's Seraphim. She could hold her lips firmly closed. Mrs Browning's was not the case of an empty sounding vessel, for she was not empty. She had many things to say, and some of them were worth saying; but by her own action she depreciated their value. She poured the liquid out of her vessel so that it drenched the recipient; yet all the time she was trying to satisfy his thirst (p. 247).

Bald is poised on the verge of a new understanding of Elizabeth Barrett Browning's work, an embarrassment at her 'prolixity' mixed with a recognition of what she had 'to say'.

It was to be Virginia Woolf who would initiate the first feminist recuperation of Elizabeth Barrett Browning's poetry in her essay '*Aurora Leigh*' in *The Common Reader: Second Series* (London: Hogarth, [1932] 1965). Woolf describes the decline in Elizabeth Barrett Browning's critical status:

> ... fate has not been kind to Mrs Browning as a writer. Nobody reads her, nobody discusses her, nobody troubles to put her in her place. One has only to compare her reputation with Christina Rossetti's to trace her decline. Christina Rossetti mounts irresistibly to the first place among English women poets. Elizabeth, so much more loudly applauded during her lifetime, falls farther behind. The primers dismiss her contumely. Her importance, they say, 'has now become merely historical' (p. 202).

Aurora Leigh and Elizabeth Barrett Browning come to signify, for Virginia Woolf, both an acknowledgement of and an attempt to overcome the 'mythic masks' placed upon the woman writer. Woolf goes on to say:

> Nothing is more striking when at last she broke the prison bars than the fervour with which she flung herself into the life of the moment (p. 207). ... we may suspect that Elizabeth Barrett was inspired by a flash of true genius when she rushed into the drawing-room and said that here, where we live and work, is the true place for the poet. At any rate her courage was justified in her

own case. Her bad taste, her tortured ingenuity, her floundering, scrambling, and confused impetuosity have space to spend themselves here without inflicting a deadly wound, while her ardour and abundance, her brilliant descriptive powers, her shrewd and caustic humour, infect us with her own enthusiasm. We laugh, we protest, we complain – it is absurd, it is impossible, we cannot tolerate this exaggeration a moment longer – but, nevertheless, we read to the end enthralled. What more can an author ask? But the best compliment that we can pay *Aurora Leigh* is that it makes us wonder why it has left no successors. Surely the street, the drawing-room, are promising subjects; modern life is worthy of the muse (p. 213).

Woolf is obviously ready to claim Barrett Browning as a precursor of her own writing, in subject matter and in the forging of a feminist poetics of writing. Her essay is the originary reference point of an increasing number of feminist re-readings and reclamations of Barrett Browning in the second half of the twentieth century.

Cora Kaplan's 'Introduction' to *Aurora Leigh* (London: Women's Press, 1978) is a paradigmatic contemporary feminist reading of Barrett Browning, registering both the potential radicalism and resourcefulness of her poetics and the problematics of her ideas in the chasms they expose between the contemporary and the Victorian:

> Barrett Browning makes the condition of the poem's very existence the fact its protagonist is a woman and a poet. Aurora's biography is a detailed account both of the socialisation of women and the making of a poet.... In spite of its conventional happy ending it is possible to see [*Aurora Leigh*] as contributing to a feminist theory of art which argues that women's language, precisely because it has been suppressed by patriarchal societies, re-enters discourse with a shattering revolutionary experience.... *Aurora Leigh* is more than a single text. It is different as it is read and understood at each separate point in history, as it is inserted into historically particular ideological structures. There is a danger in either blaming the poem for its political incoherence by relegating those debates to history or in praising it only for the euphoria with which it ruptures and transforms female language (pp. 10–12).

These potentialities were expressed more plainly by the Marxist-Feminist Collective (of which Kaplan was a member) in the year preceding her edition of *Aurora Leigh*:

... the question posed in *Aurora Leigh*, openly, discursively, rather than invisibly stitched into the design of the poem, is this: can woman be at once the speaker/writer of her own discourse and a desiring, choosing subject in her own right? In any text written by a woman the author has tacitly assumed the role of speaker. Female literary production breaks the cultural taboo against women as public speakers, a taboo felt by almost all women who defined themselves as writers in the nineteenth century. Instead of weeping Barrett Browning urged: 'Curse and write'. Yet the social and public silence of women after puberty was central to the construction of femininity, a term Elizabeth Barrett Browning hated. The central contradiction for female authors as producers of their own speech is suppressed or displaced in the work of Austen and Brontë. By making her heroine a poet Barrett Browning breaks what is virtually a gentlemen's agreement between women writers and the arbiters of high culture in Victorian England that stated that women could write if they would only shut up about it.

'Women's Writing: *Jane Eyre, Shirley, Villette, Aurora Leigh*' in *1848: The Sociology of Literature, Proceedings of the Essex Conference on the Sociology of Literature*, July 1977, ed. Francis Barker and others (University of Essex, 1978), p. 202.

From these initial radical readings of Barrett Browning other feminist critics have been able to expand into more detailed understandings of the impact which *Aurora Leigh* and the political poetry had on feminist poetics. Sandra M. Gilbert provides an exemplary reading in her article 'From *Patria* to *Matria*: Elizabeth Barrett Browning's Risorgimento' (*PMLA,* vol. 99 [1984], pp. 194–211) in which she suggests 'that through her involvement with the revolutionary struggle for political identity that marked Italy's famous risorgimento, Barrett Browning enacted and reenacted her own personal and artistic struggle for identity, a risorgimento that was, like Italy's, both an insurrection and a resurrection' (p. 194). She goes on to argue that:

by using metaphors of the healing and making whole of a wounded woman/land to articulate both the reality and fantasy of her own female/poetic revitalization, Barrett Browning figuratively located herself in a re-creative female poetic tradition that descends from Sappho and Christine de Pizan through the Brontës, Christina Rossetti, Margaret Fuller, and Emily Dickinson to Renee

Vivien, Charlotte Perkins Gilman, H.D., and Adrienne Rich. In fusing supposedly asexual politics with the dreams and desires of a distinctively sexual politics, these women imagined nothing less than the transformation of *patria* into *matria* and thus the risorgimento of the lost community of women that Rossetti called the 'mother country' (p. 195).

The movement from 'asexual' to sexual politics in Barrett Browning's verse, pointed to by Gilbert, is intriguingly acknowledged by Angela Leighton in her *Victorian Women Poets: Writing Against the Heart* (Hemel Hempstead: Harvest Wheatsheaf, 1992):

> As a poet, [Barrett Browning] learned to distrust the iconic postures of romance in favour of a socialised and contextualised account of desire. She perceives love, not as a conclusive emotional absolute, but as a mixture of lust, ambition, rhetoric, fear and, above all, conventionality. Hers is thus essentially politicised poetry, not because politics is its dominant subject matter and not because she shows herself in any sense a political radical ... but because the tensions between desire and fact, between the individual and the system, can be felt in it (p. 87).

Such readings of Barrett Browning fulfil the potential of her verse to challenge the prescribed arenas constructed for women's poetry. As Kaplan acknowledges, Barrett Browning's poetry will continue to disrupt these, the gendered discourses and the feminist theories which are applied to her writing. The historically political in her work will never allow her poetry to settle into being exemplary for contemporary feminisms – but this in itself makes the investigation of the spaces between her work and contemporary theory all the more important.

Marjorie Stone's recent feminist analysis of Barrett Browning seems to support this assumption. Stone reads Barrett Browning's work with a close attentioin to the politics of both gender and literary form (reflecting concerns Barrett Browning herself raised in *Aurora Leigh*). Stone suggests that:

> *Aurora Leigh* has typically been approached as a *Kunstlerroman* reflecting Barrett Browning's own poetical development. While there is much to support this approach, it is also a generic classification that has tended to perpetuate the traditional focus on Barrett Browning's life rather than her art, meanwhile obscuring two important dimensions of her greatest work: first, the narrative sophistication apparent in Barrett Browning's dramatic

representation of Aurora's consciousness and formation, and second, the extent to which *Aurora Leigh* was written and read as a work of polemical 'sage discourse' in the tradition of Carlyle and Ruskin's prophetic writings on the tribulations of their times . . .

. . . both the composition and the reception of *Aurora Leigh* point to Barrett Browning's close ideological affiliations with Victorian feminist activists. Moreover, the apparently conservative and class-bound elements of her writing need to be viewed in the context of surrounding textual ironies (like the man she married, she is often an intricately ironic writer), and in the larger historical context mediating the production and reception of her works.

(Marjorie Stone, *Elizabeth Barrett Browning* (London: Macmillan, 1995), pp. 12, 14.

This reading of Barrett Browning represents a confident and developed feminist critique in which the mythic masks of the female writer can be seen to be challenged not only through sexual politics, but through the ironies and literary strategies Barrett Browning herself employs.

SUGGESTIONS FOR FURTHER READING

Editions

There are no satisfactorily annotated complete editions of Elizabeth Barrett Browning's poetry. The most complete edition remains *The Poetical Works of Elizabeth Barrett Browning* (London: Oxford University Press, 1910) and similar reprints, including *The Complete Works*, ed. Charlotte Porter and Helen A. Clarke (1900). Also useful, though sparsely annotated, is *Aurora Leigh and Other Poems*, introduced by Cora Kaplan (London: Women's Press, 1978). The edition of *Aurora Leigh*, ed. Kerry McSweeney (Oxford: Oxford University Press, 1993), is the most accessible annotated edition of the poem currently available.

Biography, Letters and Criticism

Virginia Woolf, 'Aurora Leigh' in *The Common Reader* (London: Hogarth, 1932). Important as an initial feminist reading of EBB's work.

Dorothy Hewlett, *Elizabeth Barrett Browning* (London: Cassell, 1953). A thorough biography.

Cora Kaplan, 'Introduction' in *Aurora Leigh and other Poems* (London: Women's Press, 1978). Sets out the boundaries and difficulties of feminist readings of EBB.

Marxist-Feminist Collective, 'Women's Writing: *Jane Eyre, Shirley, Villette, Aurora Leigh*' in *1848: The Sociology of Literature, Proceedings of the Essex Conference on the Sociology of Literature*, July 1977, ed. Francis Barker and others (University of Essex, 1978). One of the most radical and forthright feminist readings available.

Sandra M. Gilbert and Susan Gubar, *The Madwoman in the Attic: The Woman Writer and the Nineteenth-Century Literary Imagination* (London: Yale University Press, 1979). A seminal work on women's writing in the period, containing especially useful material on *Aurora Leigh*.

Dolores Rosenblum, 'Face to Face: Elizabeth Barrett Browning's *Aurora Leigh* and Nineteenth-Century Poetry', *Victorian Studies*, vol. 26 (1983), pp. 321–38. Useful contextual arguments.

Nina Auerbach, 'Robert Browning's Last Word', *Victorian Poetry*, vol. 22 (1984), pp. 161–73. Examines borrowings, connections and appropriations across EBB and RB, suggesting that RB turned EBB's voice into his own after her death.

Sandra M. Gilbert, 'From *Patria* to *Matria*: Elizabeth Barrett Browning's Risorgimento', *PMLA*, vol. 99 (1984), pp. 194–211. Begins to read EBB's feminist poetics in conjunction with her politics.

Philip Kelley and Ronald Hudson (eds.), *The Brownings' Correspondence*, ten volumes to date (Winfield: Wedgestone Press, 1984). The most comprehensive collection of Browning letters.

Angela Leighton, *Elizabeth Barrett Browning* (Brighton: Harvester Wheatsheaf, 1986). An excellent study placing detailed readings in a theoretical framework.

Dorothy Mermin, *Elizabeth Barrett Browning: The Origins of New Poetry* (London: University of Chicago Press, 1989). Contains detailed readings of most of EBB's major works.

Angela Leighton, *Victorian Women Poets: Writing Against the Heart* (Hemel Hempstead: Harvester Wheatsheaf, 1992). Examines EBB and seven other Victorian women poets.

Marjorie Stone, *Elizabeth Barrett Browning* (London: Macmillan, 1995). A well-informed critique which employs feminist literary criticism in sustained readings of the poems and EBB's career and reception.

Julia Markus, *Dared and Done: The Marriage of Elizabeth and Robert Browning* (London: Bloomsbury, 1995). A very challenging account of EBB's life, invalidity and relationship with Robert Browning. The claims this text makes regarding EBB's worries over her racial inheritance are discussed in the Introduction to this volume.

Joyce Zonana, 'Elizabeth Barrett Browning's *Aurora Leigh* and Feminist Poetics' in Angela Leighton (ed.), *Victorian Women Poets: A Critical Reader* (Oxford: Blackwell, 1996). A complex and highly developed account of *Aurora Leigh* from a feminist perspective which usefully takes stock of previous feminist readings of this text. This collection also reprints Gilbert's essay above.

INDEX OF TITLES

ACKNOWLEDGEMENTS

———

My thanks to Dr Maureen Alden, Dr Jennifer Fitzgerald and Dr John Thompson, and to Amanda Graham for pointing me towards critical texts, and to Howard Davies for his intelligent proofreading. Any errors in the textual apparatus remain, of course, entirely my own.

POETRY
IN EVERYMAN

Amorous Rites: Elizabethan Erotic Verse
edited by Sandra Clark
Erotic and often comic poems dealing with myths of transformation and erotic interaction between humans and gods
£4.99

Selected Poems
JOHN KEATS
An excellent selection of the poetry of one of the principal figures of the Romantic movement
£6.99

Poems and Prose
CHRISTINA ROSSETTI
A new collection of her writings, poetry and prose, marking the centenary of her death
£5.99

Poems and Prose
P. B. SHELLEY
The essential Shelley in one volume
£5.99

Silver Poets of the Sixteenth Century
edited by Douglas Brooks-Davies
An exciting and comprehensive collection
£6.99

Complete English Poems
JOHN DONNE
The father of metaphysical verse in this highly-acclaimed collection
£6.99

Complete English Poems, Of Education, Areopagitica
JOHN MILTON
An excellent introduction to Milton's poetry and prose
£6.99

Women Romantic Poets 1780–1830: An Anthology
edited by Jennifer Breen
Hidden talent from the Romantic era rediscovered
£5.99

Selected Poems
D. H. LAWRENCE
An authoritative selection spanning the whole of Lawrence's literary career
£4.99

The Poems
W. B. YEATS
Ireland's greatest lyric poet surveyed in this ground-breaking edition
£7.99

All books are available from your local bookshop or direct from:
Littlehampton Book Services Cash Sales, 14 Eldon Way, Lineside Estate,
Littlehampton, West Sussex BN17 7HE *(prices are subject to change)*

To order any of the books, please enclose a cheque (in sterling) made payable to
Littlehampton Book Services, or phone your order through with credit card details (Access,
Visa or Mastercard) on 01903 721596 (24 hour answering service) stating card number
and expiry date. *(Please add £1.25 for package and postage to the total of your order.)*

In the USA, for further information and a complete catalogue call 1-800-526-2778

WOMEN'S WRITING
IN EVERYMAN

Poems and Prose
CHRISTINA ROSSETTI
A collection of her writings, poetry and prose, published to mark the centenary of her death
£5.99

Women Philosophers
edited by Mary Warnock
The great subjects of philosophy handled by women spanning four centuries, including Simone de Beauvoir and Iris Murdoch
£6.99

Glenarvon
LADY CAROLINE LAMB
A novel which throws light on the greatest scandal of the early nineteenth century – the infatuation of Caroline Lamb with Lord Byron
£6.99

Women Romantic Poets
1780 – 1830: An Anthology
edited by Jennifer Breen
Hidden talent from the Romantic era rediscovered
£5.99

Memoirs of the Life of Colonel Hutchinson
LUCY HUTCHINSON
One of the earliest pieces of women's biographical writing, of great historic and feminist interest
£6.99

The Secret Self 1: Short Stories by Women
edited by Hermione Lee
'A superb collection' The Guardian
£4.99

The Age of Innocence
EDITH WHARTON
A tale of the conflict between love and tradition by one of America's finest women novelists
£4.99

Frankenstein
MARY SHELLEY
A masterpiece of Gothic terror in its original 1818 version
£3.99

The Life of Charlotte Brontë
ELIZABETH GASKELL
A moving and perceptive tribute by one writer to another
£4.99

Victorian Women Poets
1830 – 1900
edited by Jennifer Breen
A superb anthology of the era's finest female poets
£5.99

Female Playwrights of the Restoration: Five Comedies
edited by Paddy Lyons
Rediscovered literary treasure in a unique selection
£5.99

All books are available from your local bookshop or direct from:
Littlehampton Book Services Cash Sales, 14 Eldon Way, Lineside Estate,
Littlehampton, West Sussex BN17 7HE (*prices are subject to change*)

To order any of the books, please enclose a cheque (in sterling) made payable to
Littlehampton Book Services, or phone your order through with credit card details (Access,
Visa or Mastercard) on 01903 721596 (24 hour answering service) stating card number
and expiry date. (*Please add £1.25 for package and postage to the total of your order.*)

In the USA, for further information and a complete catalogue call 1-800-526-2778

SHORT STORY COLLECTIONS
IN EVERYMAN

The Strange Case of Dr Jekyll and Mr Hyde and Other Stories
R. L. STEVENSON

An exciting selection of gripping tales from a master of suspense
£1.99

Nineteenth-Century American Short Stories
edited by Christopher Bigsby

A selection of the works of Henry James, Edith Wharton, Mark Twain and many other great American writers
£6.99

The Best of Saki
edited by MARTIN STEPHEN

Includes Tobermory, Gabriel Ernest, Svedni Vashtar, The Interlopers, Birds on the Western Front
£4.99

Souls Belated and Other Stories
EDITH WHARTON

Brief, neatly crafted tales exploring a range of themes from big taboo subjects to the subtlest little ironies of social life
£6.99

The Night of the Iguana and Other Stories
TENNESSEE WILLIAMS

Twelve remarkable short stories, each a compelling drama in miniature
£4.99

Selected Short Stories and Poems
THOMAS HARDY

Hardy's most memorable stories and poetry in one volume
£4.99

Selected Tales
HENRY JAMES

Stories portraying the tensions between private life and the outside world
£5.99

The Best of Sherlock Homes
ARTHUR CONAN DOYLE

All the favourite adventures in one volume
£4.99

The Secret Self 1: *Short Stories by Women*
edited by Hermione Lee

'A superb collection' The Guardian
£4.99

CLASSIC FICTION
IN EVERYMAN

The Impressions of Theophrastus Such
GEORGE ELIOT
An amusing collection of character sketches, and the only paperback edition available
£5.99

Frankenstein
MARY SHELLEY
A masterpiece of Gothic terror in its original 1818 version
£3.99

East Lynne
MRS HENRY WOOD
A classic tale of melodrama, murder and mystery
£7.99

Holiday Romance and Other Writings for Children
CHARLES DICKENS
Dickens's works for children, including 'The Life of Our Lord' and 'A Child's History of England', with original illustrations
£5.99

The Ebb-Tide
R. L. STEVENSON
A compelling study of ordinary people in extreme circumstances
£4.99

The Three Impostors
ARTHUR MACHEN
The only edition available of this cult thriller
£4.99

Mister Johnson
JOYCE CARY
The only edition available of this amusing but disturbing twentieth-century tale
£5.99

The Jungle Book
RUDYARD KIPLING
The classic adventures of Mowgli and his friends
£3.99

Glenarvon
LADY CAROLINE LAMB
The only edition available of the novel which throws light on the greatest scandal of the early nine-teenth century – the infatuation of Caroline Lamb with Lord Byron
£6.99

Twenty Thousand Leagues Under the Sea
JULES VERNE
Scientific fact combines with fantasy in this prophetic tale of underwater adventure
£4.99

All books are available from your local bookshop or direct from:
Littlehampton Book Services Cash Sales, 14 Eldon Way, Lineside Estate,
Littlehampton, West Sussex BN17 7HE (*prices are subject to change*)

To order any of the books, please enclose a cheque (in sterling) made payable to
Littlehampton Book Services, or phone your order through with credit card details (Access,
Visa or Mastercard) on 01903 721596 (24 hour answering service) stating card number
and expiry date. (*Please add £1.25 for package and postage to the total of your order.*)

In the USA, for further information and a complete catalogue call 1-800-526-2778

CLASSIC NOVELS
IN EVERYMAN

The Time Machine
H. G. WELLS

One of the books which defined 'science fiction' – a compelling and tragic story of a brilliant and driven scientist
£3.99

Oliver Twist
CHARLES DICKENS

Arguably the best-loved of Dickens's novels. With all the original illustrations
£4.99

Barchester Towers
ANTHONY TROLLOPE

The second of Trollope's Chronicles of Barsetshire, and one of the funniest of all Victorian novels
£4.99

The Heart of Darkness
JOSEPH CONRAD

Conrad's most intense, subtle, compressed, profound and proleptic work
£3.99

Tess of the d'Urbervilles
THOMAS HARDY

The powerful, poetic classic of wronged innocence
£3.99

Wuthering Heights and Poems
EMILY BRONTË

A powerful work of genius – one of the great masterpieces of literature
£3.99

Pride and Prejudice
JANE AUSTEN

Proposals, rejections, infidelities, elopements, happy marriages – Jane Austen's most popular novel
£2.99

North and South
ELIZABETH GASKELL

A novel of hardship, passion and hard-won wisdom amidst the conflicts of the industrial revolution
£4.99

The Newcomes
W. M. THACKERAY

An exposé of Victorian polite society by one of the nineteenth-century's finest novelists
£6.99

Adam Bede
GEORGE ELIOT

A passionate rural drama enacted at the turn of the eighteenth century
£5.99

All books are available from your local bookshop or direct from:
Littlehampton Book Services Cash Sales, 14 Eldon Way, Lineside Estate,
Littlehampton, West Sussex BN17 7HE (*prices are subject to change*)

To order any of the books, please enclose a cheque (in sterling) made payable to
Littlehampton Book Services, or phone your order through with credit card details (Access,
Visa or Mastercard) on 01903 721596 (24 hour answering service) stating card number
and expiry date. (*Please add £1.25 for package and postage to the total of your order.*)

In the USA, for further information and a complete catalogue call 1-800-526-2778

DYLAN THOMAS
IN EVERYMAN

Collected Poems 1934–1953
edited by Walford Davies *and*
Ralph Maud
The definitive edition of five
published volumes of poems:
18 Poems, Twenty-five Poems,
The Map of Love, Deaths and
Entrances *and* In Country Sleep
£4.99

Under Milk Wood
edited by Walford Davies *and*
Ralph Maud
The definitive edition of 'A Play for
Voices', conjuring up the dreams
and daily business of an imagined
Welsh seaside town
£3.99

Portrait of the Artist as a
Young Dog
introduced by Aeronwy Thomas
Ten marvellously evocative stories
which show the exuberance of
youth maturing into a fine celeb-
ratory compassion and ironic relish
for the eccentricities of common
life
£2.99

Selected Poems
edited by Walford Davies
Seventy of Thomas's most
memorable poems spanning
his lifetime
£3.99

Collected Stories
introduced by Leslie Norris
The complete range of Thomas's
stories, from sombre fantasist to
comedian of suburbia
£5.99

A Dylan Thomas Treasury:
Poems, Stories and Broadcasts
selected by Walford Davies
Poetry and prose which embrace
touching childhood reminiscence
and a spiritual yearning. Selection
unique to Everyman
£4.99

The Loud Hill of Wales:
Poetry of Place
selected by Walford Davies
Poems and prose illustrating
Thomas's crucial relationship
to Wales
£3.99